A

IS FOR

ATHEIST

A IS FOR ATHEIST

An A to Z of the Godfree Life

ANDREW SNEDDON

PITCHSTONE PUBLISHING
Durham, North Carolina

Pitchstone Publishing
Durham, North Carolina
www.pitchstonepublishing.com

Copyright © 2016 by Andrew Sneddon

Library of Congress Cataloging-in-Publication Data

Names: Sneddon, Andrew, 1971- author.
Title: A is for atheist : an A to Z of the Godfree life / Andrew Sneddon.
Description: Durham, North Carolina : Pitchstone Publishing, 2016. | Includes
   bibliographical references.
Identifiers: LCCN 2015050303 (print) | LCCN 2016000094 (ebook) | ISBN
   9781634310697 (pbk. : alk. paper) | ISBN 9781634310703 (epub) | ISBN
   9781634310710 (pdf) | ISBN 9781634310727 (mobi)
Subjects: LCSH: Atheism—Dictionaries.
Classification: LCC BL2747 .S647 2016 (print) | LCC BL2747 (ebook) | DDC
   211/.803—dc23
LC record available at http://lccn.loc.gov/2015050303

Contents

Introduction

Once upon a time I believed in god. I grew up in a family that went to church fairly regularly. Less regularly I went to Sunday school. As a teenager I was particularly earnest about religion, as teenagers can be. I once gave a presentation in French class about my faith. The other students clapped, which was unusual. I remember discussing religion with other students. Most of us just took it for granted, but it was clear that there was an appeal to belief that was born of more than lazy habit. Religion seemed to raise and answer important questions. Where do we come from? Why are we here? How should we live our lives? Religions famously address these topics. My friends and I recognized this.

This does not mean that religious life made us comfortable. It didn't make me comfortable. It scared me, injecting uneasiness into what should have been a straightforward middle-class life. For one thing there was the weirdness of it all. A three in one god? Desert miracles thousands of years ago, then silence? Mysterious plans that would justify the arbitrary cruelty found in the world and in biblical stories? All very strange. For another there were the distasteful things that were asked of me. The religion in which I grew up was not terribly oppressive, but it clearly did not treat women as equals to men. Should I really accept this? I had no appetite for spreading the word, despite my belief. Tithing was obviously a scam; my belief wasn't so blinding that I couldn't see that.

Worst of all was hell. Or rather, worst of all was the idea of eternal punishment, along with a rather complicated body of ideas that accompanied this idea. Eternal suffering is one thing. Eternal suffering as punishment for failing to live up to religious demands—for sinning, in short—is another. Being threatened with such torment for the sins of my ancestors is an even bitterer pill to swallow. And some sins have to do with mere belief, not with action. Regardless of what you did, you could end up in hell for thinking the wrong way! I found the overall picture of my life as a high stakes yet baffling test deeply disturbing.

Now my life is better. In no small part it is better because I have given up on religious belief. Some of the old questions remain, but not many. The real concerns that my teen self faced have been transformed by a better understanding of the kind of thing I am and the kind of world I live in. My life is not a test, and neither is yours. Realizing this can be quite a comfort.

If that were all there was to becoming an atheist, there would be no need to write this book. But that's not the end of the story. Religious belief is very common, to such an extent that those who reject it are suspect, even despised. Once in a while a religious spokesperson, such as a pope, says something like this:

> Openness to God makes us open towards our brothers and sisters and towards an understanding of life as a joyful task to be accomplished in a spirit of solidarity. On the other hand, ideological rejection of God and an atheism of indifference, oblivious to the Creator and at risk of becoming equally oblivious to human values, constitute some of the chief obstacles to development today. *A humanism which excludes God is an inhuman humanism.* (his italics)
> — Pope Benedict XVI, "Caritas in veritate," encyclical, June 29, 2009

As criticism of atheism goes, this could be worse. Still, it's pretty pointed: atheists are insensitive to values. Atheists offer an inhuman form of life. The message is that atheism should be resisted. If Benedict were correct about atheism, the reason to reject it wouldn't be peculiar to Catholics. It would pertain to anyone who worries about genuine values and wants to reject inhuman doctrines. Yikes!

This used to make me angry. Words like these are an insult to the many good people who are not attracted by religion but who are upstanding members of their communities. Whatever "inhuman" might mean, these people aren't it. They are humane, kind, compassionate, the very sort of humans we want as neighbors.

Why would the pope, of all people, smear these people in this way?

However, I have now reconsidered my anger. After all, consider the life of a pope. These people are brought up in thoroughly religious contexts. They never meet nonbelievers in any sustained way. They are taught doctrines and immersed in traditions that urge rejection of atheism in ways ranging from mild to murderous. Given a life like this, what should we expect popes to say about atheism? Everything they know—everything!—gives them reason to be concerned about it. They don't know any better.

Popes, of course, are not alone in this. Most people grow up in ways thoroughly permeated by religious ideas, including distrust of nonbelief. They don't know which of their neighbors are atheists. We have no marks, no defining habits, for all that unites us, essentially, is an absence. In short, lots of people are ignorant of what it's like to be an atheist.

This book is an attempt to shed some light on this for the curious. Atheism has a bad reputation that it does not deserve. Much of this is fueled by misunderstanding. I aim to rectify this with understanding, or at least the first steps toward it.

If I am correct about the understanding of atheism among the religious, then one thing should immediately be clear: we should not trust what the religious say about atheists and atheism. It's not because they are ill-willed; generally they aren't. It is because they literally do not know what they are talking about. They don't know atheists and have not studied atheism, so they are in the dark. Authority here falls first and foremost to atheists.

The same danger lurks with regard to what atheists have to say about religion. Fair enough. But there is a general difference between believers and nonbelievers here. The vast majority of atheists were not brought up as atheists. Some were, but most were not. Instead, they were brought up in a religious context. They know religion from the inside. This is my situation, and it is very common. And even those atheists who received their nonbelief as infants at their mothers' knees were brought up in a society that is shot through with religious ideas. How do I know this? Because, so far as I can tell, this is all societies. Even modern secular states are populated by people who go to church, understand religious traditions, and, crucially, think about things using religious ideas.

You don't have to take my word for this. The people at the Pew Research Center study religion and ideas about religion, among other things. They did a study about knowledge of religion across certain groups in the United States: atheists, Jews, Muslims, various sorts of Christians, and so on. Atheists scored the highest of all. Nonbelievers know more about religion, typically, than believers. (See the results for yourself: http://www.pewforum.org/2010/09/28/u-s-religious-knowledge-survey-who-knows-what-about-religion.)

So, by and large, atheists have personal experience with religion and thus know what they're talking about when they reject it. Believers don't have this experience with atheism. To learn what atheism is like, ask an atheist (if you can find one). In case you can't find someone to ask, or are uncomfortable asking, I offer this book.

There is a consequence of the familiarity of atheists with religion, at least for books like this. We aren't intimately familiar with all religions; no one is. Instead, we're generally familiar with one sect of one broad religious tradition. That sect and that tradition are usually what we left when we went godfree. That's the religion in our minds. This is certainly my case. We criticize most that which we know best, that which still haunts us, or at least that which comes to mind when thinking about religion. That's the nature of the scars that still itch. So books such as this can seem unduly weighted toward one religion, or one sort of religion, and unduly silent about others. Fair enough. Other religions will share some features with the one(s) that we are personally acquainted with, so our local complaints will have wider application. When other religions are genuinely distinct, our barbs will fail to find purchase. My guess is that religions tend to share important features, such that worries born of one faith apply to many, but I could be wrong.

So far I have been speaking of believers and nonbelievers, as if people could rigidly be divided into these categories. But the other things I have been saying show that reality is more complicated than this. I, like most other atheists, have been a believer. Now I am not. I have had the same beliefs, wishes, and fears as other believers. Some of these I have shed; others I have not. I still have many of the same questions as believers, and we are alike in thinking that these topics are important ones. With regard to a vast array of concerns, we are all in this together. I speak to you as a fellow curious traveler, a neighbor across the fence, not as an outsider worth fearing.

So, what is it like to be an atheist? What is in this book? Opinions, some defended, some just voiced. Jokes. Jabs. Snippets of argument about various topics. I have given the most attention to values. Not to god, or gods, not to the supernatural, not to science: values. The reason is that, well, values matter. Moreover, the most pernicious falsehoods out there about atheists concern values. It is widely thought that we are evil, to put it bluntly. More subtly, many think that we don't, and perhaps can't, value anything. Nothing could be further from the truth, as you will see. Even more subtle still, I am continually surprised by the extent to which people are drawn to religion out of concern for values and hence puzzled about atheism on this topic. It needs addressing, so that is what I have done.

Much, but not all, of what is in this book is critical. I wish it weren't, but I don't see how it can be avoided. After all, I'm trying to articulate some things about being an atheist, but by definition an atheist is someone who rejects religion, who draws away from ideas about god and the supernatural, who sees problems with large swaths of human thought because of its use of those sorts of idea. Atheism is a category defined by what it rejects; criticism is its defining feature, at least when attempts are made to say something about being removed from religious practices and thoughts about gods. Still, it's not all critical. And even the critical can be edifying, sometimes surprisingly so.

Because the topics are presented in snippets, you can start where you like. If you're concerned with god's existence, start with things like *God (or, Gods)* and *Evidence*. If you are more interested in values, start with *Values* and *Morality (or, On Loving the Good with and without God)*. Follow the topics as they please you, and ignore those that don't. You don't have to read this book from beginning to end. You don't have to read it all at all. In fact, this is a book about atheism for those who may not want to read a whole book. (You're welcome!)

Some atheists will disagree with what I say. Some will think that I have included topics that should be omitted and omitted some that should be addressed. Fine; this is only to be expected. As I have already said, what unites atheists is a lack of belief in a certain sort of thing. That's it. We don't have creeds or churches that unite us. Some atheists seem to want these types of things. Well, they can have them; I don't want them. Without such unifying institutions, disagreement about details is only to be expected.

We can welcome it. Why not? This is why I offer "An A to Z of the Godfree Life," not "The A to Z of the Godfree Life." There is no single way to be godfree. There are many.

This began as a different sort of book. I started out to offer a list of the consolations of disbelief. However, I discovered more burdens than joys, so that project was abandoned. I was disappointed, but then I reflected. People do not become atheists because it is easy. Much of the world is against it. It's easier not to go godfree and instead to participate in religious practice, to make various sorts of gestures toward religious belief, maybe even to believe. Still, some religious believers become atheists. We do this because we think it is correct. It's the truth, and religion is not. It might even be morally laudable, or even morally demanded, to become an atheist, but we need not get into that here. The bottom line, however, is that having an accurate worldview need not bring with it the easiest life. Just ask those atheists who have been threatened for their lives, or shunned by their loved ones, for being open about their doubt. Sound easy to you? It sounds awful to me.

The difficulties that come with atheism show why this sort of book is needed. Some people—both believing and nonbelieving—think that atheism has, shall we say, won, and that the appropriate thing for the godfree to do now would be to shut up about it all. Going on about religion now is just rubbing it in. It's rude. Shut up.

Well, atheists can be rude, of course. I suspect parts of this book are rude, and others will be taken as rude even if they aren't really. So be it. But the idea that the world is now a place without belief is pretty implausible. Billions of people belong to churches, temples, and mosques. Although the power of religion in the public sphere has receded, it is still very much present. The heads of major religions are covered by international news media and consulted by politicians. More subtly, people think using religious ideas and assumptions. It's a godly world in many important ways. I would be more comfortable in a world with much less religion.

Here's one small point showing just how subtly proreligion the world is. A 2011 study by Will Gervais, Azim Shariff, and Ara Norenzayan found that, in the United States, atheists are as distrusted as rapists. That's cold! We are unwelcome as friends and family members to a majority of Americans. These numbers will be better in some countries, worse in others. The point should be clear: this is not a context in which atheists have "won." It's one in which we're the losers. I would like that to change.

Still, there are joys to be had in unbelief. I found turning my back on religion a relief, and I still do. Maybe you will too. For one thing, I have different reasons to fear death than I had when I was a believer. For another, life is less perplexing than it used to be. Or perhaps I should say that it is less painfully and personally perplexing. There are lots of questions still to be answered about the world in which I find myself. They just aren't quite the same questions as when I was a believer. Those questions turned out to be misguided. To go godfree is not to have all of your questions answered. You will find some answers, but maybe not as many as you would like. Instead, to go godfree is more to trade old concerns for new ones. I think this is a trade worth making. Not everyone will agree. That's fine. Some who read this book will go godfree and others won't. What I really hope from you is understanding, and I offer the entries in this book as a good faith (*ahem*) guide to achieving this.

1
A Is for . . .

A Very Ordinary Day: A man wakes up, dresses, and goes downstairs to his kitchen. He makes breakfast for himself and his wife, then walks his dog. Afterward his wife goes to her office and the man sits at the dining room table to read and write. He makes coffee midmorning. At lunchtime he has a small meal in the kitchen, then takes a walk into the nearby town. When he returns he does more reading and writing. He starts to cook, and before he finishes his wife comes home. They eat then go to the gym. They watch television and go to sleep.

Many of the man's days are like this. Variations include eating out; some involve trips to the movies; others involve yardwork, more shopping, and, if he's lucky, travel, and if he's unlucky, trips to his office away from home. Is this man a religious person?

From this admittedly dull sketch of daily affairs, we cannot tell. As it happens this is pretty much my life, and I am no believer. But it could easily be the life of someone who professes some not necessarily insignificant degree of belief in god or gods, along with related ideas such as souls, the supernatural, heaven and hell, sin, etc. This is a telling point: from our behavior, we generally cannot tell the godfree from the believers. Some atheists declare their nonbelief, but most do not. Much the same goes for religious believers.

Adding church attendance to this description changes the probabilities, given that it's reasonable to believe that relatively more believers than nonbelievers attend services. But it's certainly not definitive. Lots who do not go to church nonetheless believe in a god or gods. More interestingly, some atheists attend church; some attend church very regularly. Some will even profess belief, at least in certain contexts. There are various reasons for this. Some are closeted and want to remain hidden among all of the ordinary apparently (only apparently, of course) religious people. Some like the music. Some like the community, or participating in traditions. Some are sad in their unbelief: they know that the distinctly godly claims of religions are not true, but wish that they were, for they find them attractive (in their comfort, their beauty, their weirdness—there can be lots of reasons here too). See *Belief and Doubt* for more on this.

Piety cannot be directly seen in our behavior. This should make us wonder how much giving up religion would affect our lives. The degree of publicity with which one does this can make a difference. It's imprudent to court hatred from former friends, neighbors, family, and this, lamentably, can happen. But for lots of people atheism just won't make that much of a difference, at least to day-to-day affairs.

There are, of course, people for whom giving up religion would make a huge difference, for good, bad, or a mix. Fair enough, but this group does not include everyone. It might not even include close to everyone.

The fact that religious conviction, and lack of it, does not necessarily show up in people's behavior should also make us suspect the frequently made claim that religion and morality are closely linked. If we can't tell the ordinary good believers from the ordinary good unbelievers, why should we think that religion has a unique link to being good? The answer, of course, is that we shouldn't. See *Morality (or, On Loving the Good with and without God)* for discussion.

Absurdity (and Meaning in Life): If atheists are correct, is life absurd? Does a godfree perspective on the world doom one to an absurd existence?

It can seem so. A religious outlook grounds the meaning of our lives in god's perspective on us. Atheists think that there is no such perspective. We do not typically think that our lives are meaningless. Instead, the sources of true meaning for human life must be found within these lives themselves. Identifying these is hard work, but we are all familiar with the things that make our lives worthwhile. Happiness, pleasure, virtue, knowledge, love— these are all time-honored candidates for sources of meaning in life.

We also make unfortunate mistakes with regard to finding meaning in our lives (see *Tragedy [or, Despair about the Meaning of Life]*). The classic example is the person who devotes all of his time to a career, then wakes up one day to find his life empty. Work is a legitimate source of value in life, but it's not everything. Moreover, not all jobs are equal, and not all jobs suit all people. Sadly, other examples are just as easy to find. Looking for love in the wrong place, or the wrong kind of love, leaves lives worse than they could have been. So does immersion in trivial hobbies. And on, and on, and on.

The crucial thing to notice is that humans crave meaning. Whether we seek it in the right or wrong places, we can't help but seek it. We take it so seriously that it is common to search for ultimate foundations for the significance of our lives. The normal things around us don't seem to satisfy us; instead, we seek gods to give our lives meaning. The irony (see *Irony [and Meaning in Life]*) is that when we do this we look right past the real sources of meaning. This is, in a sense, absurd: it is a cosmic joke that our hunger for meaning causes us to misunderstand the nature and roots of what makes life meaningful. It is indeed absurd that our own nature is both the source of meaning in our lives and precisely what makes us blind to this source.

The answer, however, is not to embrace god as the source of life's meaning. That is a mistake in itself and a recipe for making other mistakes about what makes life worthwhile. Instead, to avoid the absurdity of life we should give up on god and learn to pay better attention to the human condition in all its difficult details. Atheism does not make life absurd. It saves life from the absurdity that the craving for gods creates.

Adults: Some religions explicitly portray humans as children of god. Atheists aren't, and neither is anyone else. A godfree life is one for adults, in this sense at least: we must, individually and collectively, face up to our challenges and opportunities. This means considering, choosing, and acting on everything: there are no topics that are off-limits because they belong to god alone. There is no god. We are the only ones around to take care of ourselves and each other. To think of oneself as a child of god is to put one's head in the sand, at least with regard to some challenges and opportunities. Eat of the tree of knowledge of good and evil.

Agnostic: Literally, someone who thinks that we cannot know whether there is a god. It is often used to mean a less-than-fully-committed version of "atheist." See *Godfree*.

Animals (the Human Ones): It seems to me that one of the hardest things for humans to keep in mind is that we are animals—wonderful ones, of course, but animals nonetheless. The godfree life is one for animals, for the human animals that we are. To lead this life is in part to learn to keep this in mind, and forever to be learning what the implications of our animal nature are. See *Apes, Meat Machines,* and *What's the Case for Atheism?*

Anxieties: Many people are anxious about topics that religions address. Sometimes religions address these anxieties and provide a salve for them. Sometimes religions produce these anxieties and thereby make people's lives worse rather than better. Sometimes it's both. The crucial thing is not whether religions address anxieties: this cannot be a measure of their truth, as falsehoods can often assuage our worries. Rather, the important thing is to separate genuine from false anxieties.

For example, worries which rest on mythologies—about hell, for instance—are false. Their best solution lies in dispelling their spurious foundations. Other problems are real. Sickness is real, poverty is real . . . to continue this list would be unnecessarily depressing. However, genuine concerns that receive false hope from religions are not adequately addressed. This goes even if the people with false hopes feel better about their concerns. Maybe we would all feel better about the world if we believed in Santa Claus. This hardly recommends endorsement of this belief. It certainly says nothing about whether it's true (hint: it's not, and so it goes with many of the other stories that give people comfort).

We must also be careful not to make too much of genuine anxieties. I don't really mean that we should keep things in perspective, although this is wise counsel. I mean instead that we should not assume that we share each other's concerns. Suppose that one person is deeply concerned with professional success. This is indeed one of the sources of value in life, and hence it can generate genuine anxieties. But other people need not share this concern, neither to the same degree or at all. While this person might genuinely be kept up at night worrying about professional failure, others might genuinely sleep soundly, unworried about this sort of thing. It's a mistake to assume that your deep fears are mine too—indeed, that they must be mine too.

Some people are worried about whether life is meaningful in an ultimate sense (but see *Tragedy [or, Despair about the Meaning of Life]*, *Irony [and Meaning in Life]*, *Absurdity [and Meaning in Life]* for discussion); others are unmoved. Some worry about life after death; I don't care. It's a mistake to assume that what bothers you must bother me. Think doubly, at least, about your fears: are they worth the attention that you give them, and are they generated by features of your life that others do not share?

Some religious groups reach out to people in the spirit of assuaging their fears. This can be laudable, when the people in question need real help. But it can be reprehensible, when these groups indulge and even encourage baseless fears. The mere interest in our anxieties is neither good nor bad, given the vagaries of our concerns, and hence we should not think too much of religious groups that want to offer us help.

See *Fear, Hope,* and *Perplexity* for more along these lines.

Apes: We are. Pretty great ones, but apes nonetheless. Keeping this in mind is helpful for cultivating humility (both intellectual and moral) and for warding off the felt need to explain things about our lives in terms of god and the supernatural. See *Animals (the Human Ones)*, *Humility*, *Meat Machines*, *What's the Case for Atheism?,* and *You.*

Are Atheists Fully Human?: Must we be religious to be fully human? Some people seem to think so. Atheist Ireland chairperson Michael Nugent, in an October 2012 blog post titled "Catholic Church Must Stop Dehumanizing Atheists by Saying We Are Not Fully Human," documented cases of high-ranking Catholics who equate full humanity with being religious in general and, presumably, being Catholic in particular. Particularly worrisome are remarks to the effect that atheists are not fully human. Here is an example he reports from a BBC Radio 4 interview with Cardinal Cormac Murphy O'Connor, who states:

> I think what I said was true, of course whether a person is atheist or any
> other. . . . there is in fact, in my view, something not totally human, if they

leave out the transcendent. If they leave out an aspect of what I believe everyone was made for, which is, uh, a search for transcendent meaning, we call it God. Now if you say that has no place, then I feel that it is a diminishment of what it is to be a human, because to be human in the sense I believe humanity is directed because made by God, I think if you leave that out then you are not fully human.

This line of thought makes a simple mistake. There is a difference between being a member of a group and exercising all of the capacities that are exemplified by the members of that group. Consider a different human capacity: appreciating and enjoying music. This capacity is found across cultures and throughout human history, so we can safely say that it is a typical human capacity. However, there are particular people who don't care for music. These people don't sing, dance, listen, hum, whistle, etc. Music plays no role in their lives. Should we say that these people are not fully human because they don't care for music, and hence don't participate in the making or enjoyment of music? No. (See *Wholeness* for problems with the very idea of a full, complete, or whole life.)

In case you are inclined to doubt this, try it with a different capacity. Take the capacity for murder. As with music, this is found everywhere in human history, so it is a typical human capacity. Do we really want to say that murderers are more human than nonmurderers? I should think not.

To be a human does not require the exercise of all of the capacities which humans typically have. A more promising idea is that to be fully human, one must exercise the capacities that define us as human. Presumably this is more in line with what, for example, Cardinal O'Connor has in mind. The operative premise for those who deny full humanity to atheists is the idea that religiosity is at least partially definitive of what it is to be a human. (See *Religious Spirit [or, Religiosity; Religion in General; Religion in the Abstract]* for doubts about the very notion of "religiosity." O'Connor actually worries that atheists are less than human because of a neglect of the transcendent, so see *Transcendence*.) Is this true?

Here we find a deep problem. Religious thinkers and organizations who make this sort of claim are taking a stand on human nature. Do we have any reason to think that these people and groups are in a good position to illuminate the sort of thing we are? No. These people have not studied us in any principled way, so far as I can tell. They are typically experts in interpreting certain texts that make pronouncements about the nature of all sorts of things, but without any principled study of these things themselves. (See *Space Travellers* for thoughts about studying us and our place in the world.)

Just what is it to be a human? The word "human" is used in a variety of ways, so this question is deceptively simple in its appearance. However, if we are interested in our nature, then we ought to pay attention to "human" as the name of a species. Now the question is transformed: what is it for an organism to be a member of the human species? This isn't as easy to answer as one might think. There is an ongoing discussion involving biologists and philosophers about the notion of a species, with special concern about what it is for two organisms to be members of the same or of different species. There is no settled account of this, but here's a very rough look at the foremost idea. A species is a biological group that perpetuates itself through time via production of new individual organisms. This suggests that maintenance of the reproductive capacity that perpetuates the group is at the core of species membership. Two organisms are members of the same species when, under the appropriate conditions (such as health, maturity, appropriate sexuality) they are capable of producing living, reproductively viable offspring. That is, if two organisms can produce organisms who themselves can produce more offspring, then they are members of the same species. If they can't do this, then they belong to different species, regardless of how similar they are in other ways.

There are two lessons here, if this is at all correct. One is that very specific capacities, rather than generally typical ones, can be definitive of our nature, at least so far as our species is concerned. The second is that the exercise of these capacities might not matter at all to our nature. We are members of the human species if we possess these reproductive capacities, not if we exercise them. This is good news for the celibate, such as Catholic priests and nuns.

Generally speaking, when people make claims about the nature of the world, or about the nature of particular parts of the world, such as ourselves, we should ask about the grounds on which the claims are made. These grounds should include the right sort of study of the thing in question. Religious claims are almost never made on these grounds. These mistaken and, as we all know, dangerous remarks about religion and human nature are just one example.

Atheism: Lack of belief in a god, or doctrine that there is no god, in any literal and interesting sense. See *Godfree*.

Authority: (1) The say-so of the influential and why we believe much of what we believe. The foundation of religious belief for the vast majority of people is authority. They believe because others before them believed and have passed on their beliefs. This is tricky territory.

It's easy for atheists to bemoan the effects of authority on believers. "Why do they believe those crazy old books? Why do they follow those evil traditions? Why do they listen to the pope? Can't they see that everyone believes what their parents and neighbors believe, and there's nothing more to it than that! Open your eyes! Use your brains! Think for yourself and give it all up!" I feel the force of these frustrations.

However, I also feel for the ordinary believer. The thing is, for virtually all ordinary people, the facts about the nature of the world are received just as much on the basis of authority as religious myths. The big bang? Evolution? The nature of the basic constituents of the world? We can't just open our eyes and see these things. We need education and complicated instruments that most people don't have. So if they happen to believe the truth, very often it's on the basis of what some people whom they happen to trust have to say. It's on the basis of authority.

Authority is obviously no ground for the truth of ideas, at least for those about the nature of the world. Evolution is not true because living scientists or Charles Darwin say so; it's true because of the nature of the world, including the history of organisms. But authority can be a good shortcut for acquiring information. We can't do it all for ourselves, obviously, so we have to trust others to some extent. Authority is no damn good from one perspective, and unavoidable and clearly reasonable from another, and we can't help but occupy both perspectives.

One thing that can be done is to get people to be more careful about just whom to trust, at least with regard to particular topics. Scientists should be trusted authorities about scientific topics and not about other ones. Where clerics disagree with scientists on the topics of scientific expertise, follow the reasonable authority.

A related thing to do is to teach people not just the facts that science reveals, but also appreciation of the scientific method (see *Science* for more). The hard work that goes into finding out about the nature of the world goes a long way toward demonstrating why scientists should be seen as reasonable authorities about the nature of the world.

Still, even if these things are done, ordinary people are going to have to take a lot of science on the basis of scientific authority, and this leaves them open to failing to see the difference between what scientists say and what clerics, old books, and their neighbors say. Can anything else be done?

I think so, but it requires a change of focus. Understandably, much of the disagreement between the godfree and believers concerns the nature of the world. Roughly put, atheists think that nature is all that there is, while believers add a supernatural realm to this (for more see *Evidence, Order, Soul,* and *Supernatural*). Besides this, however, there is also disagreement about how we ought to live, and here we find a chance for people really to use their own minds and earn for themselves grounds for belief distinct from those of authority. This is the domain of moral philosophy, and here no special equipment is needed.

Here is how this works. Religious texts, traditions, and spokespeople typically offer moral directives. Don't kill (except for animals, or witches, or unbelievers, or murderers . . .), don't steal (except for the property of the defeated, of nonbelievers . . .), and so on. Some of this is recognizably good advice, some is pretty bad, and some is trickier to figure out. Crucially, this is the sort of thing that people can reason about for themselves. Suppose that a religion portrays women as second-class people, as many do. This is worth questioning, especially if you are a woman. What reasons are offered for believing this? How do those reasons measure up to what you know from being a woman and from being around women? Advice premised on manifest falsehoods should be ignored. The importance of such scrutiny goes, however, for every piece of moral advice offered by religion. Even when they get it right, this does not necessarily redound to their credit, for they might get it right for the wrong reasons.

It should not automatically be assumed that reasoning about values is antireligious, although with regard to some traditions it certainly is. Some faiths invite reasoning, and such reasoning has uncovered some important things. Let's give credit where it's due. Still, such reasoning often will be antireligious. It will certainly be opposed to any religion that insists on faith as opposed to reason, as well as to any position that casts reason as itself a kind of faith (see *Faith vs. Reason* for discussion). But really, can this sort of antireason position plausibly be maintained? The demand is to stop thinking about precisely those topics that seem to matter the most. Screw that, to put it kindly.

Thinking through religious directives about values does three things. First, it calls into question religious authority about these issues. Second, and more importantly, it should help to establish just what is valuable and in just what ways we should live, regardless of what religions have to say about this. There are no guarantees here—see *Morality (or, On Loving the Good with and without God)* for some difficulties—but really, there are no shortcuts to be had here, nor even to be wanted.

Finally, and perhaps most interestingly, once religious authority about values is weakened, the same should go for what religions have to say about the general nature of the world. Suppose that religions provide a lot of dubious or even incorrect moral advice, as seems often to be the case. Why then should we think that what these religions have to say about the nature of the world is any better? The grounds of the pronouncements are the same in both cases: texts, old stories, the words of supposed authorities, everything but much actual examination of the topics at hand. Maybe this is unfair with regard to religion and morality. Maybe, but not definitely. It is definitely not unfair to religion with regard to the nature of the world. The right kind of investigation has manifestly not been done here. Once people loosen the grip of religion on values, the general religious view of the world ought to follow.

In retrospect, maybe this is not surprising. A lot of people lose their religion over concerns that a just and loving god could not do the things that happen in front of their eyes and that their clerics attribute to Him. Fair enough. This is actually a mistake—see *Evil as a Reason to Reject God* for discussion—but it's certainly understandable.

Still, this will be surprising to many. It has become vaguely fashionable to attribute to science authority over the nature of the world and to let religion have authority over values. Stephen Jay Gould famously held a version of this position. It's ironic that the wind actually seems to blow the other way: people can hone their reasoning skills with regard to values better than they can with regard to the topics of science, and after this religion's grip will be fatally weakened. Moral reasoning is the best road to the godfree life, not an education in the truths delivered by science, although that is a close second and well worth having. No wonder that the god of Genesis forbids eating of the tree of knowledge of good and evil. He knew better than many that such a meal would dispel his smoke and mirrors.

(2) Although individual people are faced with authorities of various kinds—scientific, religious, and so on—this does not mean that they are also faced with institutions that rely on authority in just the same ways. As with other topics we can distinguish between individual and institutional stances with regard to authority (see *Humility* as another example). Ordinary people with other concerns and domains of expertise might accept Catholicism on the Pope's authority and evolution by natural selection on Charles Darwin's. This is hardly to be avoided. But what about the respective institutions? How do science and religion on the whole represent the role of authority?

Religion tends to enshrine it as the foundation of belief. Divine texts, mystical experiences, the thoughts of supposed prophets are all among the typical foundations of religious edifices. Religion rests on dubious appeals to authority, one way or another.

Science is different. Authority has no special role here. As noted, evolution is not true because Charles Darwin, or anyone else, says so. It's true because of the way the world is. The basis for this belief is accessible to anyone who studies the right stuff. There are no privileged authorities about this topic, or any other. Reality does not play favorites.

The initial appearances are merely that, appearances—superficial and not indicative of the facts. Religion tends to rest on dubious appeals to authority, while the institution of science eschews such appeals. Again, this is something that could be better conveyed through science education than it currently is, and which would go some little way toward shoring up respect for science and doubt about religion. See *Science*.

2

B Is for . . .

Basics: There is lots of complex stuff out there about god and gods. Some of it is very old, some of it is being produced by our contemporaries. There are also lots of equally complicated responses to these arguments. Moreover, if you are really interested in the nature of the world, you must reckon with the mathematical complexities of ongoing physics and cosmology. At least these, and other things too. Phew! (If you are interested in these details, you will have to *Pick Up a Textbook*).

It is reasonable to think that figuring out the truths about the issues that these bodies of thought address requires some attention to these complicated details. I say that this is reasonable, but that's not the whole story. The devils (and the gods and whatever else) are not just in these complex details. I'm inclined to think that much more basic issues are more important than many people seem to think. Carelessness about basics dooms the most complex of theories. Some very complex intellectual edifices are built on nothing better than sand; the complex details do nothing to shore up the weaknesses in the foundations. Attending to these details might teach us something, but the real lessons are to be found by paying attention to the basics that have gone awry.

In this spirit, I stick largely to basics. It is very important—again, more important than many realize—to achieve clarity at the very first steps of inquiry into big issues. Only when we have such clarity in hand will we know which complex details are worth attending to and which are the empty, fantastical elaborations of journeys that started out on the wrong foot.

You think that your kind of faith might be an exception, one to which the basics don't apply? Maybe. See *Exceptions* and think twice.

Beauty: The world is beautiful in many ways. There is nothing supernatural about this, and no need to invoke gods to explain it. Religious worldviews in some ways draw our attention to this beauty and then, by casting it in supernatural light, distort it. For more, see *Enchantment*. The godfree are in the best possible position to appreciate the beauty that the world offers all by itself.

Belief and Doubt: (1) Some people are convinced believers. Some are convinced atheists. In between are various degrees of conviction, with regard to both belief and doubt. These intermediate positions deserve some attention, as it's easy to focus just on the poles of this spectrum.

First, consider a person who, if asked, would describe herself as a believer. She goes to church and takes part in related activities. However, she finds the religious doctrine to which she is exposed very hard to believe. She knows things about the nature of the world on other grounds and finds both church traditions and sacred texts difficult to take literally. Bluntly put, she finds the hocus-pocus stuff off-putting. Let's call this person a "doubting believer."

The godfree should be happy about the existence of doubting believers. Many of us counted as doubting believers at some time. Such a person is willing to think critically about the claims that at least some religions make about the world. This is a good thing, both generally and from the more specific perspective of atheism. But there is another reason that the godfree should welcome and give more attention to doubting believers. These people remind us of the many facets of religion. Doctrine is only one part of what religion gives to people. It also gives community, structure, emotional satisfaction, perhaps other things, and these are not trivial matters. They might not be redeeming matters—this is an issue for which the details matter, I think—but they should not be overlooked. Doubting believers separate these aspects of religion in their own lives, and the godfree should be attentive to these nuanced details.

Second, consider a person who considers himself an atheist. At the same time, he expresses admiration for religious impulses in general and sometimes says that he wishes to believe. This person dreams of a rational religion—a way of living a religious life without commitment to false or dubiously supernatural claims about the nature of the world (see *Science* and *Supernatural*). He imagines a future in which informed people can speak of god directly without embarrassment and without betraying ignorance of the nature of the world. Let's call such a person a "doubter who wishes to believe."

Can such people have their cake and eat it too? What is left of religion if we shear it of its supernatural aspects? I suspect not much, but maybe I'm wrong. It's understandable that people might want the community, structure, emotional satisfaction, etc. that religions offer many people. However, it's a mistake, so far as I can see, for doubters to wish to rehabilitate religion in order to get these things. You wish for community? Join a bowling club, or a musical appreciation society, or a group that goes to local restaurants every month, or all of these and more. You wish for structure for your life? These groups can provide this as well, but so can other things. If your job does not suffice, join a gym, or buy a season's pass to the theater, or make a point of going to hear bands at a local bar every Wednesday. Structure is cheap and easy to come by.

Emotional satisfaction is trickier. This will depend on your tastes. Some of you might need church, or something like it. Fair enough, but it's a mistake to think that all of us need this (see *Anxieties*). I don't. Others don't. We have looked around and found other ways to address our emotional needs. It's a failure of imagination and effort to think that religious participation offers emotional benefits that other aspects of life cannot deliver.

Besides all of this, the doubter who wishes to believe is an uncomfortable figure for the convinced godfree. Such a person seems not to get it. He appears to think that there is something respectable about the idea of god (or the soul, or the transcendent, and so on; see *God [or, Gods], Soul*, and *Transcendence*) that the convinced godfree person misses. Maybe there is, but I doubt it. In a sense the doubter who wishes to believe is more of a believer than the doubting believer. The doubter who wishes to believe is, at least in some forms, untroubled by the vocabulary and even the basic ideas of religion. The doubting believer, however, finds these very things difficult to swallow. The doubter who wishes to believe seeks an acceptable form for these things. The doubting believer's patience with these things is wearing thin. The doubting believer is headed toward disbelief; the doubter who wishes to believe is headed toward belief. This is not something that the godfree generally wish to see happen.

There is a third stance to consider. Lots of people profess no attachments to organized religions of any kind. They belong to no churches and cherish no particular doctrines. At the same time, their ideas of the nature of the world are suffused with religious ideas. When asked they will say that they believe in a god of some nonspecific sort. They think that they have souls, whatever this might mean (see *Soul*). They emphasize the importance of an admittedly vague spiritual component of life. Let's call these people "nonreligious believers."

Nonreligious believers signal a failure for both religion and, even more so, the godfree. Since these people belong to no specific church, and since they might not be attracted to churchly life at all, religions have failed these people. But since they automatically take seriously religious concepts as structuring the way they think about themselves and the nature of the world, atheists have failed them even more. We have failed to convey to such people both an accurate view of the nature of the world and some sense of the attractions of godfree living. To use a metaphor that only poorly fits this issue: we may have won this particular battle, but we're losing the war. Nonreligious believers are a sobering reminder of the hold that religious ideas have on many people. I am discomfited by nonreligious believers. I am more comfortable with doubting believers. As with doubters who wish to believe, nonreligious believers seem not to get it. They might as well be people who go to church; such is the extent that religious categories have on their view of the world.

Obviously, I don't know the mindsets of the people who are reading this book, but I find it attractive to imagine myself communicating, first and foremost, to doubting believers. You are questioners, more so than doubters who wish to believe and nonreligious believers, and this is the stance that fits the godfree life most easily. If a questioning attitude can be awakened, then I imagine nonreligious believers to be a secondary audience for this book. Welcome: I hope that there is something here for you. I hold out the least hope for doubters who wish to believe. I do not share their motivations, which strike me as a serious obstacle to a clear view of the world and themselves. Since they wish to believe, they seem to be actively working against the intellectual humility that the godfree life requires (see *Humility*, *Ignorance*, and *You*).

(2) We often speak ambiguously when we declare our religious beliefs. It is important, for mutual respect and understanding, that the religious and the godfree realize and become more careful about this.

The ambiguities in question don't always arise with other sorts of topic. When I say, "I believe in ghosts," we all know what I mean: I believe that ghosts exist. By contrast, if a person says, "I believe in the prime minister," we all know that existence is not what this person has in mind. They mean that they endorse the prime minister. The declaration of this belief serves to indicate what team the person plays on. To use a bit of jargon: where the essential job of the first declaration of belief is descriptive, the job of the second is instead evaluative.

The rejections of these different sorts of belief accordingly imply different things. To reject a belief in ghosts is to deny a claim about existence. This denial does not imply any evaluation of the very idea of ghosts. One can equally happily or sadly reject their existence by claiming, "I don't believe in ghosts." But rejection of the other sort of belief is, necessarily, to evaluate. When you avow your faith in the government and I reply, "I don't believe in the prime minister," you know what I mean: we have different views about what is good for the country. Politically speaking, we play on different teams. Crucially, we both know that the prime minister exists, and that I am not, for some odd reason, denying this.

Whatever else it is in the particular forms that it takes, atheism is above all a denial of the existence of god. Both the religious and the godfree would do well to keep this in mind. Atheism itself implies nothing about the worthiness of the idea of god. One can be, for instance, a sad atheist. From this perspective, those who believe in god have a beautiful fantasy which is, unfortunately, not true of the world. Alternatively, one can be an unhappy theist. This person thinks that there is a god but wishes that there wasn't, because he's such a bad thing.

Assertion of belief, or of lack of belief, can seem like evaluation of the value of the object of belief. I suppose that careless assertion of belief does involve such evaluation. However, there is no reason to be careless about these issues, and there is lots of reason to be careful. One can clearly deny the existence of god without implying that the religious have committed themselves to an unworthy idea (however, see *Truth [or, Truths]* for complicating considerations). Hurt feelings can be avoided and good relationships can be preserved if both the religious and the godfree become more careful about separating existence claims from assessment of the value of what is said to be or not to be.

Of course, lots of actual atheists both think that there is no god and that the gods that are offered by actual religions are bad ones. I think this, as a matter of fact. But the crucial thing is that, by and large, while one class of considerations applies to the question of the existence of gods, a different class applies to their evaluation.

Believers (or, My Sisters and Brothers in Disbelief): Although it's common to divide people into (roughly speaking) two groups, atheists and theists, believers and nonbelievers, this isn't correct. As Richard Dawkins has taken pains to emphasize, there are instead people who disbelieve in all gods and there are people who disbelieve in almost all. No one believes in all gods. For one thing, there are thousands, maybe millions, on offer in human history, and no one is interested in all of them to the extent of believing in them all. For another thing, it's conceptually impossible to believe in gods that purport to be alone in their divinity and, simultaneously, in other gods. So: we all disbelieve. The theism/atheism issue is not about belief versus disbelief. It's about the scope of disbelief: should we believe in some particular god or gods, or should we disbelieve in all rather than nearly all? For thoughts about first steps with regard to these issues see *Who Bears the Burden of Argument?*

There's irony here. It goes in and out of fashion for theists to claim that atheism is, somehow, a religion, and in particular to claim that faith is unavoidable, whether it's in a god or gods or instead in the power of reason or science to reveal the nature of the world. The claim is mistaken (see *Faith vs. Reason*). "Faith," so far as I can tell, is just another word for "belief." The irony is that the truth is exactly opposite to this sort of claim. Instead of belief being unavoidable, it's disbelief that is unavoidable. We are all, to greater or lesser extent, atheists. The departure from the baseline is made by the believer, not the disbeliever.

Bigness: There is a curious turn of phrase that religious believers sometimes use in conversation with nonbelievers. They might use it among themselves too, but its natural home seems to be to prompt nonbelievers into a kind of reflection. "Don't you ever have a sense of something bigger than yourself?" is the question I have in mind. This is not a polite inquiry, even if it is politely offered. An affirmative answer is supposed to require god, meaning that you, the nonbeliever, have simply and obviously been wrong in your atheism. A negative answer casts one as a narcissist.

It's a curious question because people so often take it seriously without thinking about it. The godfree should feel free to give affirmative answers to this question without a shadow of a doubt. No gods lurk in this territory, once we think about it. The oddity of this parlance lies in the combination of the fact that everyone thinks they understand what it means—everyone thinks it points toward god—with the fact that its literal and obvious interpretations point to nothing godly at all.

As a first interpretation, take the question as bluntly literally as possible. "Big" refers to size. Well, as a medium-sized physical object, there's lots that's bigger than a person. Take me as a pretty representative example: my car is bigger than me, as is my house. My neighbor is bigger than me. A very boring list can easily be compiled for any person.

Clearly the question is not meant literally. Maybe it is instead to be taken as an evaluative query: "Don't you recognize anything more important than yourself?" But of course atheists can say "yes" here. The needs of the many, for instance, can easily be recognized as collectively more important than the needs of one, such as myself. But besides such aggregative answers, we can hold up particular and very familiar ideals. Justice, for instance. Or truth: many of us are attracted to godfree lives out of a sense that this is where the truth lies. Such lives are often uncomfortable due to the biases of the religious. Nevertheless, we reject our own comfort, to some degree, in order to orient our lives with the nature of the world. Truth matters, and we can recognize this, even at our own expense.

All of this interprets importance in a fairly objective sense, but we can opt for less grand and more subjective options here too. Many believers and nonbelievers alike structure their lives only partly around themselves. They also devote themselves to other people with whom they have interpersonal relationships. Consider a devoted mother who would sacrifice herself for her child, or a devoted companion who would sacrifice himself for his partner. Both of these people at least implicitly recognize another person as more important, by their own lights, than themselves.

It's possible that the question is meant to get us to think about our own experiences and what they might show. "Don't you ever feel overwhelmed, euphoric, even ecstatic about the grandeur and beauty of the world? And what do you make of that? Surely god?" For present purposes, there is no reason for the godfree to lack experiences of wonder and euphoria. The world is awesomely beautiful in places. Some works of art are breathtaking. Why should we not shed tears, or break up in delighted laughter, or feel our hearts race in the presence of such beauty? This is how beauty works: by engaging our thoughts and feelings in these recognizable ways. The interpretation of these experiences in terms of god is unnecessary. In fact it's often erroneous. To attribute the wonder of some beauties even to religious ideas, never mind to the divine realm itself, will be a mistake when those works were not designed for religious purposes. This holds equally for the Rockies and the Beatles' "Paperback Writer." St. Peter's Basilica should be understood in a religious context, but the extension of this interpretive stance to all human ecstasy is a mistake. See *Enchantment*.

Finally, maybe the question is sometimes meant to have a pointedly moral meaning: "Do you think of yourself as the measure of right and wrong?" There is no reason that the godfree are forced to answer "yes" here—see *Morality (or, On Loving the Good with and without God)*. Lurking here is, at least in part, the widely held yet mistaken view that rightness and god are inextricably linked. Once we give this up, we can see that atheists are free to recognize things bigger than themselves in virtually any interesting sense without opening themselves up to charges of conceptual incoherence and the return of religion to their lives.

I say "virtually" any interesting sense. I'm allowing that one meaning of this question might be, "Don't you really (*really* really, in your heart, in the middle of the night, when your worldly troubles and the fact of your mortality creep up on you) believe in god?" I don't think that this is typically what is meant by this question. Its rhetorical point seems to be to lead us to god indirectly, via a commitment to something else, only roughly gestured to as "the big." But if we do allow this question to be understood as a clumsy probe into the sincerity of our atheism, then we should offer a negative answer. To be clear, we should not offer just a negative answer, lest we risk being misunderstood. "Don't you ever have a sense of something bigger than yourself?" "Yes, but not of god."

Here is a suggestion to the religious: don't ask this question, as it is unflattering to you. If taken literally, it suggests a serious lack of basic awareness of your surroundings. You must surely recognize all the things that are literally bigger than you and literally right in front of your eyes. (Surely?) If we take it evaluatively, the question suggests a dearth of imagination and maybe even a worrying misunderstanding of values on your part. Do you really think that the godfree don't experience beauty? Do you really think that we can value nothing other than ourselves? Take a look around and you'll discover otherwise. If anything, the question suggests that the questioner, by her own standards, is kept from embracing some sort of narcissism or solipsism only by the belief in god. I find it hard to believe that religious believers are really as insensitive to the significance of justice, truth, beauty, and the like as to need religious belief to ensure that they abide by their demands, but this is what the question suggests. If this is the wrong impression for the godfree to have, then ask a different question, one that adequately conveys the real issue.

Bless You (or, God Bless You): A form of well-wishing, most commonly said to someone who has just sneezed. Innocuous.

Atheists who feel compelled to say something when another person sneezes should feel free to use "Bless You." Why might we feel so compelled? Habit, mostly. There is a long history of such comments across many cultures. Perhaps sneezing is so noticeable and so significant as a possible sign of illness that practices of wishing people well after a sneeze have tended to arise wherever people live together. Such comments tend to be either religious or health-related.

Why is "Bless You" so innocuous? When these words are used after a sneeze, they are hardly ever meant literally. The intentions of the speaker are rarely, if ever, particularly religious. This means that, despite their religious content, there is no sneaky proselytizing at work in such utterances. The words could be swapped out for health-related ones stripped of all religious words without offending anyone.

Sometimes "Bless You" is used not in connection with sneezes but when people part. In this context it seems to mean something like "Have A Nice Day" and, as in the case of its use with sneezes, it is pretty innocuous. It's not *equally* innocuous, however. This usage is more likely to be meant literally. The godfree would never use these words in this way, except as a habit or a veil in very specific locations. This usage can be expected to make us less comfortable, but so be it. It's pretty harmless, on par with "Merry Christmas." See *Merry Christmas! (or, Happy Christmas!, for Those of a British Background)*.

Let's admit that this is not very important. At the same time, it's an interesting example of the ways in which religious ideas and habits pervade our culture. To become an atheist tends to involve having your relation to this sort of hidden godliness changed, for better and for worse.

Bodies: While most familiar religions now focus on the soul or spirit, roughly meaning our minds, so far as I can tell (see *Soul*), there is a long history of religious attention to the body. Judeo-Christian tradition actually calls for the literal resurrection of bodies, as if souls must be embodied. Contemporary faiths tend to downplay this, more or less, but the idea is worth some attention.

What should we think of the idea that we might be resurrected after death through the reanimation of our bodies? There is an obvious source of initial appeal to this idea. After all, we all know that persons are intricately tied to bodies, to put it mildly. There are important senses in which we are our bodies, by normal standards. So far, so good for the idea of bodily resurrection.

The initial appeal runs out here, however. The reason is that there are also normal standards, just as reasonable, which dissociate us from our bodies. For instance, we all know that bodies change, and not all of these changes involve changes in the respective persons. Suppose that you get a haircut: your body has changed, but, presumably, you have not. This implies that persons are not literally identical with bodies. (For an intellectual exercise, check your intuitions about whether persons change when other bodily features change: when you cut your toenails, when you have moles removed, when you lose limbs to disease or accident, when you suffer from Alzheimer's, and so on).

This is a good thing, really. We all know now that the fundamental constituents of our bodies change greatly over the course of our lives. Our cells multiply and are replaced; the atoms that compose these cells also change. So we are, quite literally, made of different stuff over the course of our lives (even if we never lose our limbs or have our hair cut). Yet we all recognize personal continuity in the face of this fundamental change. This means that there is more than one normal body per person. This obviously complicates any view that insists on personal resurrection through bodily reanimation.

This is not the end of the problems. Some of this material has been part of prior persons. Think of oxygen being inhaled, used to form body parts, then finding itself back in the atmosphere to be inhaled again. And again, and so on. Not only is there more than one normal body per person, over time there is more than one person per part of bodily stuff.

What this all means is that just what counts as "my body" is a lot more complex than a first thought suggests. Certainly given the normal ways in which we speak of our bodies, there is no one thing that counts as "my body." But with this goes the literal possibility of resurrection of people via the resurrection of our bodies. Perhaps bodies could be resurrected, but they will not line up with the persons who have inhabited the earth.

Now, I have addressed all of this as if the resurrection of the body involved the resurrection of persons—that is, of beings with mental lives, not just bodies. Maybe this is gratuitous. Maybe the respective religious traditions could insist on the resurrection just of bodies, with no assumption that persons would be brought back with them. It's an odd view—resurrection would bring to life zombies of the sort found in the movies and on television, not normal human persons—but religions are odd top to bottom, so perhaps this is no objection. Regardless, such a view gets us off the hook with regard to caring about religion—see *Soul* for discussion.

Thankfully none of this really matters, of course: there is no good reason to take seriously the resurrection of bodies or persons (or souls, or whatever). However, the difficulties that we encounter once we scrutinize the relevant ideas are important. They stand as good examples of the fact that many ideas that seem coherent or simple aren't nearly so simple, or even coherent at all, once we try to determine how they actually work. Given the lack of reflection that goes into many people's views about religion, this is ripe territory for such shadowy difficulties.

Bright: An ill-fated term developed in the early twenty-first century as an attempt to find a new and attractive synonym for "atheist." The effort backfired. See *Godfree.*

Bullshit: Thanks to Harry Frankfurt, there is now a technical definition of bullshit. It's speaking without concern for the truth or falsity of what you say. Note how this is different from lying: it is important to the liar to speak falsely and to conceal the truth. The bullshitter, by contrast, does not care whether what is said is true or false.

I think that there is more bullshit in religion than lying (see *Lies*). There can be no doubt that religion can lead to, or at least be coupled with, carelessness about truth: see *Humility* and *Truth (or, Truths)* for discussion. Still, bullshit is not the overwhelming tenor of religious discourse, at least to my ear. The pronouncements of typical believers ring of sincerity, even if they are divorced from proper care for truth. See *Sincerity.*

3

C Is for . . .

Certainty: An unreliable feeling, worth distrusting, even shunning. See *Uncertainty.*

Children's Education: Many think that children should be exposed to religion, somehow. Some people think that it's good for children. It's not uncommon for people to return to regular church attendance once they start families. Is this line of thought true? Should children be taught about religion? If so, how?

The godfree have no compelling religious reason to expose children to religion. Even those nonbelievers who attend church lack this: their own reasons for attending church are not religious, after all (see *Belief and Doubt*).

There is no moral reason to teach children about religion (see *Morality [or, On Loving the Good with and without God]*). Moreover, we have moral reasons not to indoctrinate them. Children are impressionable—a fact capitalized on by religious groups interested in shaping children's minds for their own ends. To immerse them in sincere avowal of ideas about faith and the supernatural is not only to give them false ideas about the nature of the world and about values—about the true and the good—it is also to point them away from the habits of thought and hard skills that are needed in order to learn about these things. This is surely of consequence.

Still, there are reasons to teach children about religion. Some are historical. In order to understand the emergence of civilization, we need to know about religion. Other reasons are civic, and follow from our history. Our governmental institutions have developed in a more or less religious context, and in at least some respects understanding these institutions benefits from familiarity with religion.

Still other reasons are civil. The people around us take part in religions. To understand them, in both good and bad respects, we should know about their religious beliefs and practices.

So: children should know about religion because of the kind of social world in which they find themselves. That's it. There is no deeper reason, having to do with morality or self-actualization or anything else, to teach religion to children.

Churches (or, Buildings for Worship of Gods): There are lots of these in the world. Some are wonderful, architecturally and aesthetically speaking. Others are banal or even awful. Regardless, does atheism require the destruction of these places of worship? After all, the godfree have no use for worship and its objects. But the answer is no, of course not.

Why would the buildings be spared their scorn? For lots of reasons. A godfree life neither requires nor even recommends the destruction of churches. They can be put to lots of uses other than the worship of supernatural beings. I like the idea of turning them into movie theaters since there is an old movie theater in my neighborhood that is used as a church—turnaround is fair play, after all. But my tastes don't have to settle the issue. Let's preserve the best ones as examples of ideas now given up and as imaginative and constructive achievements that are hard to match. Turn others into concert halls, or condominiums, or museums. Use your imagination. There's no need to waste them and lots of reason to use them in godfree ways, perhaps even more than we use them now. I suppose that we might as well raze the particularly ugly and hard to use ones, but imaginative effort could deliver reasons to preserve even those structures.

Some will find even this nondestructive godfree approach insufficiently respectful of these buildings. I'm of two minds about the amount of respect due to these places, which is why I take an open attitude toward their preservation as, well, something. Yes, religion can embody much that is admirable about us: our best motives, for instance. And churches are the places where these motives are recognized and even turned into action. But religion also embodies our worst aspects: our irrationality, found in belief, fear, and certain actions, for instance. And churches are the places where *this* is enacted. The good deserves respect, the bad does not. Let's call it a draw and insist on neither the curator's unchanging hand nor the wrecking ball for these buildings.

Community: We are social animals, so good communities, both big and small, are needed for us to live good lives. Many find this in church, such that leaving these churches would make their lives worse. That's a real cost of atheism. It's no defense of religious ideas, of course, and this points to the solution to the problem. Atheists can and should value communities, for our own good. If we do not belong to religious groups, either informal or institutionalized, we should find others. Join a gardening club. A theater group. A band. A club devoted to one of your favorite foods. A book club . . . need I go on?

Some atheists want their own churches. To me this sounds . . . awful, but to each their own. Tastes dictate to a large degree what sorts of communities will benefit us.

Note: the power of communities can also be bad for us, as we all know. Getting some distance from others, and from the practices and ideas that bond and bind them, can often be good. Since, to date, there are no significant godfree churches with which to replace the religious ones, it is wise to approach a life of atheism with an expectation of taking responsibility for one's own life. This isn't just prudent, it's fitting—see *Adults*.

Control: My impression is that many people seek religious help, either from gods or from their worldly representatives, when facing issues that are out of their control. Illness, loss, the mere results of a sporting competition— it's all the subject of prayers, of pleas for help, even for direct intervention by angels and demons.

Fair enough: it's discomfiting to face a loss of control at the best of times, and these pleas are often made at the worst. Who would chastise the desire for help at the bleakest of hours? Not me.

As blameless as the urge to ask for divine help might be, the ideas that support, even foster, such requests are more dubious. Are we really to believe that god, the universe, ultimate reality, or whatever, cares so much not just about humans but also about *me* that intervention in my difficulties can reasonably be requested just for the asking? Or just for the leading of a particular kind of life? Hubris!

The godfree life offers no solace here. The universe does not care about us. From this perspective we are insignificant. There is nothing other than other people to ask for help when facing challenges. This is cold comfort, of course, but such is the humility to which the godfree are committed, in principle if not in reality (see *Humility* and *You*). Life is not meaningless, of course, which we all know outside of our darkest moments (see *Tragedy [or, Despair about the Meaning of Life], Irony [and Meaning in Life],* and *Absurdity [and Meaning in Life]*). But it is not meaningful because of our grand significance in the universal scheme of things. More down to earth things account for the value in our lives.

Some things really are out of our control. It's natural to wish for any help that might be out there. Still, it's arrogant to think that we matter in such an ultimate way that the universe might be bent to our aid through requests to a divine will. It is humility to recognize otherwise.

Cult: I cannot see any differences between organized religions and cults. I don't mean this as a compliment to so-called cults.

I can imagine someone appealing to the means of transmission and maintenance of doctrines and habits to distinguish religions from cults. Cults undermine or avoid rational evaluation of their central ideas, so the argument would go, whereas religions transmit their beliefs in ways open to rational criticism.

There's something to this if we take a long look at the history of organized religions. Picture scholastic monks bent over old manuscripts and you see something like rational scrutiny of doctrine. But the view from inside a church, in my experience, bears little resemblance to this academic past. Put aside emotional blackmail effected both by parishioners and by church officials, which is common enough, and consider instead singing, chanting, and repetition, as performed both by adults and children. The deep point, as I see it, of these aspects of church life is to inculcate and reinforce ideas in ways that circumvent and perhaps even subvert rational criticism.

Suppose, however, that this argument distinguishing religions from cults is correct. It would imply that the possession and scrutiny of beliefs, such as that there is a god, is central to religious life. Yet this is something that many deny (see *Practical Religion*). Instead of belief, so it is sometimes claimed, religion is a matter of doing, of habit, of practice, of emotional engagement. To focus on belief is to miss the point, from this perspective. Fine, but this erodes the present case for distinguishing religions from cults. Either rational scrutiny of belief is central, which opens up religion to the familiar problems plaguing arguments for the existence of god, or it's not, making religions indistinguishable from cults by the standards of defenders of religion itself. It can't be both ways.

4

D Is for . . .

Death: Many find in religion a balm for the fear of death. I suspect that many hold onto religious ideas only because of this fear. This deserves a second thought.

First, no real salve can be provided by those religions that promise hell after death. I'm inclined to think that people who would prefer eternal torture to nonexistence aren't thinking clearly. Some will turn to religion out of a hope for paradise rather than hell, but this is to ask from religion a solution to a problem that it generates, not to one that just happens to be there. There is no reason to think that hell awaits other than on religious grounds. This, of course, is both intellectually dubious and morally reprehensible. Bullies, boo! (see *Heaven, Hell,* and *Paradise [Fool's; or, Whatever Gets You through the Night]*)

Second, whether death is bad needs some analysis. There are longstanding bodies of thought, both religious and godfree, which hold that it is not. Putting this aside, the fear of death for many, it seems to me, stems from a combination of a fear of change, which is a pretty common aspect of human life, and a fear of nothingness. Since fear of change is familiar, let's focus on nothingness. This in itself is not lamentable, if it's taken to mean lack of experience. Experienceless sleep is not a blight; it's very nice, if you ask me. Moreover, no one, so far as I know, begrudges the nothingness that came before they were born. It's only subsequent nothingness that bothers people, which is why I combine this issue with fear of change to account for worries about death. If nothingness before birth is not problematic, neither is nothingness after death.

This all suggests that, if we put aside spurious visions of hell and the lack of a problem that is nothingness, the issue that bothers people is the idea of coming to an end, not the state in which one ends up. Tastes will differ here, but this is something that can be faced calmly. To become godfree is, in part, to cultivate humility and acceptance of one's own finitude (see *Humility* and *You*). This takes away much of the sting of the idea of death. In other words: get over yourself and stop thinking that your existence matters in the grand scheme of things. Egomaniac!

This does not mean, of course, that there is nothing to live for and that we might as well embrace death earlier rather than later. See *Meaning of Life, Irony (and Meaning in Life), Tragedy (or, Despair about the Meaning of Life),* and *Absurdity (and Meaning in Life)* for details.

5

E Is for . . .

———————

Enchantment: Literally a feeling—of awe, of wonder. But some religiously inclined people think that a world with a supernatural dimension is enchanted. On this basis, specifically religious versions of the feeling of enchantment are warranted. By contrast, a godfree world is, in this sense, disenchanted. These people consider this a loss and lament our modern lack of enchantment, even sometimes calling for the reenchantment of the world through greater religiosity.

This idea, however, does not work. Suppose that one is enchanted by a beautiful natural vista. The Mediterranean glistens before you; the Rocky Mountains tower over you: it feels wondrous, and the feeling calls out for explanation. To what am I responding with such sublime feelings? Suppose that the answer offered is that it's the hand of god in his worldly creation. The operating assumption seems to be that the world we encounter cannot be, itself, beautiful or meaningful. Instead its beauty, and our enchantment by it, must be explained by something else, which in this case is a particular understanding of the divine.

As an explanation of the source of our enchantment, this answer fails. The reason is that our original question recurs with the answer. We are enchanted by our understanding of the divine. What, however, makes *this* beautiful, meaningful? If we insist on seeking our answer somewhere else—not in the ocean or the mountain in the first case, not in the divine in the second—then a never-ending progression of answers threatens. Such a series never amounts to an answer after all because the original question keeps recurring.

Here is the issue: if, for a feeling of enchantment with something, we insist on citing something else to explain it, then we always fail in our explanatory attempts. Something must be, itself, legitimately enchanting for our explanatory questions to be answered. But if this is the case, then the right answer to our question might well be that the thing itself is enchanting—the ocean, the mountains, and so—and not an underlying supernatural contribution.

Here is a quick godfree account of awe in something natural. It's the fit of the world with our worldly, human sensibilities, delivered by the natural processes that have produced us within this world, which deliver experiences of beauty. Natural selection has set us up to be sensitive to certain ways that things look. The distant reasons for such sensitivity are reproduction and survival. We have to recognize threats and opportunities if we want to live and have children. But the effect of having these capabilities is interest—yes, even enchantment—with things that we find around us. These sensitivities are flexible, so we can develop our tastes for colors, shapes, and their arrangements through experience and effort. We can lack these sensibilities or have failed to sharpen them and consequently be insensitive to what the world offers (just as, presumably, we might be if there were such a thing as spiritual beauty). To think otherwise is, maybe, wishful thinking, or just the mistake of searching for an explanation of enchantment in the wrong place.

See *Irony (and Meaning in Life), Tragedy (or, Despair about the Meaning of Life),* and *Absurdity (and Meaning in Life)* for more along these lines.

Eternal: Never ending. Good sometimes but not always. The godfree tend not to be hung up about whether things last forever.

Some religious belief and practice is aimed at worship of the eternal. Sometimes this is posited as a property of a personal god, sometimes it is offered as worthy of worship all on its own. For instance, some religious believers aren't particularly interested in gods. Instead they offer "ultimate reality" as their object of worship, and one of the supposedly good things about this is its eternal nature in comparison to the finite and changing things that we encounter in our normal but superficial reality. (For doubts about these notions, see *Reality [or, Realities].*) The deep assumption seems to be that things that begin and end are necessarily poorer than things that persist. This, however, is pretty dubious.

Let's start with the obvious cases. Things that are bad are better for being temporary rather than eternal. Eternity makes them worse, not better. This is precisely the point with many visions of eternal damnation: it's so awful because it's eternal, not better.

The same goes for neutral things: stretching their duration can make them worse, not better. Consider lectures (or sermons, if you are so inclined) as examples. Surely the details need not be spelled out here.

Perhaps good things are improved if they are eternal. However, that this must be the case is not obvious. Consider good experiences. Extending these (as with neutral things) can make them worse, not better: we get bored, our attention wanders, and what was once good is good no longer precisely because it has been made lengthier. Consider books that you have read or movies that you have sat through. Some of these would indeed benefit from being extended, but not all of them. Many books and movies would benefit from trimming.

Good experiences in general cannot be improved by making them eternal. For this to be the case, human nature would have to change. As we are now, good things tend to be good hand-in-hand with both their temporary status and the way humans work. There is no particular reason, however, to think that changing us to appreciate eternal things would be an improvement. Our starting point is that things are not necessarily better for being eternal, so changing us to appreciate the everlasting looks like a sideways move at best.

Why is so much made of the eternal? I suspect the fear of death and the familiar religious undervaluing of the changing world here, tarted up in grandiose terms (see *Death* and *Enchantment*). Sublimated wishful thinking is still wishful thinking, however, nothing more.

Everyone Has Their Own Religion: False, and surprisingly pernicious.

A door-to-door proselytizer came to my home recently. He started his spiel apologetically, by saying that he realized that "everyone has their own religion." This is where I cut him off. I said that I have no religion, thanked him, and closed the door. It is a mistake to assume that religion is a necessity. It is a mistake to assume that the things that motivate you also motivate all others. It is an error to think that the fears that you have are also shared by everyone else. These concerns might be widely shared, but that is much different from their being universally shared (see *Anxieties*).

Not everyone has their own religion. I don't, and the same goes for millions of other godfree people. See *Religion* and *Religious Spirit (or, Religiosity; Religion in General; Religion in the Abstract)* for more on what we don't have. You don't need these things either, so far as I can tell.

Everything Happens for a Reason (or, It Was Meant to Be): (1) False, yet oddly widespread. This idea is offered as a platitude even by those who aren't particularly religious, despite being a thoroughly religious idea. A relationship falls apart? That's god's plan, get over it. A person contracts a disease? Someone claims that there must be a reason for this, and this is supposed to make the sick person feel better. Examples are literally infinite, since reasons of this sort are supposed to lurk everywhere.

Why would we think that everything happens for a reason, or that some things are meant to be while others are meant not to be? Here's a little technical vocabulary: philosophers distinguish "motivating" reasons from "justifying" reasons. Motivating reasons are the considerations that we offer to explain our behavior. Why am I writing these words? What are my reasons? The considerations that move me to do this are, for instance, a belief that this is an important part of a parcel of significant ideas and a desire to clarify these ideas for both myself and others. Justifying reasons are the considerations that make an action worth doing in some sense, regardless of whether people ever think of these things. For instance, suppose that there is a substance Y that would protect us all from cancer. We all have reason, in the justifying sense, to take Y. But suppose that nobody knows about Y. We could not be motivated by thoughts about Y to consume it. There would be no motivating reasons specifically about Y, even while we had justifying reason to consume Y.

When we speak of things happening for reasons, it is the motivating sense that is relevant. Justifying reasons don't make things happen without being converted into motivating reasons, which means that they have to have a role in thoughts. Why would we think that there are these sorts of reasons behind, for instance, the pattern of gravel in my driveway, the number of ants in my garden, the number of blades of grass in my lawn, etc.? After all, if we take seriously the idea that *everything* happens for a reason, it pertains to such unimportant considerations as these as much as it does to more significant ones.

Should we take seriously that these things have this sort of reason behind them? One way to make this case is from the ground up. Start with, for example, human behavior that we all agree is explainable in terms of reasons. Then move to animal behavior and extend this explanatory stance. There are features of nonhuman animal behavior that call out for interpretation in terms of reasons that produce it. Why is the dog nosing around the back door? His reason is that he wants to go out. Why is that bird walking near the path and holding its wing out? The reason is that she wants to attract our attention and to draw us away from her nest. It is pretty much as easy to find reasons for nonhuman animal behavior as it is for our own actions.

The next step is to move on to nonanimate phenomena. There are, for instance, natural regularities, such as laws, and maybe these ought to be understood in terms of motivating reasons. Why is the acceleration of objects at the earth's surface 9.8 m/s^2? Maybe a reason can be articulated to explain such structuring features of the natural world. Finally, complete the extension by moving to seemingly random phenomena. Why did the branch break at precisely *that* moment, just after the children had left the yard? A divine reason can be tempting here.

For all of this to be a good pattern of inference, the appeal to motivating reasons has to earn its explanatory keep. However, from this perspective motivating reasons are lazy scroungers, to be shown the door rather than embraced with respect. The natural sciences are in the business of explaining this whole array of phenomena, and they have found no use for this extended idea of reasons behind everything. For one thing, there is no extended use for thoughts throughout the whole array of scientific explanations of natural phenomena. Human and nonhuman behavior is usefully explained in terms of thought, but natural laws and random events are not. For another, and more particularly, for this line of thought to deliver reasons behind everything, we need to be able to show the difference between a coincidence, or something that happens for no reason, and something that happens for a reason. There is no such mark of the difference throughout the natural world, and so some things must be seen as produced not for reasons but through other processes.

The other way to make this case is from the top down. Start with the idea of the world as produced by a mind, and then deduce that all particular occurrences have reasons behind them. This is simple, direct, and only as good as its starting point. This starting point, however, is famously dubious, to put it mildly.

This second general way of thinking about reasons should be attractive only to those who are explicitly committed to a view of the world as having this nature—that is, to religious believers. The worrying thing is that many people who are not overt believers take seriously the idea that everything happens for a reason, or that some things are meant to be by nonhuman, supernatural meaners. This is evidence of the deep penetration of everyday thought by religious ideas. We ought to take care to root this out, as the particular idea is a mistake and the general tendency of thought is one that leads people to further errors.

The truth is that very few of the things that happen in the world are done for reasons. Only some of the things done by things with minds happen for reasons. We all do lots of things without really meaning to. Consider eating a meal. You have motivating reasons to eat—pleasure, health, even survival. But you typically don't have a reason to chew precisely that many times, or to bite off *that* piece of bread rather than *that* one. When we scrutinize our behavior, we find many subactions without particular reasons. And this goes for us, wonderful creatures with minds that we are. Where there are no minds, nothing at all is either meant to be or not to be.

Another source of the confusion might be the conceptual complexity with which I started: the distinction between motivating and justifying reasons. We discover, for instance, that we have reason to consume quinoa because it is good for us. This reason exists before we encounter it—we don't have to "mean it" for it to be there. Nor, however, does anything else. To say that we have a reason to eat quinoa is just to say that it is good for us. Since we are thinking things, the health benefits of quinoa fit into our perspective on ourselves. It need not be made a reason by some other mind or minds. Moreover, this is the wrong sense of "reason" for the purposes of vindicating the platitude that some things are meant to be. It would be nice if English, and maybe other languages, did not lead us to this confusion by using one word in multiple ways, but there we are. Without some housekeeping in our vocabulary, we are stuck on this lexical road to dubious ideas.

(2) Sometimes the idea that everything happens for a reason gets dressed up in the misleadingly formal garb of the "Principle of Sufficient Reason." The basic idea here is the thought that everything has a cause. Lots of eminent philosophers have offered versions of this over the centuries, but typically without being sufficiently careful about sliding between "reason" and "cause." It is one thing to think that everything—at least the things that we encounter in the world—has a cause. It is a related thing to think that, due to this, everything can be explained, but it is not quite the same. Still, these ideas about causes and explanations are what the Principle of Sufficient Reason addresses. It is another step to think that there are reasons, in some sense, for everything. And it is our familiar error to slide from this to the idea that everything has a reason, in the sense of being meant to be. Causes abound, it is true. Not nearly so much reasons.

Evidence: (1) Could there be evidence for the existence of god? Are there clues in the world around us that point to the divine? Many people think so: consider purported miracles, or the claims that some make when faced with awesome natural beauty. The statue weeps blood—it's god's hand in the world! Look at the awesome beauty of the Grand Canyon! Such awesome beauty indicates that there must be a god! (For thoughts to the contrary, see *Enchantment*.)

I'm inclined to think that a god who was benevolent and omnipotent would not bother with such oblique hints as to her existence. Either she would communicate it outright, without equivocation, or she would cover up her existence altogether, and there would be no clues whatsoever that might reveal the hidden god (because, after all, she's omnipotent, so completely effective hiding will be no problem). On my view, given the lack of outright and undeniable messages, there is no evidence for the existence of god. Stop looking, you're wasting your time.

However, there is a line of thought, attributable in some form at least to Ophelia Benson and David Hume, which calls into question whether there could be evidence of god's existence in any form, including direct messages. Imagine whatever sign you like: miracles galore, messages ringing in your ears but with no obvious worldly source, the systematic fulfillment of the prophecies of any particular sacred text—or of all of them, for that matter.

The crucial question is whether this would be evidence for the existence of a god or gods.

The answer is: not exactly. Presumably at least some of us would want to explain these phenomena, and so hypotheses would be formulated. Some of these hypotheses would undoubtedly invoke ideas of the divine, in either familiar or novel forms. Fair enough: the phenomena might invite such hypotheses, depending on what form they take. But other hypotheses would eschew supernatural explanations and offer worldly ones. Powerful bodies with access to lots of technology can accomplish marvels. Corporations fit this bill. So do governments. Interestingly, so might extraterrestrials.

When the various hypotheses are compared, it will always be more reasonable to favor the worldly ones over those that invoke divine, supernatural elements. The worldly ones are intellectually conservative: they explain what we are experiencing in terms of processes that we know to be, in principle, possible. Explanations that invoke the divine, however, are akin to those that invoke magic. They explain the appearances in terms of things that seem to be impossible, and this is no explanation whatsoever. Ultimately, such explanations really do offer magic as an explanation, for there's no principled difference that I can see between what we call magic and what we call supernatural.

What is the implication of all this? To put it bluntly: there is no possible evidence for the existence of god.

It won't do to insist that there will be signs that differentiate extra-terrestrials from divine forces. Presumably aliens would accomplish their effects on us using alien technology. Now consider our own technology. It can be baffling to those of us—such as me—who don't know how it works. I have no idea how such things as cell phones and computers work. Obviously some of us do: we build these things, after all. This means that our general confidence in the fact that our technology works by mechanical principles and not magic is warranted. But the processes are mysterious to most of us, and might as well be magic. Sound reproduction is close to my heart in this regard. I have no idea how a compact disc, a cassette tape, or a vinyl record captures sound, but they do. They do it in different ways, which is almost even more incredible to me: multiple worldly yet near-magical methods for reproducing sound! What a world! It's marvelous that humans have discovered multiple ways to capture sound cheaply and easily so that, for example, the musical performances of the best musicians in the world can be reproduced in high fidelity in the homes of very poor people. This might as well be magic, but it's not.

This is only one small example from a vast array of human technological achievements. Given our own many worldly wonders, there is no reason whatsoever for us to expect to be able to distinguish alien technology from divine magic. This leaves us searching for other conceptual resources to use to sort out the better hypotheses from the worse ones. So, let me repeat: it will always be more reasonable to prefer the hypotheses that explain the puzzling appearances in terms of processes that we know to be possible over ones that seem to invoke the impossible. Suppose that biblical prophecies started to come true. We should not see this as evidence of a god or a supernatural realm. We should see it as evidence of something natural that we don't understand. This means that we should favor explanations in terms of worldly processes over those that involve the divine. At worst, when local explanatory attempts have failed, we should take seriously the possibility that aliens are doing it. This is far more reasonable than taking gods seriously.

Are religious believers troubled by their inability to distinguish god from powerful aliens? Should they be? I think that they should be (see *What's the Difference between a God and an Extraterrestrial?*). I doubt that many have thought about it. They are probably more willing to believe in a god or gods than other forms of intelligent life. This is a mistake.

This line of thought stands up against even appeals to feelings of the utmost confidence that we might have. Such feelings might be due to general purpose emotional capacities, or they might be attributed to a special purpose faculty for sensing the divine. Imagine that one is overcome by the most powerful confidence possible in the existence of god. It is as if god is directly meeting with you, mind to mind. The apparently divine presence is very powerful. Is this experience infallible? Of course not: none of our experiences are. A corporate or governmental or extraterrestrial entity could be exploiting our emotional capacities, be they general or special purpose. That's the kind of thing we are—trickable. We know this; although science might reinforce this aspect of our view of ourselves, it's something we know on more commonplace grounds as well. A stick immersed in water looks bent, but it is not. Painters have used *trompe l'oeil* techniques to trick our eyes for centuries. The ceilings of the Vatican museums are full of examples, if you want to see some. More sadly, we can be absolutely convinced that someone loves us when they do not. The lesson is this: even the most overwhelming feelings of confidence in the presence of the divine are not evidence for the existence of god. They are better evidence for something else.

(2) As if all this is not enough, there is a deeper problem. The addition of supernatural explanations to our understanding of the world would undo everything we have already figured out and make further science impossible. It would render all natural laws invalid, thereby making it impossible to theorize about mechanisms responsible for diseases, etc. The reason is that we could never rule out the possibility or actuality of mysterious, supernatural causes in our attempt to explain how things work.

Imagine that you are trying to figure out what causes a particular kind of cancer. You suspect gene mutations, such as BRCA 1, which led Angelina Jolie to preemptively undergo a double mastectomy. Genes and cancer are thoroughly natural phenomena. If we added supernatural things to our understanding of the world, we could never figure out that something like BRCA 1 was responsible for cancer. We could suspect it, but that's all. The reason is that when we had narrowed down the class of possible natural causes to gene mutations, we would still have the whole realm of possible supernatural causes to reckon with. We have no means of assessing these or of narrowing them down, so it would always be an open question whether and which supernatural causes were at work. This would leave us always wondering what the cause of this sort of cancer is.

This problem is encountered not just when we face problems like cancer. It thwarts our efforts at understanding normal, healthy natural mechanisms. Imagine a period of greater anatomical ignorance than our present day. We don't know how blood circulates through the body. We are trying to figure out the answer, and we suspect that the heart is responsible. Note: this is the correct answer. We can't conclude this, however, if supernatural things have to be included in our study of blood circulation. Even if it looks like the heart is responsible, it might really be supernatural causes. If you had a way of controlling supernatural causes you could run experiments to test supernatural hypotheses. But we don't have any way of controlling the supernatural. This means that you are stuck: you can't conclude that the heart is responsible for blood circulation because you can't rule out supernatural forces.

This pattern is also found when we consider inquiry into laws of nature. If we add supernatural phenomena—gods, spirits, angels, demons, souls, and so on—to our understanding of the world, we can't formulate laws. We could not, for instance, figure out that bodies attract each other proportionately to their mass. This would be to confine our inquiry to natural mechanisms to explain, for instance, the tides, or the falling of apples from tree branches, or the movements of the planets. If there are supernatural forces at work in the universe, these must be accounted for as well. But we have no ways of studying these (contrary to the claims of many charlatans), which means our attempts to understand tides and apples must stall.

The overall problem should be clear. The addition of a supernatural realm to our ways of thinking about the world in which we find ourselves paralyzes any principled attempt to understand ourselves and our universe. No knowledge of natural laws, no understanding of disease mechanisms, no natural knowledge.

The good news—well, it's good from my perspective at least—is that science does in fact exist. We have successfully formulated natural laws and figured out some things about natural mechanisms such as hearts and BRCA 1. This is significant: supernatural phenomena have been demonstrated to have no use in our principled understanding of the world. (This inference pattern is known as *modus tollens*, in case you care, and has been known to be perfectly valid for millennia. Those who want to know more can *Pick Up a Textbook*.)

Skepticism about science is unfortunately rampant, even in sophisticated countries with lots of access to science education and technological marvels. Perhaps this is a failing of science education— for more see *Science*. But maybe it's clear thinking on the part of those who take the supernatural seriously. All inferences made by scientists are unwarranted and hence presumptuous if there is a domain of gods, souls, and so on in addition to the natural world. Those who believe in gods and souls should be suspicious of science. Those who take both science and the supernatural seriously don't understand the implications of this combination.

Let there be no mistake: when I call the science-deniers "clear thinking," I do not mean to condone their skepticism. They really have it the wrong way round. It's the belief in the supernatural that is presumptuous; no beliefs in gods, souls, etc. are warranted, and hence there is no good reason to be suspicious of science here.

(3) Let's ignore what I have just said. Suppose that we have worked hard to explain something. We have run out of naturalistic candidates to do the job, so we are ready to entertain supernatural explanations. However, because of how explanation works, this strategy will have a surprising effect. The result of turning to what looks like the supernatural will instead result in expansion of our ideas about nature, thereby squeezing out the supernatural.

Here's why: explanation is subject to an "intelligibility constraint." That is, we construct explanations by spelling out intelligible steps/principles/ mechanisms . . . etc. to explain something. For instance, suppose that you want to explain how it is that someone has red hair. To do this you need to shed light on the mechanisms by which hair is grown, and among these which are responsible for color. You might also want to get into the genetics of hair: how the hair growth mechanisms are built by genes, how these genes are put together through reproduction, and so on. Maybe other topics, broken into other mechanisms, would need to be addressed too. Crucially, what is "intelligible" is importantly shaped by what we already know/understand, in the sense of what we have put a concerted effort into understanding. To continue with the example: for those with no familiarity with genetics, spelling out the role of genes in producing red hair will not make sense. Such a person needs to learn something else before the hair explanation will be intelligible.

Here is what this means for thinking about god and evidence: when we supplement a given view of nature with an intelligible explanation, we have really just shown that our earlier view of nature was incomplete, and now we have a better view of what the natural really is. There is no room for the supernatural in our explanatory efforts after all. And this means that there's no way for positive world-based evidence to be provided for the existence of a supernatural god.

To insist on the super- or nonnatural in spite of this is to insist on mystery. See *Mystery* for concerns about this idea. As soon as we see the details about how something works—as soon as we dispel mystery—that thing has a role in nature. This is just another way of saying that science and philosophy are hard work and that, for now at least, the project of understanding the world is not finished. Atheism is devoted to intellectual humility (see *Humility*), perhaps above all else.

Evil as a Reason to Reject God: (1) I gather that many people lose their faith in god due to worries about his character. God is supposed to be good, so goes the thought, but the world is so clearly evil and could so easily be improved upon that there can't really be such a god. Much ink has been spilt elaborating upon and defending against this worry, which is known as the problem of evil. Fair enough, I suppose, but I am not much moved by it.

Here is the reason. The primary problem I have with the idea of god is not about the quality of his character but about his very nature. God is typically thought to be supernatural, and that's the problem. There is no good reason to take seriously the idea that there are supernatural things (see *Evidence* and *Supernatural*). This means that worries about good versus evil are a bit beside the point.

Many traditions portray god as omnipotent, omniscient, and benevolent. The fact that the world is full of evil, both in terms of human activities and in terms of the suffering due to nonhuman causes, poses a problem for this conception of god. Something has to go. If god is all-powerful and all-knowing yet allows this evil to happen, perhaps he is not good after all. If god is good and knows about this evil, perhaps he cannot prevent it and hence is not omniscient. If god could prevent it and is good, perhaps he does not know about it. Defenses of this notion of god against the problem of evil typically take the form of explanations of why the evil that we see is compatible with the existence of a god with these characteristics. Very few have been inclined to argue that the world is not full of evil. Wise, that.

Suppose that these defenses fail. This would not imply that there is no god. It would imply that there is no omniscient, omnipotent, and good god. Perhaps all supernatural beings are malevolent. Perhaps they are mentally incompetent. Maybe they are deeply limited in their abilities yet deeply pained by our situation. All of these options offer the existence of the supernatural along with the vast evil we see in our world.

The problem of evil is an in-house problem only. The move from worries about evil to atheism is unduly hasty. The real problem with theistic worldviews is not the evil we see in the world, but the supernatural domain that such views countenance.

(2) A particularly problematic response to the problem of evil is to point to god's plans or to purportedly divine standards of goodness that are different from our worldly standards. It is wrong for us to cause the suffering of millions of people and animals, but not for god to do so. Why? No plausible answer has been given, or could even be provided. We are supposed to stop thinking about the evil once the idea of a distinct set of values for god is on the table. This, however, is unacceptable. It is special pleading combined with necessarily problematic appeals to mystery (see *Mystery*). It is especially problematic for any religion that offers moral prescriptions, which is, I would wager, all of them. These religions seem to claim to understand morality, on the one hand, while disavowing the possibility of real understanding of morality on the other. Moral prescriptions for humans are offered very confidently, dogmatically even. God, however, is let off the hook with a different and mysterious morality. Double standards? No thanks.

Exceptions: There are, of course, exceptions to the things that I say about religion. Maybe not all religions emphasize faith, or the supernatural, or souls, or sin (see *Faith vs. Reason, Supernatural, Soul,* and *Sin*). Maybe some don't link moral values to god's will (see *Morality; or, On Loving the Good with and without God*). So be it: this is the cost of my strategy of eschewing some fine-grained details and sticking to more basic issues (see *Basics*). Inquiry goes on, and on. Fair enough.

Do you fall into one of these exceptional categories? Are your religious beliefs sound on the basics and nuanced in the important, difference-making details? Is your religious practice exempt from the worries that I present? From those presented by others? Is your religious tradition the outlier that gets it all right rather than one of the myriad problematic ones? I haven't met you, but I will say "no." If you belong to one of the familiar major monotheistic religions, then the answer is certainly negative. This applies to, literally, billions of people. Mathematics is on the side of my hunch: there just aren't that many people who fall into exceptional categories.

Do you, somehow, believe in a god or gods? A soul? The supernatural? Do you use the concept of the spiritual? Of sins and the sacred? Then you are not an exception. That's how important the basics are: regardless of the particular details of your beliefs, practice, or tradition, if you accept even one of these fundamental notions, then you are not exempt from the worries raised by the godfree. Sorry.

Experience: There is no doubt that some religious believers think that they experience god through the things they encounter in the world. "Some" must be emphasized here—not all claim such experience of god. There should be little doubt that approaching the world from a religious perspective leads one to interpret what one finds there in religious terms. This is fine, so far as it goes. It is to be expected. What it does not provide is some sort of experiential claim for the existence of god. Just as apparent perceptual experiences can be mistaken, so can this sort of religious experience. Perceptual experiences can be double-checked. We regularly separate the false appearances from the true ones. Religious experience needs this sort of procedure in order to deliver a case for the existence of god. Otherwise, all we can say is that many people experience the world in religious terms, as if there are gods there. Feelings of certainty don't suffice to make things so, as we all know.

6

F Is for . . .

Faith vs. Reason: (1) Very few of us are raised godfree. I wasn't, although the religious touch of my parents was thankfully very light. Given this, how do people like me find our way to atheism? It's somewhat complicated I'm sure, but at the core of the process is something like this: we learn a few things, reflect on our religious beliefs, and eventually decide that they do not match the world. To simplify things even further: reason leads us away from faith.

Are reason and faith really in conflict, as this potted reconstruction of my personal history suggests? Well, it depends on just what we're talking about. "Faith" is particularly tricky. My impression is that this is widely taken to be a matter of personal avowal and belief, of positioning oneself on the side of god as a matter of personal loyalty, maybe even of heartfelt devotion. It strikes me much like joining or supporting a team: not the conclusion of an inference, but something else (see *Reason* for more on inferences). In this broad sense, faith does not depend on deliverances from reason, nor does it invite its critical powers, so yes, they are opposed.

I have no doubt that there are other senses of "faith" that stand in different relations to reason. Certain church traditions, for instance, have long had a place for scholarly scrutiny of texts and doctrine. These traditions place faith and reason side by side, to some extent. To just what extent? That's a hard and important question. Perhaps such study happens within limits where reason is not welcome and where "blind" faith reigns. To the extent that this is the case, even these reason-friendly religious traditions oppose reason with faith at important junctures.

Books such as this one are invitations to reason about the ideas that religion offers. If you think that this means that it poses a danger to faith,

64

then you are correct. It's also an opportunity, if you ask me. Religion addresses important questions. The truth matters here. Faith without reason is reckless, for that's a good way to commit yourself to the wrong ideas about important issues. More careful reason (warning: this is a euphemism for hard work; see *Pick Up a Textbook*) is surely the more appropriate and cautious tack to take with regard to such important things.

(2) One might think that all of this is so obvious that it should go without saying. I'm inclined to agree, and yet I'm the one saying it. Why? Because it has become fashionable to claim that reason and faith do not really clash because a commitment to reason really rests on a foundation of faith. What a strange idea! It's false, of course, but it's worth some scrutiny to see why.

The argument goes like this: when we think about the things about which we can reason, we discover that reason itself is not among them. We cannot demonstrate the legitimacy of reason by argument, for this is to use reason itself. Instead, a commitment to reason rests on an unreasoned foundation. Instead of being rational, the commitment to reason is itself an article of faith. So: the rational life does not displace faith. And once faith is on the scene, we need not direct it only at reason. Faith in god appears to be just as legitimate as faith in reason.

Should we believe this argument? No, and here is why: this line of thought confuses multiple senses of both "faith" and "reason," so it does not work. We need to be more careful about just what we're talking about when we use the words "faith" and "reason." Once we take the appropriate care, we see that there are indeed important sources of conflict between faith and reason, just as it is has seemed to most people.

Specifically, there are two ideas of "faith" and two ideas of "reason" being confused in this argument. On one hand we might mean these as structuring features of our lives overall. On the other hand we might mean particular strategies and attitudes that we can take toward particular topics. The typical sense of "faith" is the second one. When we talk about faith, we mean a stance one can take toward the idea of god. The relevant sense of reason is also the second one: when we are worried about possible conflict between faith and reason, we mean "reason" as an optional approach to take toward certain ideas. This sense of "reason" does not rest on the relevant sense of "faith," which means that they can conflict. As it happens, reason in the second sense can be defended with reason—reason in the first sense—and this means that the original argument does not even get off the ground.

Here are the details. First, reason is unavoidable. If you want to get food from your plate to your mouth, you must abide by reason. We can reconstruct the process as an inference. The particulars are boring, but here they are nonetheless: I am hungry, meaning I want food in my belly. If I want food to end up in my stomach, then I must get food to my mouth. If I want food in my mouth, then (barring dumb luck or the benevolence of others) I must move food from somewhere else to my mouth. There is food on my plate. If I don't move it to my mouth, then (barring luck and benevolence) I will starve. Therefore I must move the food from my plate to my mouth. We could add more details about bodily movements, but I think the point is clear: renounce reason and we die. It is not that we think this process through when we eat. It is that rational measures are built into us by nature. To renounce reason altogether is to give up such natural achievements.

The reason that this is the case is that means-end relations are vital to living, and the understanding of such relations is part of what the faculty of reason does. Still, it is true that reason in this sense, as an unavoidable feature of life, is not open to rational justification. Not that it needs it: if we die without something, we hardly need an argument to see the value of that thing. As a structuring feature of life, reason rests on something other than reason. We accept it out of literal need. Hence there is something to the idea that reason rests on faith and hence cannot conflict with it.

However, the nonrational foundation of reason as a structuring feature of life is not "faith" in the normal religious sense. The normal sense of "faith" is not intrinsically connected to worldly need. We obviously can survive without it; I do it every day. If need is involved in the normal sense of "faith," it is a kind of need tied to our immortal survival in the afterlife. And this, clearly, is a nonstandard notion of need. The bottom line is that reason as a structuring feature of life does not rest on faith in the sense in which religious believers mean it.

Besides this general, overarching sense of "reason" and (maybe) "faith," we use these in more particular ways. The recommendation to adopt a stance of faith toward god is obviously meant against a background understanding that not everyone adopts this stance. We are capable of taking it or leaving it. It is one attitude toward such issues among others. Likewise, reason in a more particular sense is an attitude—or, more precisely, a strategy—which one can take or fail to take toward exactly the same topic. As particular stances toward god, clearly reason and faith differ and, presumably, can conflict. But this sense of reason clearly does not rest on the conflicting sense of faith. The avoidable kind of reason does not rely on the avoidable kind of faith.

More pointedly, this sense of reason is justifiable by reason itself. Rational justification of reason as a particular strategy toward a particular topic can take two forms. First, we might justify it in general terms: reason famously concerns relations between ideas (read David Hume for a classic treatment of this topic), and the stance of reasoning about a particular topic is defensible in general terms by pointing out how it promises to chart the relations between ideas.

For example, suppose that a teacher wonders why some of her students are overweight while others are not. She watches them for a while and realizes that the healthier students all play hockey at lunchtime. She suspects that something about this activity is keeping these students healthy. Further inquiry teaches her about caloric intake and output, cardiovascular health, and related issues. She has reasoned her way from an observation through a web of interrelated ideas.

Generally speaking, the ideas in question might be those inherent to the subject itself (the students and their weight), and they might be those that relate this subject to others (such as what the students do in their spare time and more general ideas about physiology and health). For any topic, if such things are available to be thought about, then the topic is one to which reason applies. That this is the case with regard to god and religion is obvious. There are lots of ideas to think about here. We have all done some of this reasoning.

Second, we can justify the particular strategy of reason in more local terms, by clarifying and assessing the strengths and weaknesses of some particular idea. The persuasiveness of such a case will depend on its details, which can be assessed only after the case is constructed. Still, that such a local case can be made should be clear. Here is an example. Imagine that someone tries to persuade you to change religion from your current church to a life of devotion that requires you to give up all your possessions and to renounce your family members as wicked. This particular argument would deserve particularly close scrutiny if you were going to give it a chance to work on you. This is reason at work.

Either way, reason as a particular strategy allows for rational justification and gives no solace to the defender of faith in the normal sense of a particular stance toward god. To ask for more in the way of justification than either these general or local arguments is to change the topic. It is to move from the potential justification of reason as a particular possible stance toward god to the issue of the justification of reason in general. This admits no such justification, but neither does it rely on anything like the normal sense of faith. When we focus on the meanings most germane to the issue, reason and faith can certainly conflict, and reason is open to rational justification in a way that provides no comfort to defenders of faith.

Here is a potential justification of faith that allows much of what I have said so far. For faith to be preferable to reason with regard to belief in god, this must be a belief the strengths and weaknesses of which cannot be assessed (for such assessment is one of reason's jobs) and which exhibits no relations between ideas either internally or externally (for this is the other job I have allowed for reason). Reason then would have no job to do with regard to this topic, and hence faith could have free rein (and reign).

This is a version of the idea that science and religion concern different topics, so see *Questions* for a more direct discussion. In its present form— this is just baloney. So far as I can tell, no religion has ever offered a god completely featureless and completely detached from other issues. This would be a god about whom nothing could be said—for example, she is neither good nor bad, great nor small. It would also be a god with no jobs, such as arbiter of morality or originator of the universe. To offer this sort of god is to wallow in a particularly pure mystery (see *Mystery* for misgivings about so doing).

So: to urge faith over reason (or under, as its foundation) with regard to god is not on. It is at least a willful refusal to think about the issues here—issues which, by the standards of religious belief itself, are of the utmost importance. It might also be a way for the powerful to inculcate and reinforce blindness in the innocent for their own gain. Both the godfree and the well-meaning believer should work against this more sinister possibility.

(3) Some of you might not be convinced by the conceptual distinctions that I have just waded through. Do you still suspect that reason and faith don't really conflict because reason requires faith? If so, then let's come at this from a different angle. Here is an example to show how much the religious themselves will rest on faith yet resist reason. To do so is just to admit that there is a conflict between them.

Sometimes people appeal to god in an explanatory spirit. Why, for instance, do the tides go in and out so regularly? An attractive answer to many over the centuries has been that god does it. This is to treat certain sorts of worldly phenomena as evidence of the existence of god. (For worries about this, see *Evidence*, but for now let's examine this on other grounds.) For many people, this will be the end of their line of thought. There is a little bit of reasoning here: an inference is being made to answer a question, one which involves moving from an observed phenomenon to, in this case, an unobserved explanatory postulate. But that's the end of it for most people.

What's going on here is that something divine is being invoked to explain something worldly. In most people's hands this looks like real reasoning, but the appearances are actually deceptive. People stop their reasoning just by invoking the god they already happen to believe in. A quick inference is made, then faith steps in and stops the reasoning.

As it happens, even more reasoning is invited here. To use the divine to explain the worldly does not automatically mean that your preferred god is the best divine explanation for the job. Suppose that you appeal to a single, general-purpose god to explain the tides. Why should we merely infer that god does this? Why not argue from the regularity of the tides to the activities of a god specifically of the tides? This would be a tide spirit who pushes and pulls the waters of the world but who has no other jobs. And now that we think of it: why should we infer either a single general-purpose god or a single tide god? Why not argue from the tides to particular gods (or angels, or souls, or whatever you want to call them) for each wave? The regularity of the tides would be explained through the coordinated activities of these billions of tide gods.

Here's the point so far: when god is offered as an explanation of something, we are involved in reasoning. This sort of reasoning takes work. Crucially, alternative explanations must also be examined to sort out the strong ones from the weak ones. In the present case we can see that there are various forms that the explanatory appeal to god can take. Reasoning is needed to determine which one is the best. The work isn't over when we cite god as the explanation of something. It's just beginning.

The fact is that for most people, the citation of their preferred god to explain something is the end of their reasoning. They don't pursue the details because they don't really care. They are not interested in really explaining the tides, or anything else about the world. They are giving voice to their faith instead. Faith steps in and blocks reason. This would not be the case if reason and faith were really so interrelated as some seem to think.

There is good reason (by which I mean bad reason) for people of faith to resist really reasoning about gods and the world. These people recognize what we all really know: that faith and reason conflict in a deep way. To see this, let's continue with the tide case. Why should we cite any kind of god as the explanation of the regularity of the tides? Perhaps instead of gods it is the perfectly natural, although hidden and, let's say, strange activities of extraterrestrials that make the tides happen in the way that they do. Or, maybe it is neither gods nor aliens but mindless natural processes, such as gravity that do it. (In case you weren't sure, this is the correct answer, at base.) Reasoning is required not just to sort out the best godly answer from the other godly ones; it is needed to show that our explanation needs to cite god at all.

Despite the appearances presented by explanatory appeals to god, typically people just rest on faith, not the union of faith and reason. It's no wonder: although the history is complicated, meetings of faith and reason tend to go badly for faith.

Family and Friends: (1) It's strange that, at least in North America, valuing of families has been framed as a religious topic. Any godfree person can sincerely avow that families are good (other things being equal, of course). Moreover, we can do it directly: it's families themselves that are good, not families because god says so. See *Enchantment, Morality (or, On Loving the*

Good with and without God), and *Values* for discussion. So: let's reject the rhetoric that ties the worth of families to religious interests.

(2) If you come from a religious family or a religious community in which you have lots of friends yet find yourself tempted by a godfree life, you are in a potentially tricky situation. Your family and friends might, well, not exactly welcome your change, but at least accept it. Or they might shun you. At worst they might try to kill you. This is not an idle worry, unfortunately. There is not much that can be said in general to address your particular situation. Except maybe this: it is worth being careful about evaluating the truth or falsity of particular ideas, and it is doubly worth being careful about how we give voice to these assessments, if we ever do.

One of the things to be careful about is the beauty, the appeal, the value of the idea in question. A system of thought can be beautiful or admirable in its content, yet false. This means that people can be committed to ideas that would be great if they were true, but which happen to be unfortunately false. Those in love, maybe literally, with their religious ideas at least see them as beautiful. When we reject these ideas, we risk conveying the sense that there is no worthwhile appeal in them. This need not be the case. The genuine appeal of some ideas accounts for the fervor with which they are held, pushing questions of truth and falsity to the side. So: be careful about the feelings of the believers whom you love and who love you. Hopefully this will make coming out as an atheist relatively easier, if not easy. See *Belief and Doubt* for more.

The flipside of this issue is the quality of the motivations of the believers in your life. People are tempted by ideas about gods and by religious practices in a variety of ways. Many of the psychological sources of religion are blameless, well-meaning, even just outright good. Careless criticism of religion can include either accidental or deliberate yet hurtful impugning of the good hearts of people that you love. There is no good reason to do this.

Let's acknowledge the correlatives of these points. Many religious ideas are not beautiful; they are ugly, harmful, worth shedding from human life. Likewise, some psychological sources of religion are either mixed, both good and bad, or outright morally problematic. It's legitimate to criticize religion and believers on these grounds, but don't expect them to like you for it, even if they are your family members or your best friends.

Fear: The cause and effect of many people's attachment to religion. Religion does not do well on either count.

Let's not dwell on the fact—to which I can personally attest—that religious belief engenders fear. Many people give time and money to disreputable organizations because they are afraid of something like eternal damnation. This fear is a groundless effect of pernicious myths. Shame on these institutions for indulging this fear by promulgating these stories and then profiting from the resulting fear. They should be shunned. End of story.

More interesting are fears that seem to be the cause of religious ideas and activities without being their effect as well. For instance, apparently the ancient Mayans were afraid that the sun would become stuck in the underworld after it set and would not return the next day. They had rituals to "help" the sun reappear in the morning. In other words, they developed religious beliefs and practices around this fear.

There is a lot to learn here. Presumably hardly any of us share this fear, but it must have been gripping for the Mayans. One lesson is that the vividness of a fear is no indication of whether it is a worthwhile fear to have. We can be terrified of things that do not warrant this response. Another lesson is that the vividness of a fear is no indication of how widely it is shared. The ancient Mayans were presumably deeply moved by their worry about the sun, but it is nowhere near to a universal human fear. The same goes, however, for fears prevalent in early-twenty-first-century sophisticated societies. Their vivacity need not indicate universality. Your deeply compelling fear of death, for instance, implies nothing about deep human concerns all by itself. Maybe it's just you. Suppose religion gets you through the night. This doesn't imply anything about other people. I sleep fine, godfree sleep, thank you very much.

We must be especially careful about assuming that fears that are produced by religion are universal. Let the ancient Mayans be our guide here. Presumably some Mayans worried about the sun only because others had developed habits of thought and action around bringing back the sun in the morning. Should we be worried about the sun just because these

Mayans were deeply afraid that it would not rise? Of course not. The same goes for eternal damnation and other contemporary religion-based fears.

We must be careful when thinking about religion and fear. There are dangers that come with offering false hope. There are dangers born of the salving of fear with fantasy. When people believe falsehoods that make them feel better, they might miss out on important aspects of reality. They might think that they have to do things on the basis of these fantasies that they don't really have to do. Suppose that the fantasy that assuages my fear calls for legal prohibition of abortion, which would be bad for women. Or the destruction of nonbelievers, which would be bad for lots and lots of people. It's hard to recommend divorcing dealing with fear from reality, surely.

See *Hope* for more along these lines.

Foxholes: A so-called foxhole is basically a hole in the ground—a slit, a small trench, a ditch—occupied by a soldier in order to defend something. When you are in a foxhole, you are pretty much trapped. If people are advancing upon you or firing at you, you have two choices: stay put and let the aggression come for you, or leave the hole for the open air and make yourself a more obvious target. It's a grim choice. Soldiers in foxholes can't help but have their mortality on their minds. Their lives are either immediately at risk or subject to threat at any time.

It is sometimes said that there are no atheists in foxholes. When we consider, literally, those soldiers who find themselves in these holes, it's easy to see why. When faced with the constant prospect of violent death in a muddy hole in the ground, who could help but wish for miraculous help? Who wouldn't ask for divine aid? The more general suggestion being made by this saying is that while we might entertain lack of belief in god when we are safe and comfortable, when life really gets hard—and it will—we can't sustain this. When we look death in the eye—or the bank manager whom we owe a great deal, or our departing lovers, and so on—atheism falls by the wayside. When push comes to shove, we all believe, and we all ask for help.

So goes the suggestion. We all know that this isn't true. Ask Hume, ask Hitchens, ask around more generally among those who face death.

Let's put aside such exceptional people at least and examine the point that seems to be made here. The temptation to seek help from god when faced by difficulties is very common. Maybe it's universal. I suspect that it's very common when people feel that they lack control over their problems (see *Control*). All of this is natural, blameless, perfectly understandable. What is not so acceptable is the suggestion that this sort of change in conviction is desirable. This goes for both religious and more general standards. Do religions really endorse statements of faith made only in desperation, in the face of a lifetime of rejection of such ideas? Is that all it takes? Consider a deathbed avowal of love from someone who has voiced their cold rejection of you for years. How seriously should you take it? Does it change everything, as if the years of hatred had not happened? Should it change anything?

More generally, why should we value anything said under such dire pressure? We all know that testimony gained under duress, especially that verging on torturous, is worthless. Ordinary people will say anything when the thumbscrews turn. The waterboard is no friend of truth. Foxhole theists are as dubious as confessions beaten out of the accused.

There's another saying that pertains here: hard cases make bad law. It is unwise to judge the normal, the typical, by what pops up in the unusual, for the unusual is not representative of the usual. Just think about the meanings of the words and you will see the point. Well, the atheist who recants in the foxhole—or in the face of death, or under the knife, or in response to a threat—is in an unusual situation. This person's life—the myriad moments that constitute the norm—is one of nonbelief. The desperate moment is different from this, maybe with regard to belief, but certainly with regard to desperation. A godfree life is no more fraught than a religious one; I'll bet that, other things being equal, it's less so. So to put all weight on the foxhole moment at the expense of the others is unwarranted. Yesterday counts, at least for me.

Put another way: a foxhole god is no god at all.

Freethinker: An old name for atheists, still used by some. See *Godfree*.

7

G Is for . . .

Gift: An example of the widespread reach of religious ideas through our language, and from there through our thought.

Just what is a gift? Let's say, at least provisionally, that it is something that one person gives to another typically without expectation of compensation and often in a spirit of good will to the recipient. Moreover the thing that is given is meant to be a good to the recipient, in some sense. A free punch in the mouth is no gift, under normal conditions.

Gifts are common. We give them to each other all the time. There is nothing interestingly religious about this. But there is a use of the term "gift," along with such related terms as "gifted," that does depend on a religious framework if it is to make literal sense. A child to whom musical ability comes naturally might be described as "gifted." A few extra days of life with loved ones before a disease kills someone might be called a "gift." The recipients of these good things are obvious. But the nature of the supposed giver of the gift is not at all clear. Who are we to take the source of the gift to be when "gift" is used in this way? Supposing that the doctors and music teachers are not whom the speakers mean (see *Thank God!* for related issues), there is no worldly giver of musical ability and life, and other goods. This way of speaking only makes literal sense if we are speaking of nonworldly givers. Presumably, for some, this is exactly what is meant: talents, time, and many other things are gifts from god, or gods, to us.

Put aside all the problematic aspects of taking this literally (for example, the divine favoritism). This is the sort of deep feature of our everyday thought to which the godfree typically become attuned. It is desirable for atheists not to use this sort of language once they become aware of its religious baggage. Desirable, but not terribly important. Still, it's not nothing.

See *Language* and *Zounds!* for related topics.

God (or, Gods): (1) I'm tempted to say that, as an atheist, I have nothing to say about this topic. But that's not quite right.

First things first: I reject the existence of gods. What this amounts to will depend on what "god" means. What "god" means, however, turns out to be a very slippery matter. This goes for believers more than nonbelievers. I will disbelieve in any reasonable definition of "god" that you have to offer, unless you can give me reasons to believe. The particular details need not matter much, as we shall see. Believers (see *Believers [or, My Sisters and Brothers in Disbelief]*), on the other hand, typically believe in one or a few gods, and you would think that this would involve having a particular idea of just what it is that you believe in. For some it does indeed; good for those people for being clear on this. But for a surprising number of people, the nature of the god in which they believe is rather muddy. Procedural guff often arises in conversations with these people (see *Guff*), which just isn't good enough for a topic that is admitted by all to be very important.

In the major monotheistic traditions, god is typically thought of as a supernatural person with certain characteristics: omniscience, omnipotence, benevolence. This is a perfectly legitimate and important way to think of god. Atheists often have exactly this notion of god in mind as the subject of their disbelief. Lots of problems arise due to god's supposed characteristics (for example, see *Evil as a Reason to Reject God*), but particularly problematic is the idea of something outside of nature. I am inclined to think that every reasonable characterization of god must involve the supernatural, and that hence we can reject them all for this one feature. The other purported characteristics of god just don't matter that much. See *Supernatural*.

When pressed, believers who start with this familiar notion of god often change to a more austere notion. God isn't really a supernatural person. Instead, some cast god as the supernatural source of everything without being thought to be a person. God is "absolute reality," some say. In a similar vein, some say that god is love, and again mean this without endorsing the idea of god as a person. Fine, but let's be open about the extent to which adhering to this sort of austere notion involves giving up on the idea of god found in Christianity and Judaism and Islam and Hinduism, and in many other religious traditions. Such austere gods cannot command anything, for instance. They cannot make anything, or forgive . . . and the list could go on.

On the other side are gods who are definitely persons but who are more worldly, less perfect than what is offered by our contemporary monotheistic traditions. Such are the gods of ancient Greece, Rome, and Egypt, for example. I think of these as "muscular" or "comic book" gods, since they are so similar to our contemporary representations of superheroes. Not that many people in my part of the world believe in muscular gods, so far as I can tell, but as with the other sorts we can reject them due to their supernatural nature.

Some traditions speak of "nature" gods—gods of water, earth, and so on—and these seem to be exempt from antisupernatural scruples. Fair enough. But I don't see how there is anything like a conception of "god" here. Are nature gods subject to natural law? If so, then they are just things in the world like me and you (and my dog, and my car . . .) and hardly worthy of the term "god." If not, then they aren't part of nature after all, and can be rejected along with the other supernatural notions.

All of this is, of course, an exercise in finding literal notions of "god." I recognize that much use of this term is probably not literal at all, but metaphorical. Fine, but that need not trouble the atheist. We can all construct metaphors out of familiar ideas without committing ourselves to the existence of those things. Try it for yourself: do a little research on unicorn metaphors, for instance, and you will put yourself into precisely this position. See *Symbolism (or, Analogy, Metaphor)* for more.

(2) "God" is the lynchpin idea in a whole network of ideas. These other ideas are not necessarily closely related, or related at all. It is one thing for god to be the origin of the world, another for god to offer immortality. The purported roots of morality in god's perspective are only tendentiously related to these other topics. Surely this list could be lengthened (beauty, meaning of life . . .). Considerations that hold for one job of god don't necessarily hold for another. Criticisms of god in connection with one idea don't necessarily pose problems for the others. Some notions of god

are well suited to one of these, others to others. Anyone who takes ideas about god seriously has to put in some time disentangling these threads. Both believers and the godfree often run these issues together a bit too haphazardly. For more on just the topics mentioned in this paragraph, see *Eternal, Origins, Morality (or, On Loving the Good with and without God), Beauty, Meaning of Life, Tragedy (or, Despair about the Meaning of Life), Irony (and Meaning in Life),* and *Absurdity (and Meaning in Life).*

Godfree: Atheism has a labeling problem. "Godfree" is my label of choice. It strikes my ear as more carefree and baggagefree than "atheist," which I also like. "Agnostic" is fine if a little wishy-washy. Does anyone hate self-proclaimed agnostics? But it's not a label that suggests fun, which is a problem. Much the same goes for "nonbeliever." Atheism brings with it burdens and benefits, one of which is ridding yourself of the troublesome thoughts that come with believing in god. Or, if you prefer, the thoughts of a troublesome god. To give this up is to become godfree. Phew! What a relief!

"Secular humanist"—okay, I guess. I'm not entirely sure what it means. This is a problem: if I were to use it, I would have to pin down its meaning and then explain it to others. No thanks. "Freethinker" avoids the issue. Lots of religious believers are freethinkers, in the literal sense, about lots of topics, maybe even about god. The freethinking connotation will be clear only to those who know the historical and cultural associations that this term has. Lots of people lack this knowledge, leaving one having to explain oneself again. What explanation "godfree" requires, it can't be about its basic meaning: that it wears on its sleeve.

Which leaves "bright." I was sympathetic to the relabeling initiative (obviously), and also to the attempt to find a fun term. But it's a bad choice because it's loaded: its contrary is "dim," which has no complimentary overtones and which hence cannot help but be unwelcome. "Godfree" has no obvious contrary, and certainly not a pejorative one. So—it's godfree for me.

Golf: One among many activities with which to fill the days you used to spend in church.

Guff: (1) I am a professional philosopher. I encounter a lot of nonsense in this line of work. Guff. Gobbledygook. Bullshit. Baloney. Writing and speaking that revels in obfuscation rather than clarity. Technicalities can be hard to understand, but legitimate ones serve clarity of understanding rather than obscuring it. Consider mathematical and logical notation: nothing could be more conducive to clarity of expression of ideas, and nothing can be more difficult to understand before one receives the appropriate training. This training makes the clarity clear; not so with some other vocabularies, for which no clarification is possible.

My impression is that writing about god, the supernatural, faith, and related ideas is particularly beset with guff. I won't name names, but I will enjoin believers not to tolerate this. These topics are important, so they are worth thinking clearly about. Any sermon or lecture or article or book that seems to be impervious to clarification probably is, and should be shunned on this account. Use whatever bullshit detector you have at your disposal. Since these topics are highly important, it is just as important not to accept guff about them. Set your bullshit detector to a very discriminating level lest you fall prey to lack of clarity of thought. The importance of these topics does not imply that we should be less than normally discriminating about them. On the contrary, it means that we should accept only those ideas that have the highest degree of support. Guff is unworthy of these topics and an insult to you and your belief.

(2) So far I have been addressing the substance of religious ideas. But religious discussion is susceptible to a different sort of bullshit, one that does not arise elsewhere with nearly the same frequency. Whereas substantial guff is a problem everywhere, religious conversation, writing etc. has a disturbing predilection for changing the subject. You're talking to someone about god and they seem to mean one thing, then when problems arise with that idea they say that they didn't mean that at all and rather meant something else. When you try to pursue that idea, it turns out to be not the real topic either. Some thinkers even enshrine this problem at the core of their theology as a virtue: god is ineffable, so that nothing can literally be said about "him" (he's not literally a "he," so this pronoun is misleading, and so on). Let's call this "procedural" guff, since it has to do not with the content of ideas but with how one handles them.

Do I need to point out that this won't do? If your subject matter keeps changing, you risk not saying anything. If you commit yourself to ideas that cannot be said, then by definition you are not saying anything when you talk about them. Strictly speaking we can't even believe in that about which we cannot speak or think, for belief requires something to be believed, and this line of thought offers us nothing.

Good faith conversation accepts that topics can be discussed, pinned down, clarified, accepted, and rejected. To give up on these things is to give up on adult discussion of the topics at hand.

See *Symbolism (or, Analogy, Metaphor)* for related difficulties in religious discourse.

8

H Is for . . .

Habit: Relatively automatic repetition in both behavior and thought, and the root cause of many people's ongoing attachment to religion. No defense of god, the divine, and associated ideas, institutions, and practices. *See Tradition (or Custom).*

A religious life is often shot-through with religious habits. There are habits of action: of going to particular places at particular times, of making certain gestures, of doing things with food, or money, or devices. There are habits of thought: of silently speaking to god, of framing topics in religious terms. Some habits are individual, others are widely shared and institutionally enshrined—think of recognizable rituals.

One of the barriers to leading a godfree life is giving up all of these habits. It can be disorienting and uncomfortable to make these changes, especially all at once. As with any other attempt to give up habits, people backslide.

Fair enough. I didn't say it would be easy. If it helps, you'll probably develop new habits to replace the old ones. And you might discover that the shedding of some of your religious habits is liberating. I can't promise that this will be the case, but it's not uncommon.

Hamlet's Advice:

> *There's more to heaven and earth, Horatio,*
> *Than are dreamt of in your philosophy.*
> —Hamlet (1.5.166–7)

Fair enough. Intellectual care and openness are wise counsel (see *Humility*). Even the most vivid imagination has limits. But this advice cannot be taken seriously as a defense of the supernatural, of mystery, at the expense of the hard work of study of the world. Wallowing in mystery is intellectually and, sometimes, morally problematic (see *Mystery*).

As for well-developed religious ideas, Hamlet's rebuke applies to them just as much as it does to overheated enthusiasm for the latest scientific deliverances. The lesson of the slow progress of science must surely be that there is more to nature than is dreamt of by lovers of the supernatural. Take Hamlet's advice as a prophylactic against presumption, not as a principled resting place for faith.

Heaven: None, in any religiously interesting way. Wishful thinking.

The idea of heaven is subtly dangerous. The promise of an incomparably excellent and everlasting life after this one can lead us to undervalue our current, actual lives. It can lead people to accept misery at the hands of others, either directly or indirectly, out of a sense that this life is temporary and that better times will come. This is a dangerous mistake. One might well hope that a world without the idea of heaven would be a more just one.

It can also lead us to undervalue the high points of our present, actual lives—the only lives we will have, from the godfree perspective. Think about your life: have you had moments of such bliss that they could not be improved upon? I am inclined to say that I have. Certain tastes, specific musical moments, particular vistas, and lots of touching moments with my wife come to mind. I know that, from the perspective of logical possibility, any good moment could be made better. To think otherwise is a failure of imagination. But I also know that, limited creature that I am, for real life purposes these moments really are as good as they get. This is no indictment, for they are wonderful. This is all the heaven worth wanting. To expect even better than this after one's death is obviously greedy and unobviously risky. The risk is that we fail to appreciate the swirl of the music, the lover's touch, the Rockies' grandeur in all their worldly glory, for our attention is partly elsewhere.

Hell: None, in any religiously interesting way. "Other people," the grim Sartrean joke goes, and while he has a point, thinking of worldly hells shows how different they are from the typical religious version. Conjure up the worst thing that you can imagine on earth—rape, torture, faculty meetings—and that is what the godfree experience as hellish. Thankfully these are all temporary, compared to the unending ordeals of the religious version. Perhaps they are also tragic in their finitude; there is no hope of eternal bliss to wash away these painful incidents. Still, it's hard to make a compelling case that the religious version of hell is not worse than whatever worldly travails we suffer. (But what's so great about eternity? See *Eternal*.)

Surprisingly, the religious idea of hell is just as much wishful thinking as its idea of heaven. It is patently moralistic wishful thinking, rather than the desperate and self-oriented version that delivers heaven. It's one thing for a fear of death and a weariness of life's challenges to generate the idea of an everlasting paradise. It's quite another to hope that the wicked get their comeuppance forever and horribly. The truth is as it appears to be: sometimes people get away with wrongdoing. Sometimes they profit from it so successfully that they live out their days in a way that kings would envy. That's it. There are no fires or pitchforks waiting for them after the grave, literally or metaphorically.

As with the idea of heaven (see *Heaven*), the notion of hell has its risks. Besides the fear it causes—real and significant fear, many of us former believers will tell you, and despicable given its epistemic credentials—the idea of hell can lead to worldly acquiescence in others' evil. They will get their eternal punishment and we will get our reward, so why bother fighting them here? Such subtle undervaluing of worldly justice is a palpable shame. It's so insidiously effective that the evil might well have invented the notion of hell to get them off the worldly hook. Of course the germs of this idea lie deeper in our psychology than this suggests, but certainly the crooked and powerful stand to benefit from it.

You love the good and lament the bad? Then renounce the idea of hell and insist on worldly justice.

Holidays: Many holidays, even ones recognized by secular states, are either overtly or historically religious. It's right there in the word: holy-day. This puts atheists in a bit of a bind (see *Xmas*). The bottom line is that we can participate with a clear conscience (well, mostly). Still, it would be nice for there to be more secular holidays, or secular substitutions for religious ones. These vary by country, but in Canada, where I live, thank goodness for such occasions as Labour Day, Remembrance Day, Robbie Burns Day (why not?), and so on. I will be happy to trade religious holidays for secular ones. Heck, I'd like two secular holidays for every religious one that we give up, if possible. Why not?

Hope: Is this a hopeless worldview that I offer? Religion offers many things: an ultimate meaning of life and death, everlasting life in lieu of mortality, the ultimate punishment of wrongdoers. A godfree world offers none of these things. Does it thereby condemn us to despair?

Well, there are hopes and then there are hopes. Whether the godfree life is hopeless will depend on what you value and fear.

Consider a schoolchild who, day in and day out, suffers at the hands of bullies. Every morning this child awakes and thinks, "I hope they leave me alone today." This is a hope that is generated by the fears that the child faces.

Whether the godfree life offers hopes in this sense will depend on what you fear. If you grew up fearing hell, as I did, then the adoption of a perspective that promises nonexistence when you die is a hopeful one, in that it assuages this fear. If, however, you fear nonexistence, as many people seem to, then atheism offers no hope. The grim reality is that with death you will cease to exist; to live godfree is to be forced to accept this and live with it. See *Death* for more.

Now for the other sense of "hope." Suppose that I get up some morning and think, "I hope that someone gives me a cupcake today." This is a free-floating hope, born not of fear but of my taste for baked goods.

A godfree life might offer the sorts of things that match your tastes. If this is the case, then it might well be a hopeful worldview for you. But your tastes might not sit well with atheism. Should this be the case, then a godfree life will not strike you as a hopeful one.

Here, I think, is the rub for lots of people: regardless of the more objective credentials of either atheism or some variety of religious belief, some people have tastes for the things that religion offers and some do not. Some have a taste for critical reflection and the pursuit of truth over comfort; others do not. Instead of conviction that some idea is true, hopes, fears, and tastes form the foundation of many people's religious orientations.

No univocal case can be made for the idea that a godfree life will be an easy one, or one that offers what you want. Truth and desire easily come apart, as we well know. So no promise can be made that a godfree life will offer you hope. It might, but it might not. You might be so out of touch with reality that the world cannot please you. So be it. This can hardly be taken as indictment of the world.

For more on the purported roots of religious hope, see *Eternal, Tragedy (or, Despair about the Meaning of Life), Irony (and Meaning in Life), Absurdity (and Meaning in Life), Heaven,* and *Hell.*

Humanism (or, Secular Humanism): A belief or theory that turns away from ideas about god or the divine or the supernatural and instead invokes ideas about human capacities and experiences to address at least some questions that are typically addressed in religious terms. See *Godfree.*

Humility: (1) Having a modest view of one's own importance. At its core, atheism is humble, and its most central virtue is humility, while a religious view of things is arrogant. Humility is especially important in science. And yet plenty of atheists and scientists are jerks, full of themselves, while plenty of religious people are humble, and even explicitly hold humility up as an ideal. Something's got to give, doesn't it?

Well, does it, really? I'm not so sure. We have to distinguish what we're ascribing humility to. We are all used to ascribing this to persons, which is perfectly reasonable. Let's call this "personal" humility. However, we can also speak of humility at the level of institutions. Let's call this "institutional" humility, and its opposite "institutional arrogance." I mean a variety of things by speaking of traits ascribed to institutions rather than persons. I mean, on one hand, the traits that certain institutions hold up as worthy for individuals to strive for. But I also mean these traits to be ascribed to the institutions themselves. Regardless of the traits of the people who participate in these institutions, the institutions can have this sort of characteristic themselves. They have this by virtue of the views to which the institution is devoted and the methods by which these views are pursued and protected.

Lots of atheists and scientists are jerks (see *Jerks*). They lack personal humility. Nevertheless, atheism and science are devoted to humility. As institutions, their core trait is humility. By this I mean a variety of things. For one, they represent humans as not particularly important in the scheme of things. For another, and more importantly, they are committed to the value of hard work in figuring out the truth about the nature of the world, the nature of us, and about what is important—that is, about values. Part of this emphasis on hard work is ongoing awareness of the possibility of being wrong. Arrogance, both personal and institutional, gets in the way of this hard work by assuming an unduly firm grip on one's grasp of the truth and hence overlooking the constant possibility of error.

This is particularly important to grasp with regard to science. As an institution, science is set up to check, and double-check, etc., the data with regard to the things that scientists study. Sometimes particular scientists emphasize temporary results too much, forgetting both to be cognizant of the possibility of error and to fess up when mistakes are revealed. This is personal arrogance. But the humility to which their institution is committed protects us all against such errors. Institutional humility endures when personal humility fails.

Ironically, the institutional humility of science can even endure *because* the personal humility of scientists fails. Scientists who are full of themselves compete against each other for accolades within science. This means putting in lots of hard work, doing lots of double-checking, all for the glory.

What about religion? Humility and arrogance are found there in complex ways. Many religions explicitly encourage personal humility; this cannot be denied. But both overtly and incidentally, they tend also to encourage personal arrogance. And they tend, as institutions, to be arrogant.

Here's why I say this. There are two sources of the institutional arrogance of religion. First, it tends to represent humans as very important, from the perspective of god, or the universe, or ultimate reality, or whatever. This is, obviously, arrogant. I'm arrogant, for instance, when I represent myself as quite important, after all. Well, that's what religion does for humans in general. And, as it happens, it's false.

Second, religions tend to denigrate the value of hard work in figuring out the nature of the world, including values. Instead, religions tend to claim that, through revelation or mystic experiences or divine texts, or whatever, they have a certain view of the nature of the world and of what is important. These particular views have invariably turned out to be deeply mistaken, and the presumptive certitude of religions is a big reason why these errors have been made.

Here is the bottom line: all scientists could be jerks, yet the institution would still embody substantial and methodological humility. All believers could be humble and yet religion itself would still be intellectually presumptuous and unduly aggrandizing of us and our place in the world.

When questions of humility and arrogance arise with regard to atheism and religion, let's put aside the jerks and the saints and instead ask ourselves which of these is committed to the possibility of error, to the value of hard work in figuring important things out, to the relative unimportance of people. Which portrays itself as having a firm grip on truth regardless of hard work? Which portrays people as, in some central way, the point of it all? Don't let the jerks and the simple good people mislead you: as institutions, atheism is humility embodied, and religion could hardly be more arrogant. It's easy to be seduced by a view of self-importance and little intellectual work, of course, but it's worth resisting.

(2) So far I have spoken of both personal and institutional humility and arrogance. But maybe it's not on to speak of institutions themselves as literally having these sorts of character traits. Maybe only individuals can be humble or arrogant. This would mean that there's something wrong with the point made above.

Fine. Suppose that we can't speak of institutions as having character traits. Nevertheless, consider science and religion with regard to personal humility and arrogance. One of these institutions regards truth as hard work and humans as insignificant from the point of view of the universe at large. The other sees humans as, in some sense, the point of it all, and truth as easily found in certain texts or in the pronouncements of certain people. Which is more likely to lead individuals to be humble, both morally and intellectually? I take it that the answer is clear.

(3) Here is a different route into the same topic. Let's get more fine-grained about humility. On one hand there is intellectual humility—being humble about what we know and how we find out about it. On

the other hand there is personal humility—being humble about one's own importance. A godfree stance is committed to both intellectual and personal humility. Knowledge is a hard-won achievement. It takes lots of hard work, both to acquire this knowledge and to ward off error in its pursuit. Consequently we should not be too confident about what we think we know. As for our view of ourselves: it looks like we are an insignificant species in an unremarkable corner of the cosmos. It's not all for us. Not even close.

Religions tend to undermine such intellectual and personal humility. They represent humans as quite important in the scheme of things, typically. And they represent knowledge about the nature of things as easy to come by—it's in the word of god, or divine prophets. All we have to do is to consult the appropriate texts or spokespeople, which is not particularly hard to do.

Of course, sometimes religions recognize limits of human knowledge, thereby counselling intellectual humility. This is a good thing. But just as often they put the possibility of such knowledge off limits, shrouding it in mystery (see *Mystery*), which is a bad thing. The hard work of intellectual inquiry is not lauded enough by the religious.

For some reason such intellectual humility as is found in religions tends not to lead to personal humility. The religious worldview is shot through with the idea of the significance of us as a species and as individuals, of our places in god's plan, as mysterious as it might be, of divine reasons for everything that happens to us. Self-aggrandizing, no?

A possible slogan for the godfree stance: let's get over ourselves.

(4) Nietzsche is famous for having said that god is dead. It is much less remarked that he followed this up by saying that since we killed him, we must become gods to become worthy of our act. This, however, is exactly the wrong way to think about the godfree life. This should be clear once we free ourselves of the metaphorical hyperbole and note that we did not literally kill god. This means that, literally speaking, there is no remarkable act of which to be worthy. Instead, there is a growing (I hope, at least) realization that an accurate view of the world has no room for the familiar idea of a god. There are no supernatural origins of either morality or the natural realm, especially personal ones. The implication of this dawning

realization should be an increased humility, not an increased sense of our own worth and power. It's a big world, and it's not about us in any interesting sense. Figuring out worldly truths and appropriate actions is harder than a religious view entails, not easier. Atheism is not a religion of either humanity or the self. It's not a religion at all, and it has no room for gods of any stripe.

For personal implications, see *You.*

9

I Is for . . .

Ignorance: (1) Sometimes people look for unexplained, or purportedly unexplainable, phenomena as evidence for the existence of god. Someone's disease oddly disappears. A statue starts to cry. Heck, there is the bald fact of the existence of the universe. We don't know, from a normal or naturalistic perspective, how this sort of thing came about, so god must have done it!

This way of thinking commits one argumentative error and one other sort of error. First, this sort of argument is known as a fallacious appeal to ignorance. From the fact that we don't know something, nothing in particular can be inferred except that there's a question that we don't yet have an answer to. The existence of gods needs evidence specifically of this, gods' existence. A mere gap in explanation doesn't bear on that at all.

Second, this sort of argument shows an odd sort of impatience. Science and philosophy are hard work. It might take centuries for the details of specific issues to be worked out. Jumping from lack of an answer about something to the existence of god is undue impatience, as we see from the long record of arguments of this sort that have subsequently been eliminated by eventual provision of the explanation in question.

(2) Why do people make the second error, the error of impatience? Let's put aside the case of people who are impatient about everything. Why do some people insist on hastily inferring the hand of god in events that have not yet been explained? I suspect that many people find not knowing things uncomfortable. It's not even the prospect of all the hard explanatory work that is off-putting. It's the lingering question itself that calls for resolution. Consequently the easy, but incorrect, answer is very tempting.

This is the wrong view to have of ignorance. We must be more careful with it. On one hand we should recognize the labor that might be required to provide accurate answers to our questions. On the other hand we should just learn to live with not knowing things. An important part of atheism is to acknowledge and embrace ignorance, indeed to insist on it, both our own and that of our species as a whole.

(3) Bliss; see *Paradise (Fool's; or, Whatever Gets You through the Night)*.

Irony (and Meaning in Life): Does life have meaning? Does atheism imply that life has no meaning? It's not unreasonable to worry about this, but it is mistaken. Not only does a godfree life have meaning; the only way for appeals to god to confer meaning on our lives is if it is possible for an atheistic worldview to deliver meaning to life.

The worry seems to be something like this: not everything that we want is worth wanting. We have all regretted buying worthless pieces of crap. This point reverberates throughout our lives: not all plans are worth devising; not all commitments are worth making; not all ways of life are worth living. When we reflect on these possibilities, or, even worse, when we experience disappointment along one of these dimensions, it can be appealing to seek out an ultimate foundation for the various sources of value in life. Maybe the things worth wanting are the things that god wants; maybe the plans worth making are those endorsed by god, etc. This way of thinking tries to ground the meaning of life in god's perspective on our lives.

As stated, this does not work (see *Tragedy [or, Despair about the Meaning of Life]*) for details. In order to understand the problem, all that we need to do is to pay attention to some conceptual distinctions. Some things are, to use a little jargon, *instrumentally* valuable. That is, these things are valuable as instruments, or tools, for achieving other things. Things with instrumental value have a kind of value that is derivative from the value of other things. Consider a hammer. This is valuable if you want to drive nails into something. Driving nails into, for example, a window frame is valuable if you want to keep the winter wind out of your house. This is valuable if . . . We might go on forever with this sequence of explanations (but we might not, as we will see). As we pursue this sequence, our attention moves from our quotidian activities to questions of the deepest significance to us. But so long as our answers cite only more instrumental values, we fail to find a final answer to our original question. We fail, in fact, to answer any of these questions. This is what generates the worry about the meaning of life. Our fallibility leads us into errors about what is meaningful. Who's to say that anything is meaningful? Maybe god?

Maybe, maybe not. I'm inclined to say that, on the one hand, we all can say this, god or not, and that, on the other hand, it's not typically up to us, so that nobody can say that anything is meaningful. More conceptual distinctions are needed. Instrumental value is not the only kind of value that there is. Some things are not valuable merely as tools to accomplishing other things. Instead they are valuable in and of themselves. These things are *intrinsically* valuable. Consider again the hammer, the nails, and the window. Driving nails into a window frame can keep wind out of your house, but this does not seem to be worth doing in and of itself. However, certain sorts of experience seem to be worth having or worth avoiding regardless of their relations to other things. Keeping the winter wind out of your house is valuable if you want to be warm rather than cold. Warmth is a pleasant experience; cold not so much. Pleasure is, I'm inclined to think, intrinsically valuable. Displeasure is intrinsically disvaluable. These things are worth wanting or avoiding in and of themselves. Nothing more is needed—other than understanding of human experience—to explain what is worthwhile about these experiences.

Anything can be instrumentally valuable. For this, all we need is some goal that the thing in question is a tool for achieving. Not everything, however, is intrinsically valuable. The hard thing to do is to figure out which things (or experiences, or actions, or whatever) are valuable in and of themselves. This is a hard thing to do, but it's not impossible. Answering this question requires us to pay attention to our lives and the things that seem to give them meaning. Some of them will only be instrumentally valuable, but others will, I think, turn out to be intrinsically valuable.

So far as I can tell, people turn to god to explain the source of meaning in our lives when they realize that not everything is valuable in itself. The assumption seems to be that things cannot be truly meaningful unless they are valuable in a grand sense (to put it as vaguely as possible). Let's call this *ultimate* meaning. Maybe these people think real value has to matter eternally, from the perspective of the universe as a whole, and that god's perspective is the appropriate perspective for accounting for this sort of meaning. Regardless, we can now see that this sort of move is premature. The crucial distinction is between things that are derivatively valuable and things that are valuable in themselves. Those things that are valuable in the second sense don't need to be valuable in any sort of grand or ultimate sense. Instead, they just need to really matter, and this can be delivered in a very down-to-earth sense.

In fact, the idea of intrinsic value is needed for god's desires, plans, etc. to matter in a way that can deliver meaning to our lives. Suppose that the value of some action or object always needs to be explained in terms of something else. This would mean that nothing really matters. For our wants to matter, they would have to be related to something else, such as god's wants. But the value of god's desires would also have to be related to something else to matter. This follows from our starting point, which is the idea that the value of something must always be explained in terms of something else. In order for there to be meaning in our lives, something must be of intrinsic value rather than merely instrumental value. But there's nothing in the idea of intrinsic value that restricts it to god's concerns. So far as we call tell from these ideas themselves and the sorts of things to which they apply, our wants, plans, etc. can be valuable in and of themselves just as much as god's can be.

Here is a more precise way of putting this point. Consider the form of a desire god might have about us:

God: wants for us that X.

This desire is one that we can have for ourselves:

We: want for us that X.

We can fill in this form to generate examples:

God: wants for us that we live happy lives in an earthly paradise

We: want for us that we live happy lives in an earthly paradise.

If god's desires about us can have intrinsic meaning, and if they are desires that we can also have, then our own desires can have intrinsic meaning. The same will go for our plans, commitments, ways of living, etc. There is nothing about god's having them that gives them intrinsic meaning that cannot also apply to our having them. (See *Morality [or, On Loving the Good with and without God]* for more on related issues.)

Given all of this, here is the first irony concerning meaning in our lives. God's perspective can give our lives meaning only if we don't need god in order to give our lives meaning. This is just to say that intrinsic value is all that is needed for our lives to have meaning, and that this is not limited, conceptually, to god's concerns. The implication is that the nonexistence of god does nothing to threaten the meaning of our lives. So long as certain things are worth pursuing in and of themselves, our lives can have meaning. I think that pleasure is worth pursuing and that pain is worth avoiding. I think that knowledge and interpersonal relations are also worth having in and of themselves. Figuring out whether this is true, and what else might really matter, requires that we attend to our natures and to the sorts of things that seem to matter in our lives. It does not require, on its face, any sort of divine contribution.

When we start to think about our own experiences of value, we find the second irony concerning meaning in life. We want things, and yet experience sometimes brings with it disappointment, which in turn can lead us to wonder about the nature of the things that really matter. This sort of experience can lead us to think that god grounds the true meaning in life. It's due to our nature and our experience that we crave meaning and, in turn, seek out ultimate foundations for meaning in our lives. But the irony is that the true source of meaning is internal to our lives and our place in the world. It is not to be found in any sort of divine, ultimate perspective on us and our concerns. Our natural concern for meaning can lead us, ironically, to turn away from the things that really matter.

On second thought, maybe our lives really are tragic. It's not that a godless world implies that our lives don't mean anything, as the original fear held (see *Tragedy [or, Despair about the Meaning of Life]*). It's that our inclination to take the idea of god seriously misleads us about the nature of the things that really matter. Our craving for meaning leads us to misunderstand the nature of true sources of meaning by turning our attention to the divine. Rather than delivering meaning to our lives, the idea of god robs us of it, and this is indeed tragic.

See also *Absurdity (and Meaning in Life)*.

10

J Is for . . .

Jerks: Lots of atheists are jerks. So are lots of religious people. Neither belief nor nonbelief corners this market.

It's particularly problematic when we are jerks toward each other in discussions of the merits and demerits of religion. We should try to stop this. Maybe I come off as a jerk in some entries in this book. Maybe I have been a jerk in places. I'm sorry about that.

We can all acknowledge that a jerk is a bad thing to be. We should also acknowledge that the gods of many religions are jerks. This goes for the gods of major current monotheistic religions just as much as for the multiple gods of ancient Greece or Egypt. Eternal damnation for someone else's acts? Calls for the destruction of unbelievers? Plagues? Famines? Games with the lives of mere mortals? And on and on . . .

In its classic form, this is known as the problem of evil, a problem for the credibility of many religions. See *Evil as a Reason to Reject God* for discussion.

11

K Is for . . .

Knowledge: Does atheism offer this? Somewhat yes, somewhat no. The acquisition of knowledge is hard. We don't know everything. Atheists get this more than those who seek false certainty in religion. A love of truth does not necessarily come with a grasp of it. Rather than knowledge, the godfree are well advised to hone their *Humility* and to learn to love *Ignorance*.

12

L Is for . . .

Language: (1) Our everyday language, at least in the case of English, is shot through with religious concepts and preconceptions. This cannot be overstated. Some of the subtle effects of giving up religion come with creeping awareness of the extensive reach of the worldview of the divine. This is a perennial theme of philosophy in general: we do well to be reflective about the very ideas that we take for granted. Doubt everything. Really, everything.

The pervasive spread of religious ideas through our language has two implications, somewhat at odds with each other, but there you go. One is that, due to the common and basic role of these ideas, we often frame thought about important topics in religious terms, or with religious presuppositions, without realizing it. Getting these presuppositions out in the open can be very useful for making progress in understanding these topics. The other is that our use of explicitly or implicitly religious language often implies nothing about a speaker's actual religious beliefs, or lack thereof. The common terminology is often useful for communication due to our linguistic conventions, not because of the deep faith of the speaker. For examples see *Gift* and *Zounds!*

(2) Much examination of religious ideas and ways of speaking, both formal and not-so-formal, overextends its reach. It presupposes the reality of the divine and portrays the issue as how best to talk and think about it. This is premature. Our approach should instead be more tentative. What sorts of things about the divine can plausibly be said as, for example, explanatory hypotheses, and how do they measure up to other, nondivine explanations? The supernatural must earn its way into our thought and

talk, just like other ideas—no free rides for religion, regardless of our inclinations. This can be difficult, given how far religious ideas intrude into the starting points for important questions, but that's the way it goes nonetheless. I suspect that, rather than being about real features of the wider world, religious talk often gives voice to issues that are purely psychological. These concerns need not have worldly answers or even correlates: see *Anxieties*, *Fear*, and *Hope*.

Lies: Deliberate deception through misrepresentation of the truth.

Religious doctrines are all false. Does this mean that we should think that religious spokespeople are liars. No. Certainly some are, even about the core tenets of their faiths. They espouse things that they think to be false, in various hopes—of keeping their jobs, increasing donations, and so on. But generally I think that religious authorities believe what they say they believe and are hence mistaken but not deceptive.

They are not, however, necessarily *simply* mistaken. See *Bullshit* and *Sincerity*.

Love: I won't try to define love. You know what it is.

I resent it when god is equated with love. I doubly resent it when love is offered as evidence of the existence of god, or when the rejection of god is somehow seen as a rejection of love. It isn't, in either case. Atheists can truly love, and truly value love. There is no god, but, thankfully, there can be, and is, love.

13

M Is for . . .

Marriage (as a Model for Godfree Living): (1) There is much religious interest, at least in North America, in marriage. Religious groups speak up for so-called traditional marriage and against same-sex marriage. Bigots, sure, but this is not why I bring this up. I bring up marriage because, ironically, it provides a useful model for understanding what a godfree life is like.

I don't know particularly much about the history of marriage, but it pretty clearly has very often been governed by religious norms, institutions, and laws. But currently, in very many countries, we have the existence of purely civil marriage: marriage as governed by civil norms, institutions, and laws. In fact, in places where both religious and civil institutions conduct marriage ceremonies, it is often the civil practices that take precedence. The religious ceremonies might have personal or even some social significance, but it's the civil standing of the relationship that really matters. In case you doubt this, just see what happens when marriages in these places dissolve. It's the legal apparatus of the state, not the church, that clearly matters.

What should we make of all this? The institution of marriage is complex, so I won't pretend to provide an exhaustive study of it, but nevertheless important lessons can be learned. We find here a kind, or array of kinds, of interpersonal relationship that, for millennia, has been known to be deeply important to people. It's so important that we wish to design significant parts of our societies around it, by making official codes that are enacted through official procedures. In many places and at many times, this has been done by religious authorities, which is unsurprising given the long history of mutual engagement of religious and more broadly social affairs. This goes for the history of the society of which I am a part, and it goes for many others. In mine and some of these others, the religious and the civil have grown apart with regard to many aspects of human living. Marriage is a good example. It was hardly possible to think of marriage in nonreligious ways in these societies; now the purely civil takes precedence and the religious aspects of marriage are both optional and eschewed by many.

This pattern of change has not destroyed marriage. Sure, people think of it differently today than in, say, early in the twentieth century. But marriage is very old, and many changes in thought and practice have occurred to it in, for example, the long history that unites Europe and North America. In a nutshell, the recent change is from something important conceived of in religious terms to something important conceived of in nonreligious terms.

This is a pretty good model for the move from a religious life to a godfree life. The things that once mattered to you still matter. They don't matter in the same way, and some of the old things don't matter at all anymore. But things still matter, both old and new. Life goes on, in some ways much as it did before (see *A Very Ordinary Day, Standards,* and *Values*).

It can seem baffling, maybe overwhelming, to consider a change from a religious life to one of nonbelief. Fair enough, when taken in such general terms as this. When wondering what this change is like, and what a godfree life is like, think of marriage. What once was thoroughly religious is now distinctly civil and, officially, godfree. This is a significant change, yet people get married as they did before, which is no change at all.

(2) Arguably there is a second lesson here. When such important aspects of our lives as marriage are freed from the dogma-ridden grip of religion, they are open to constructive reconsideration and redesign. Same-sex marriage would be unthinkable in North America if it were still taken to be a thoroughly religious matter. Anyone who thinks otherwise is deluded. But marriage has been freed from religion, and this institution is being made more fair as a result. Given the tenuous relationship between religion and morality (see *Morality [or, On Loving the Good with and without God]* for details), this is the sort of thing that can be expected as more and more of human life is freed from religion. So maybe things do change after all. Only for the better? I'm not so naïve as to really think that. But maybe.

Meaning of Life: (1) In some senses "yes," in others "no." See *Tragedy (or, Despair about the Meaning of Life), Irony (and Meaning in Life),* and *Absurdity (and Meaning in Life).*

(2) Kai Nielsen has remarked that people who say that if god is dead, nothing matters are spoiled children who lack real compassion for others. He has a point, but it's one that is worth refining. This is more apt to be true of atheists who say this rather than theists. The religious believer who says this might well just be naïve, inexperienced, uninformed. We should not assume that theists understand what it is to live a godfree life. But most atheists have seen the issue from both sides. If such a person still claims, especially without argument, that a secular world includes nothing of consequence, then he is indeed a spoiled child. The atheists who get off the hook are those who have never had a religious worldview, and hence who have not arrived at their secular viewpoint through reflective scrutiny of the nature of the world, of values, and of related issues. These people might be spoiled children, to be sure, but we can't tell from their endorsement of this sort of value nihilism. They might instead be naïve or depressed.

Meat Machines: Anything that is made of meat and operates according to mechanical principles is a machine made of meat. Well, that's us. We are meat machines.

Religion tends to come with a view of human nature. When we reject religion, we should also think twice about our understanding of the kind of thing we are. A religious view of human nature typically includes such ideas as spirits and souls (see *Soul*). These are concepts of supernatural things. When we reject the supernatural, these go with them (see *Supernatural*). This should leave us wondering just what kind of thing we are.

In contrast to supernatural phenomena, a godfree viewpoint sees the world as operating solely according to natural principles. We are wholly a part of this world. Natural principles are, broadly speaking, mechanical principles, if we include in "mechanics" the practical aspects of chemistry, biology, and physics. This means that we are natural machines. We aren't unique in this: *anything* reasonably complicated is a natural machine.

Presumably religions hit on such supernatural ideas as the soul and the spirit as a way of accounting for the nature of our minds. Well, no such supernatural ghosts are responsible for thinking. It is our brains that do this, and these are made of meat. Perhaps the most striking feature of humans is our capacity for thought. This is accomplished by our meaty noggins, not by anything ethereal or divine. We are, more than anything else, meat machines.

Keeping this in mind should help to curtail the vanity that religion indulges, even encourages (see *Humility* and *You*). The whole universe was designed for the likes of you? You have a divine spark inside you that other things don't? You can live forever while everything else is lost to the sands of time? Get over yourself. You are the product of imperfect but wonderful mindless natural design, not magic. In this sense you are just like all the other creatures in the world.

As soon as the idea of meat machines comes up, some people start to worry about ordinary features of human life. You think we are meat machines, so you think that we don't have minds! Can't feel! Can't really love! Aren't responsible for our behavior! (for more see *Love* and *Responsibility*). Of course not. What I mean is that these are things that meat machines do. We are wonderful machines, but we are machines nonetheless. This means that if we are to understand love, responsibility, and the rest, we have to explain them in, broadly, mechanical terms. Self-understanding is mechanical understanding. Magic, which is what religion offers, is out. Once again, this is where the hard work of the sciences (and philosophy and other disciplines) is unavoidable.

The kneejerk worry that seeing ourselves as machines diminishes us speaks to the extent to which broadly religious patterns of thought permeate our lives and structure the ways not just in which we think of ourselves but also in which we pose the very questions that we want to answer about ourselves. See *Language*.

This is where atheism gets you: to seeing yourself as a machine. This can be jarring, and some people will never like it. This does nothing to undermine this view of ourselves, since the world has not been designed for our happiness. Other people, however, will like this idea fine. I do. I'm happy, even proud, to be a machine made of meat.

Mercy: Thought highly of, but tricky, and not so clearly great as people think.

What does "mercy" mean? Part of mercy is releasing someone from a dire situation. Think of so-called mercy killing. This is to kill someone because their physical condition is so bad that continued life is worse than death. Other things being equal this sort of mercy is indeed good. What's not to like about being released from a terrible situation?

Here's something: when the person who releases you from your peril is at the same time responsible for that threat, the mercy is not so good. Why should we love the people who remove their boots from our throats? I can think of many more appropriate responses. To call this "mercy" and to hold it up as laudable is perverse, maybe laughably so.

This, however, is exactly what religions do with regard to god. God is the one who sends you to hell. God is one acknowledged source, in many religious traditions at least, of worldly problems such as disease and office meetings. When the gods offer us ways out of these terrors they are worshipped as merciful. But this is the mercy of a tyrant, not of a saint. This is the mercy of the cat who lets the bird fly away. To ask the bird to love the cat is a bit much. Maybe the idea of god is one worth admiring. If this is the case, god's mercy will have nothing to do with it.

Merry Christmas! (or Happy Christmas!, for Those of a British Background): A problematic greeting, not altogether easy to use or to receive. I avoid it as much as possible. It's a religious greeting, after all. To direct it at the godfree, or to expect to hear it from them, is insensitive to our tastes at least, and maybe even to more sensitive aspects of our lives. Religion has been a source of pain and fear to many of us, so don't expect us to love it when explicitly religious terms are directed at us.

At the same time, with a little thought we can hear this as it is meant—as an inclusive and warm wish offered in a not-particularly-freighted way. We can even sincerely wish Christians a merry Christmas. To say it sincerely from a godfree perspective is to mean, "Enjoy your particular traditional festivities." To say it insincerely is to mean something like, "I don't really hope that you enjoy your hypocritical lip service to a factually and morally dubious religious background." We might mean that sometimes, but we don't have to. We can be expansive in our wishes for others to enjoy themselves in whatever forms they value. To be godfree is not necessarily to be generosity-free.

Is "Season's Greetings!" better. Yes, frankly, despite being a bit wishy-washy. It's fair to all who celebrate various things at the same time of year. Fairer still is for us to wish each other what we like, so long as we mean it generously and extend to each other some courtesy regarding tastes. The godfree can say "Same to you" in much the same spirit as Christians say "Merry Christmas!"

Some Christians are not flexible about their holiday greetings. Some want "Merry Christmas!" to be said by all, regardless of taste, belief, or tradition. To argue for obligatory "Merry Christmas!" is not open-minded or generous. It is a mild form of bullying. The more you have doubts about the value of "Happy Holidays!" the more suspect your "Merry Christmas!"

Overall, this is one of the least important things for believers and godfree alike to worry about.

Miracles: There are none, in any literal sense. This means that they can't, literally, have any divine significance.

Many religions and religiously minded people take seriously the idea that miracles happen. Sometimes these are offered as evidence for the existence of god (see *Evidence* for discussion). But just what is meant by a "miracle" is typically left unexplained. When we reflect on the possibilities, we discover problems.

Perhaps the most common understanding is that a miracle is something impossible that nevertheless happens. Its impossibility implies that it must be due to special—that is, godly—causes rather than mundane ones. This is arguably the way to understand Christ's feeding of multitudes from a few loaves and fishes, or his producing wine from mere water, or his healing of people who suffer from fatal illnesses with a mere touch. Note, however, that it's not just any sense of "impossible" that matters here. God is constrained by logical possibility (see *Morality [or, On Loving the Good with and without God]* for discussion) and arguably by her own nature. Can god cause himself not to exist? Not if the ontological argument is to be believed (see *Ontological Argument*). So some things are impossible even for god. The sense of "impossibility" that matters for miracles is natural: it is impossible, by natural law, for one to turn water into wine (without other things, like sugar and yeast, being involved, over a significant period of time). On this understanding, a miracle is a happening that is contrary to natural law. The miraculous is the naturally impossible that nevertheless happens.

This way of understanding the miraculous suffers from a misunderstanding of what natural law is. Our formulations of laws of nature are descriptions of general, relatively abstract features of the world. They are devised by observation of what happens, and their import is to probe the structure of what is naturally possible. Anything that happens, on this view, is naturally possible. Nothing that happens can be a violation of natural law. If laws of nature were like criminal laws—codes devised by agents that things could choose to follow or to break—then, in principle, things that happened could be contrary to these laws. But that's not what natural laws are like. Natural laws follow the things that happen, rather than having a mindful source independent of these things. Nothing that happens is contrary to natural law; nothing that happens is unnatural. And hence nothing that happens is literally miraculous in this sense.

Sometimes, rather than the naturally impossible, people classify as "miraculous" things that we don't understand. If we can't explain it, it's a miracle! For instance, when someone has a health problem that disappears without treatment, people often call it miraculous. This often goes hand-in-hand with the first definition of "miracle": the reason we can't understand something is that it's due to god rather than to the natural principles we codify as laws of nature. Regardless of these links, the concept of the miraculous as the inexplicable provides no evidence of anything at all, worldly or unworldly, other than the limits of our understanding. This is a version of a fallacious inference from ignorance (see *Ignorance*). From the fact that we don't know something—which is what calling something inexplicable amounts to—we can only infer that we don't know that thing, not that it has a particular source, nature, or cause. This sort of inference goes beyond the fact of our ignorance and hence requires specific evidence independent of our current inability to explain what has happened. And note: once an explanation is provided, this sense of "miraculous" is dispelled, which is a very strange thing to happen, once we reflect on the use to which people put the idea of miracles.

Further ways of invoking miracles water down the idea to such an extent that it's surprising that people take them seriously at all. People call uncommon things "miracles," even when we know how they happen and when they are perfectly explicable in natural terms. It's a miracle that I won the lottery! It's a miracle that the tornado missed my house but destroyed all my neighbors' houses! But the fact that something is unusual implies nothing supernatural about its nature or origin. To make such an inference betrays lack of understanding of both the nature of the world and of basic statistics.

Finally, the weakest use of "miracle" ties it to things that merely catch our attention. Consider "the miracle of birth." Hardly anything could be more common or natural—there are seven billion of us, for goodness' sake!—and we know how babies are made. The only thing "miraculous" about conception and birth is that people are enthralled by it. There's nothing special about it other than our interest in it, and so there's nothing about human reproduction that indicates anything divine.

It is probably the case that there are abstruse notions of "miracle" other than these. But such notions are not what is meant by any typical, real-world invocations of the miraculous, and hence they cannot vindicate claims of miracles made by ordinary people. Moreover, it is far from clear that such technical versions would warrant our attention in arguments about the supernatural. If miracles are consistent with natural law, for instance, then they are natural, regardless of what else might be said about them. The natural provides no grounds for belief in the supernatural. Given this, it is worth assuming that when people claim that something is "miraculous," this should be taken with at least one grain of worldly, skeptical salt.

Moral Math (or, Good vs. Bad Effects of Religion and Atheism): Has the contribution of religion to the world been generally positive or generally negative? What about particular religions? And what about of those who give up religion? Can we answer these questions at all accurately?

Well, we can certainly make a start. The good and bad consequences of at least particular religious institutions have been tallied and debated by both defenders and opponents. I think the case is pretty decisively negative for these institutions, but we can all admit that this is tricky territory worth handling with care. I'm aware of the dangers of bias (and I hope that others are too). The important (and gruesome, and lamentable) details can be found elsewhere. Instead, let's get in mind some general principles of doing this sort of assessment and some perspective on the stakes.

Perhaps the most important general principle is this: when assessing the consequence of beliefs, institutions, ways of life, both the good and the bad must be taken into account. It's too easy for defenders to focus on the good alone and opponents just on the bad, and to rest their cases there. This won't do, on simple mathematical grounds. This should be so obvious as to be uncontroversial, but it's forgotten often enough that it's worth emphasizing.

This general principle yields some interesting nuances. One is that the good and the bad can be complexly interwoven. Consider the Catholic Church in Africa. It has long opposed the use of condoms as birth control, and this influence has significantly contributed to the spread of AIDS in certain African countries. This is a bad thing. But the Catholic Church also has healthcare initiatives around the world, including Africa. Some Catholic hospitals and healthcare workers provide valuable care for people suffering from AIDS in Africa. This is a good thing. But how much credit does Catholicism deserve for addressing a problem that it has helped to perpetuate? Less than for other goods, it seems to me. These sorts of complexities make the assessment of the contribution of such institutions to the world even more difficult to assess than it might seem at first glance.

A related nuance is that it must be acknowledged to be acceptable to ask questions about the bad that we all produce, even for those of us who also produce good things. The good does not make the bad disappear, except perhaps in very special cases. Nor does the bad erase the good, of course, although we might well wonder whether the bad is generally more serious than the good.

As an analogy, consider a doctor who murders his neighbor. As a doctor this man has a generally life-preserving, even life-saving, history. But the murder is a significant moral evil. It's so serious that we can certainly reasonably ask whether the doctor's good contributions to the world are outweighed by it. We can also legitimately wonder whether it is acceptable to associate with this person. And I take it that we would generally find it clear that this would be a very dubious person to hold up as a moral ideal. This analogy, of course, means that these questions apply to all major religious institutions and traditions, and probably to most minor ones as well. The answers might turn out to be positive ones, but we certainly cannot assume that this will be the case.

Doing the moral math is even trickier for atheism. There are very few, if any, institutions and traditions that count as explicitly godfree. We have no creed that unifies us, no churches at which we officially meet. Maybe there have been governments that have been completely religion-free, but this is very hard to assess. Some have substituted more secular targets for the machinery of belief that religion deploys (for example, rigidification and enforcement of dogma), making these religious in spirit if not in name. And we cannot assume that people who appear nonreligious really are— see *A Very Ordinary Day*. This goes for complex traditions and institutions as well. Hence the contribution of atheism to the world is very hard to pin down with any accuracy.

At the end of the day, does any of this matter? Only sort of. We should want people, traditions, institutions, and so on to be, on balance, morally good, not bad. This goes without saying. But in the case of religion and atheism, the central question is one of truth. Is it true or false that there is a god, a divine realm, supernatural beings, and the like? An organization with a bad track record could nevertheless hold and represent the true answer to this sort of question. So, strictly speaking, the moral math just does not speak to the truth or falsity of claims made in discussions of religious topics. Good results don't themselves deliver true beliefs.

Morality (or, On Loving the Good with and without God): (1) This is a big topic. I suspect that for some people it's *the* big topic. I am routinely surprised by the frequency with which this topic arises in discussions of the existence of god. The implications are many. Some are familiar: that you can't be good without god, that you should believe in god if you take morality seriously. Others are more disturbing, even sinister: for example, that some people who seem to be good are so detached from the nature of goodness that it takes belief in the supernatural to keep them on the straight and narrow. There is a lot to straighten out here. Much of what I have to say will be familiar to anyone who has taken a certain sort of philosophy course. Or it should be; I'm routinely surprised by how much confusion there is to be found on this topic, despite the time-honored and easily found lines of thought that clarify things. The roots of what follows are found in Plato, for goodness' sake! That's pre-Christian philosophy! And yet the arguments seem to be unfamiliar to many. They are good and important arguments, so here it all is—once again for those who have heard it all before, but, puzzlingly, the first time for many.

What is the relationship between god, or religion, and morality? Lots of people assume that the religious life is the morally good life, and that increases in attention to religion correspond with increases in virtue. Consider New Year's resolutions: sometimes people who want to be morally better resolve to go to church more often. Consider also politicians who (let's say sincerely) publicly consult with religious figures when facing a big decision, such as making amends for a personal wrongdoing or invading a foreign country. The popular associations between ideas of god, religion, and morality are legion. Are they also sound?

Why might people associate god with moral values? Certainly religions tend to be a source of ethical advice. These teachings are a mixed bag, as we all know. Look up what major religious texts have to say about slavery or shellfish in case you want a hint. Regardless, all this advice is one reason for people to link god with goodness. Let's put this aside, as I suspect that it is merely an incidental reason. What deep, principled reasons might there be for thinking that morality and god are intricately connected?

The most important answer lies in one of the jobs traditionally ascribed to god: that of origin of everything. It is common, at least within certain important religious traditions, to claim that god created the heavens and the earth. One way of understanding this, both more and less literally it seems to me, is to think of god as the creator of everything. This must include moral values, so the thought goes. God created us, god created the earth, god is the source of the universe, and part of all this is moral values. So, by virtue of the job of creator of everything, god must be the source of morality.

The practical steps that people sometimes make when they link religion and morality would make sense if god were the origin of morality. If you want to be a better person, maybe you should go to church more often. If you are a politician wondering about making public amends for your shortcomings or about the moral justification of the war you are inclined to enter, maybe you ought to seek religious help. Since god is the origin of morality, religious experts ought to know a thing or two about moral values.

As it turns out, this is all very problematic, for a variety of reasons. Here's why. The basic version of this view of morality is typically referred to as "divine command theory." Suppose that we ask someone committed to this idea why, for example, killing people is wrong. The person might well answer, "Because god says so." God's command is offered as the foundation, and hence explanation, of the moral status of a familiar sort of action. The focus on commands is, however, unduly limited. The person might well have said, "Because god does not want you to do that" or "Because god hates killing." Here it is god's feelings that are the foundation of the wrongness of killing. In general, divine command theorists portray god's perspective as the source of moral values, regardless of how this perspective is expressed.

This is certainly a natural way to understand the idea that god is the source of everything, including moral values, but this does not mean that it's a convincing idea. Let's think through its implications. Consider first the meanings of moral terms such as "good" and "right." Whatever else these might mean, surely if something is good then it is worth liking or pursuing, or we have reason to like or pursue or promote this thing. Likewise, if some action is right then it is decisively worth liking or promoting, or we have decisive reason to like or perform it. The same goes for our terms for negative evaluation: the bad is what is worth disliking, and the wrong is what we have decisive reason not to perform.

Now consider the usage of these evaluative concepts. For example, take the claim that torturing children for fun is wrong. Fair enough, it seems to me—this is unlikely to be a controversial moral judgment. Nevertheless, we can meaningfully ask why it is wrong. In virtue of what precisely is torturing children for fun wrong? Why is it worth disliking? What gives us decisive reason not to do this sort of thing? The likely and correct answers to this question will offer details about torturing children for fun: the pain, the damage, the lack of redeeming effects—these are the sorts of thing that answer our evaluative questions.

Here is the important implication of this for present purposes. The divine command theorist cannot say any of this about torturing children for fun. This means that the divine command theorist can't give the right answer to these questions. By the standards of the view that it is god's perspective that is the source of moral values, it is false that torturing children for fun is wrong because of the details about the kind of thing that it is. Instead it is wrong because of god's perspective on this action.

Let's be clear about these implications. By normal standards, torturing children for fun is wrong because of the kind of thing it is. Divine command theory requires us to give up this idea. Instead it is wrong because god says so, and not because there is something inherently problematic about torturing children for fun. Until and unless god says otherwise, we should not think that torturing children for fun is wrong.

Even more strikingly, if god said otherwise, then torturing children for fun would not be wrong. The pain and the damage are only bad if god makes them bad. If god likes them or commands us to do these things, then they become good and right.

This is but one example of ordinary moral reasoning. In *all* cases it is the facts about particular sorts of objects, actions, and states of affairs that give these things their particular evaluative status. It is details about these facts that we offer to explain our moral judgments. And in *all* cases, the divine command theorists cannot offer these very details. The true answer, by the standard of divine command theory, must always cite god's perspective, not the worldly details.

So far so bad for divine command theory, I'm inclined to think. Here's why. On one hand we might think that what this reveals is merely that divine command theory requires a revision of ordinary thinking about morality. We can't assume, after all, that we already understand morality before we scrutinize it. We must be open to the possibility of discovery that requires a change in our habits of thought. Fair enough, but note that divine command theory does not require mere here-and-there change. It requires us to give up any answer to a moral question that cites ordinary worldly details as making something good or bad, right or wrong. That is, so far as I can tell, a wholesale revision of moral reasoning, which of course needs considerable defense. Instead I'm inclined to take a firmer stance: it's not just that we think that, for example, it's the worldly details that explain why torturing children for fun is wrong. Rather this is something that we know. We might not know all of the particular details, but we know that they are the sort of thing on offer to explain why this is wrong. And since divine command theory requires us to give this up, divine command theory must be wrong.

This is only the tip of the iceberg for views that root morality in god's perspective. Think about the view of the world and god's commands that

112 • A Is for Atheist

the divine command theorist offers. When god says that something is good or bad, right or wrong, this is not rooted in the nature of the world. There is nothing about the world, by the standards of this view, that makes things good or bad, right or wrong. It is god's will that imbues the world with value. This should be emphasized: it is *only* god's perspective that is the source of value. God can make *any* particular thing good or bad, *any* action right or wrong. The implication is that god's commands, feelings, etc., and with them all of morality, are arbitrary by the standards of divine command theory. This is just to say that gods cannot have reasons for their pronouncements about value, because this view implies that there are no possible reasons. The world is evaluatively neutral; gods can say "good" or "bad" as they please, since there is nothing about the world to which such pronouncements should answer. Ironically, despite seeming to offer firm foundations for moral values, divine command theorists take precisely this away.

Now, this might seem like a rather austere problem. Not everyone cares about the solidity of the foundation of moral values. But it implies problematic things about god. Indeed, this is the other side of the coin for divine command theorists: their view not only makes a mess of our understanding of moral values, it also makes a mess out of our notions of god. Atheists don't have to care about this, of course, but religious believers do.

Here are the problems. Divine command theory robs us of the idea of god as a moral authority, and with this as someone or something worth listening to. Consider first the normal notion of an authority about something. This is someone who, essentially, is an expert about a particular topic. An authority about the wildflowers of Cape Breton knows a lot about these flowers. With this knowledge come certain powers of judgment. The wildflower authority, on the basis of her knowledge, can judge whether a particular flower is a typical one for a given place or a rather rare one. Those of us who are not experts have reason to take seriously the wildflower authority's judgments precisely because of her command of the relevant body of knowledge.

Here is the problem: divine command theory implies that god cannot be this sort of authority about morality, and hence that we do not have this sort of reason to take seriously divine pronouncements about values.

The reason is that if god's perspective is the source of moral values, then there is no body of knowledge about values for god to be an expert in. God's pronouncements are arbitrary, remember—whatever she says goes, with regard to moral values. The Cape Breton wildflower authority is an authority because of her command of a body of truths. But by the standards of divine command theory, there are no moral truths analogous to these botanical ones, and hence there is no opportunity for god to be this sort of authority. The wildflower expert can be right or wrong about Cape Breton fauna. By contrast, divine command theory implies that there is nothing for god to be right or wrong about. With such knowledge goes much of the reason to listen to god about values. Divine command theory takes away the possibility of god being an expert about values whose judgments we should listen to because of this expertise. No truths entails no knowledge, no knowledge implies no expertise, no expertise implies no reason for us to pay attention to god's pronouncements. Morality's arbitrariness, according to this view, isn't such an austere problem after all.

This is still not the end of the problems with views that offer god's perspective as the foundation of moral values. One might be tempted by this sort of view out of respect for god. She is so powerful that she is the origin of value itself. Ironically, however, divine command theory undermines our capacity to compliment god and divine pronouncements.

One of the things that is commonly said of god is that he is good (or great, or wonderful, etc.). Correlatively, people can be inclined to say that god's will or pronouncements are good (or worth heeding, or whatever). In both cases what is meant is what it sounds like: god is being complimented using such words as "good" in their normal sense.

Here is the problem. If we root moral values in god's perspective, then we lose the ability to say complimentary things about him and his will. At best we end up saying something empty. Suppose, for instance, that by "good" we mean something like "commanded by god." A believer might commend a way of acting, such as giving to charity, by saying that god commands us to do this, or loves this way of acting, for example. This grounds goodness in god's commands directly, but it takes away our ability to assess god's commands themselves. By the standards of this sort of view, someone who claims that god's commands are good is really saying that god's commands are commanded by god. The assessment of god's commands has disappeared with this translation. This person turns out not to be saying anything of interest at all about god's commands. Divine command theory turns our compliments about god into empty statements with no evaluative content whatsoever.

This is the best-case scenario. The worst is that any view that makes god's perspective the source of moral value turns our attempts at compliments into insults. Yikes! Here is how: suppose that by "good" we mean "loved by god." Now consider the claim that god is good. Normally this is meant as a compliment. But by the standards of divine command theory this claim means something like god loves himself. It is very hard to hear this as a compliment. When we speak of people loving themselves, we sometimes mean it descriptively, but at least as often we mean it pejoratively. "Oh, he's so in love with himself!" is not a compliment. It's a claim that the person is a narcissist. Completely accidentally then, divine command theory risks turning our compliments about god into insults. Do theists really want to say, when they claim that god is good, that he loves himself? I find it hard to believe that this has ever been the intended meaning of an assessment of god as good.

This can be usefully connected to the earlier thoughts about seeing god as a moral authority who is worthy of being taken seriously. If god's goodness amounts to self-love, we lose our grip on why we should worship, or even respect, god. God's goodness could, by normal standards, be offered to explain why we should worship her. But this underpinning of our respect is eroded by divine command theory. A supernatural narcissist is not worthy of our respect, never mind our devotion. The pronouncements of such a figure are worth summary dismissal, not serious consideration.

I can imagine defenders of divine command theory balking at this point. The assumption has been that when we say of god that she is good, we are saying the same sort of thing as when we compliment our neighbor as good. Maybe this assumption is incorrect. This would mean that when we compliment god, we are saying something quite different from normal uses of "good" and associated terms. At the very least we are judging god by a special standard that does not apply to other things. God's will is the standard for judging other things as good, but not god himself.

Maybe. However, maybe not. There are at least three problems with this sort of view. The first is that it is, so far as I can tell, just false. People don't mean something different when they compliment god; they mean generally the same sort of thing as when they compliment people. This way of saving divine command theory implies that we use a deep double standard when assessing god versus assessing people. This just seems not to be the case.

Now put aside this worry. Let's assume that we do, or should, employ this sort of double standard when assessing god and divine commands. Suppose that we ask about the details of this standard. If it's not god's will, just what is it that makes god and his perspective good? We have two broad options for answering this question, neither of which is good news for divine command theory.

The first option for answering this question offers particular qualities of god as establishing his goodness. In virtue of what is god good? Maybe it's his love. Maybe it's his benevolence, or mercy (tricky—see *Mercy*), or whatever; the particular options are numerous, but their details don't matter right now. What matters is the idea of explaining god's goodness in any terms whatsoever. If we specify details about just what makes god, then in effect we build an account of goodness that conflicts with divine command theory. Suppose that it's god's love, benevolence, and justice that make him good. Since this is supposed to be an account of god's goodness that is different from divine command theory, we are to understand the value of these characteristics as independent from god's perspective on them. God's love is good regardless of what god thinks about it, for instance. But this flies in the face of the account of the origin of value offered by divine command theory, making its account of other sorts of value that much more tenuous.

Moreover, these characteristics can be found elsewhere. People can be loving, just, and benevolent. Aren't these characteristics good when we have them too, regardless of what god thinks about them? After all, when we speak of god being just, benevolent, or loving, this is usually understood to be meant in the same sense as when we speak of humans in these terms. A defender of divine command theory could insist that when we speak of god's love, we are, for instance, speaking metaphorically and hence not of love in the same sense as when we speak of each other (alarm bells should go off here—see *Symbolism [or, Analogy, Metaphor]*). This, however, should be unsatisfying to all believers who understand such statements literally.

It is also essentially to retreat to unexplained mystery with regard to god's goodness; see *Mystery* for concerns about this in general.

This brings us to the second option. Instead of trying to specify details about god's goodness, one could insist that god is just good and that there is nothing that can be said or understood about this. This is full-on embrace of mystery, which is a problem (remember, I just referred you to *Mystery*). More to the point, however, it does not do the job that it should be doing. The reason to seek a distinct standard of goodness for god was to preserve a complimentary sense of "good" for him. This is what divine command theory threatened, after all. But an unexplained sense of goodness is not complimentary either. Consider what this strategy involves. It requires that we think that god is good not because she is loving or just or benevolent . . . or whatever. There is nothing that can be offered to shed light on god's goodness. This is just a way of saying that we don't really know what it means to say that god is good, but we're confident that it means something nice.

Crucially, to say that god is good cannot be understood to be anything like what it means to say that a person is good. We can explain this—or, at least we can using normal patterns of evaluative thought and talk, which are threatened by divine command theory. People are good because, for example, they are honest, courageous, etc. Not god, if this strategy is adopted. And so the claim that god is good is robbed of all its content. The compliment is empty, which is no compliment whatsoever. It's nice to want to pay a compliment to god, but surely it is a meaningful one that is intended.

Here is where we stand: the view that claims that god is the origin of values faces a host of problems. Some concern our idea of god. Others concern the ways in which we speak and think about values. A religious believer could, in principle, bite the bullet and acquiesce with deep revision on both sides. Few have, in fact, wanted to do this. Moreover, I'm not sure that such revision is really acceptable with regard to values. If what's at stake is not just how we speak and think of values but what we know about values, then the adherent of divine command theory who insists on revision here is committing herself to error.

All of these problems go away if divine command theory is given up. Suppose that god is not the origin of values. Instead, god says that certain things are good or right because they really are good or right, independently of god's perspective. This allows us to say the normal things about values— for example, that torturing children for fun is wrong literally because of the nature of torturing children for fun. God could not make this right; its value is independent of his perspective. If this isn't just the way we tend to speak about values but something that we know about values, then any account of the relation between god and morality had better deliver this view of things or it will be false.

This way of seeing the relation between god and morality saves morality from arbitrariness. God's pronouncements and feelings about values are no longer free-floating. They are grounded in the real values of things. When god loves something, it is a response to its independent goodness. This allows for god to be a moral authority in the normal sense: he is a perfect expert about values. He can be this because, let's say, he is omniscient and because there is a body of information about values that is independent of his perspective that he can have perfect knowledge of.

Finally, and relatedly, this view of god-morality relations delivers a natural and ordinary sense in which people can say complimentary things about god. Suppose that you want to say that god is good. What does this mean now? It means that there is a standard of value independent of god's perspective to which god measures up perfectly. People can be good by the same standard, but not to the same extent. If moral values are not determined by god's will, then we have a simple and natural way of understanding how we can say normal complimentary things about him that many want to say.

So: theists have multiple reasons to think that morality is independent of god. There are three things to note about this independence. First, there is no reason to think that religious devotion or activities have a special link to information about being good. Many religious people do know a lot about what is right and wrong, but it's not because they are religious (or, at least not directly). It's because they have a lot of experience of the world and the kinds of lives that people live, so they have learned a thing or two about what is valuable. Crucially, if we want to be better people or to understand morality better, we should also pay attention to the world and our activities in it. Churches and religious texts are probably not a particularly good way of doing this. They are certainly not a uniquely good way.

Second, atheists do not give up morality along with a belief in the existence of god. Morality, even by believers' standards, should not be thought to depend on god. So the rejection of god implies nothing about the existence and authority of moral standards. We can be good without god. We can arguably love the good more directly if we give up thinking about god. It is just a mistake to think that, without god, anything goes.

Finally, some religious believers might be uncomfortable with the idea that moral values are not created by god. Besides the lines of thought already examined, which should show the importance of separating morality from god, all I can do is offer some partners in crime. For some this will make the situation better, but for others this will make it worse! So be it.

God is constrained by an independent realm of moral values. If something is by its nature wrong, then god cannot make it right. Likewise, the truths of math and logic are also outside of god's power. He is constrained by these also. So it shouldn't seem so strange to think of morality as not dependent on god's perspective—it's not alone.

Let's start with logic. Consider a valid pattern of inference: *modus ponens*. *Modus ponens* has this form:

Premise (1): If A then B

Premise (2): A

Conclusion: Therefore B.

What this is saying is this: if A implies B and A is actually the case, then B must also be the case. If we believe that A implies B and that A is the case, then we should also believe that B is the case. We are justified in inferring B from these premises. The form of this argument guarantees, 100%, the truth of the conclusion provided that, when filled in, the premises are true.

Here is an example with the variables filled in:

Premise (1): If people care about religion, then I will sell a million copies of this book.

Premise (2): People care about religion.

Conclusion: Therefore I will sell a million copies of this book.

The form of this argument guarantees, 100%, the truth of the conclusion provided that, when filled in, the premises are true. Alas, the truth of the premises is not guaranteed. I wish that people's interest in religion meant that I would sell a million copies of this book, but it probably doesn't. Too bad for me, but it does nothing to impugn logic and the validity of *modus ponens.*

God cannot make *modus ponens* invalid. God cannot make it the case that B does not follow from these two premises. Suppose that B was not the case despite A being the case. This would mean that the first premise was false: A does not in fact imply B. A and not-B means that A does not imply B, which is just the denial of Premise 1. People caring about religion but not buying my book, which is the combination of Premise 2 and the Conclusion, also shows that Premise 1 is false. God cannot hold premises with this form true yet make the conclusion false. With the conclusion automatically goes the truth of the first premise, whether god likes it or not.

That math is not dependent on god is even easier to show. Consider a simple equation: 2+2=4. God cannot make this false. Let's be clear about what the claim is. It is not that god can't give the symbols different meanings that make the equation false. We can all do that. We can stipulate, for instance, that the symbol "2" stands for the quantity 2.5, meaning that 2+2 equals 5, not 4. This is a point about language, not about math. The mathematical issue is about quantity. "2" stands for the quantity two, which can be represented with dots: $(\cdot\,\cdot)$ God cannot make the conjunction of $(\cdot\,\cdot)$ with $(\cdot\,\cdot)$ equal anything other than $(\cdot\,\cdot\,\cdot\,\cdot)$. That's how these quantities go together. If we are faced with a result of $(\cdot\,\cdot\,\cdot\,\cdot\,\cdot)$, then it wasn't $(\cdot\,\cdot)$ and $(\cdot\,\cdot)$ that were combined. The quantities—the dots—just won't work like that, regardless of what we or god say about this.

The upshot is that we should think of god as constrained by independent domains of various sorts of truths—at least morality, math, and logic, but maybe others. For some religious believers this will be hard to swallow, but that's just too bad: this is how the phenomena work. For others, placing morality in a context of other constraints on god will make it easier to accept that morality does not depend on a divine perspective. Atheists, of course, have no special problems with what to accept here. Crucially, both believers and the godfree can directly love the good.

(2) All of this shows that theists and atheists alike should think of morality as independent of god. What it doesn't show is how this works, and this is something that people should have questions about. We understand what it's like to be given rules by an authority figure, and this is what it would be like if morality were determined by god's will. But what is morality like if it's not dependent on god's will? Here are a few words about this.

The first thing to do is to recall what it means to use evaluative terms. If something is good then it is worth liking or pursuing, or we have reason to like or pursue or promote this thing. If some action is right then it is decisively worth liking or promoting, or, equivalently, we have decisive reason to like or perform it. The bad is what is worth disliking, and the wrong is what we have decisive reason not to perform. This gives us our first hint about what moral reasoning looks like without god: we have to look around, at ourselves and the world in which we operate, and try to determine what we have reason to do and what we have reason not to do. Consider torturing children for fun once again. Do we have reason to like this or to dislike it? To answer this we need to collect some details. Fun is good, so that provides a consideration in favor of liking this act. We know this from our experiences of fun. But torture involves pain and damage, and we know from our experiences of those that they are bad, and can be really bad, so we have reason to dislike those. And so on, on through the details, drawn from our own experiences, from others' experiences, and from whatever other sources of information turn out to be useful.

John McDowell has emphasized that, with regard to understanding moral reasons, morality works much like other aspects of human experience. Take fear as an example. We all know that there are things that are worth being scared about, while other things scare us but aren't really scary. It's important to be able to tell the difference. This requires that we sort out fear-reasons. That is, we have to see which things scare us, then try to figure which are worth being scared of. This requires attention to particular properties of the triggers of our fear experiences. Suppose that I am afraid of the sound of thunder. Thunder is the sound of massive electrical discharges from the sky to the earth, and this can be lethally dangerous, so this is a reason in favor of fearing thunder. But very few people are actually harmed by these discharges, which is a reason not to be afraid. Loud noises are useful signals for tracking danger—a reason to take fear of thunder seriously—but this signal is grossly over warning, which is a reason not to be afraid of it. And so on, with regard to the ways in which thunder enters our lives. The present lesson is that it is a mistake to try to make morality absolutely unique. In many ways it functions like other aspects of our lives. It doesn't have to be any more mysterious than they are.

In some ways this is so familiar that it barely bears saying. This is what we do all the time, pretty informally, when we puzzle our way through figuring out what we have reason to do. At the same time it is worth spelling out because some people do this much more formally. When we think through our reasons for response and action with regard to very particular things, we are doing what is known as "applied ethics." When we stand back and think more abstractly about our reasons for action, we are doing "normative theory." These are studied by philosophers and professionals in other academic disciplines, and have been, one way or another, for centuries. Other sorts of ethicist study even more abstract features of morality; this is the body of study known as "metaethics." Literally millions of godfree words have been written about these topics, and millions more will follow. This is obviously not the place to delve into this territory in detail.

The bottom line is this: if you want to really know about how godfree morality works, there is no getting around some hard work. Pick up a text book! (See *Pick Up a Text Book* for more on the importance of this activity.) There is no getting around doing this work, and, in fact, religious devotees have often committed themselves to doing exactly the right sort of scrutiny of values. Since the work is hard, lots of people will be morally flawed regardless of their religious tendencies. I offer no guarantees of goodness. Suspect those who do.

(3) Tying god to morality, depending on how it is done, makes at least two other mistakes. One is a misrepresentation of human motivation. Many religious thinkers either explicitly or implicitly think that people will not pursue the good or avoid the bad without a threat to their eternal well-being. Toe the line or go to hell! God is offered as a divine police officer whose job is to keep people on the straight-and-narrow despite their more natural self-centred, even murderous, tendencies. But human motivation is

not like this. For one thing it is much more complicated. For another many people have no problem seeking the good and avoiding the bad, or, to put it in a more down to earth way, they have no problem putting aside their own interests for the good of others. When you put these ideas together you get the altogether realistic possibility of people being simultaneously moved in self-interested and other-serving ways. Doing the good is a tricky task, but people do not in general need a ghostly threat to make them do this.

The second and related mistake is to assume that moral demands require a divine foundation in order to be authoritative. The last mistake concerned what moves us; this one concerns the source of the authority of moral reasons. Suppose there is no god—does this mean that we have no reason not to own slaves? Not to torture? Not to steal, lie, etc.? One might think that moral reasons disappear along with god. Sure, torturing causes immense suffering, but this suffering does not provide any reason to act in particular ways without divine backing.

The mistake here is not peculiar to religious thought. The core error is to assume that we need a general account of the authority of moral reasons over and above the nature of those reasons themselves. The reason not to torture is, let's say, the suffering. When you doubt this, what is needed is not a story about god or a theory about the authority of moral reasons. What is needed is for you to reacquaint yourself with the nature of suffering. *That* is the reason not to torture, but you can't really be expected to get this if you don't have a clear view of what suffering involves.

This point generalizes: particular worldly facts provide moral reasons, and there is not necessarily anything general to be said about them. To insist on a general account is a mistake. And this means that the absence of god makes no difference to the authority of moral reasons. Pain makes torture wrong, not pain backed up by God. When you doubt that you have moral reasons to do anything ever, you have lost a grip on your moral math and need to redo your ethical sums. This is just to say that the hard work gestured at above cannot be shirked.

Let's make this more specific using a bit of technical vocabulary. We can distinguish between first- and second-order issues (questions, reasons, bodies of discourse, and so on). Take tennis as an example. First-order questions about tennis are directly about tennis. A question about the mechanics of a forehand is a first-order question. Second-order tennis questions are about first-order tennis questions and only indirectly about tennis. A question about questions about forehands is a second-order tennis question.

Here's why I bring this up: in at least some forms, god is invoked in order to provide a second-order theory about moral reasons. The first-order reason, for example, that torture is wrong invokes its suffering. But the supposed second-order reason that this first-order reason holds is, for example, that god wills it to be thus. The crucial thing to note is that first- and second-order questions (issues, etc.) are different sorts of questions. If you want to know about the mechanics of forehands, you have to pay attention to the first-order tennis questions. The second-order ones are about a different topic—they are about thought about tennis and tennis specifics, such as forehands. Likewise, if you want to know what makes things right and wrong, you have to attend to the first-order moral issues. The second-order moral issues are about different topics—they are about thought and discourse about right and wrong, and only indirectly about right and wrong.

Here is another way to make clear the error that is made here. We must distinguish two issues. On one hand there are the reasons that things are right or wrong—these are the first-order reasons. On the other there are questions about how these considerations get to have the status of reasons; this is second-order territory. One reason, for example, that torture is wrong is the suffering that it causes. But one might have questions about suffering: can it really provide reasons not to do such things as torturing? What gives it this authority over us? God is sometimes invoked to answer this question. Why? And why should we think that the second-order perspective is necessary for the first order to have the role that it does? The move might be generated by an implicit assumption that nothing can be a reason all by itself. Instead, something like divine intention must be cited to explain the authority certain considerations have. But this won't work. It generates an infinite regress that means nothing is ever a reason: see *Tragedy (or, Despair about the Meaning of Life), Irony (and Meaning in Life),* and *Absurdity (and Meaning in Life)* for more in this vein. Say that pain makes suffering wrong. The present line of thought suggests that the reason that pain has this role is something else, such as god's wishes—they are the reason that pain can be a moral reason. But the present line of thought also suggests that god's wishes need their status as reasons vouchsafed by something else. This is because *nothing* is a reason all on its own, including god's thoughts. This third thing would need its status as a reason delivered by something else, and so on forever without ever concluding, which means that nothing is really a reason. To avoid this regress we must admit that there is no logical necessity for reasons to derive their authority from other considerations: some reasons are reasons on their own. This goes, when we attend to the details, for some first-order reasons. The implicit source of the search for something else to vindicate all reasons should be given up, not indulged.

Not all religious thought posits god in a second-order spirit. Some offer gods as directly making things right and wrong. This is just divine command theory, and I have already examined the problems with this position. However we posit god in moral theory, there are problems with tying right and wrong closely to a divine perspective.

(4) The relations between morality and prudence deserve some consideration (big topic: *Pick Up a Textbook*). Prudence is the domain of self-interest. To act prudently is to do what is good for you, in some way. Morality is the territory of right and wrong more broadly understood. One religious line of thought arranges prudence and morality in one way, while an important godfree pattern of argument arranges them differently. The religious idea is the presumption about motivation just examined, that people need to be threatened with hell in order to be good. This grounds our reasons to be good in our thoughts about our own well-being. The world does not include a hell, however, so it might seem that atheists remove an important motivational prop from morality, and perhaps the foundation of moral reasons altogether, by severing this link between morality and prudence. However, as we have just seen, we should insist on the possibility of both moral motivation and moral reasons distinct from our concern with our own well-being. Morality does not have to be rooted in prudence; we can be directly good. Of course there might be worldly links between morality and prudence, but we need not insist on this in general, nor on the supernatural link in particular.

Prudence provides a good model for demystifying morality. Some people—lots of people—can't comprehend how anything can be morally required or prohibited without a god. This is a puzzle about the possibility of moral reasons. But consider prudential reasons—that is, our reasons to do things that serve our own well-being. This is clearly grounded in facts about us, our nature, our interests, and the world in which we find ourselves. This is not at all mysterious. The worldly ground of moral directives is, in principle, no more and no less mysterious than that of prudential directives. Godfree morality is no more mysterious than godfree self-interest is. (The same goes for reasons to believe things—epistemic reasons—but I won't belabor the details.)

(5) Suppose that you are an atheist who, along the lines provided above, takes seriously objective moral facts without god. When you speak about these issues with people who assume that there are tight links between god and morality, or who at least take the possibility of such links seriously, you might well be asked for examples of objective moral facts. I have made the mistake of offering examples of objective moral facts—for example, by pointing out that pain is bad, or that slavery is wrong—in response to this question. These are good, simple candidates for moral facts. If there are any moral facts they are, after all, objective facts. However, the people asking this question don't really want examples of objective moral facts. To take the question at face value, as respectful as this might seem, is a mistake, as I have regretfully learned. What these people want is an explanation of how any moral facts could be objective, which is a much more difficult thing to provide. One way of getting into it is to go through something like the discussion of possible links between god and morality that I have already provided. Another way of getting into it is through the concerted study of secular ethics. As indicated above, there is lots to look at about particular moral issues and more general considerations of right and wrong from a godfree perspective. Serious study of this territory requires not just familiarity with accounts of how we should act in particular contexts or in general. It requires that we pay attention to challenges to the proffered accounts of both of these things. Either way, this is not the stuff of a few sentences in response to a request for examples of objective moral facts. It is hard work, and I doubt that the understanding can be had short of putting in hours of labor. So be it. The important thing is for the godfree to be sensitive to the real interest behind the request for objective moral facts, and for the tempted believer to be sensitive to the ways of articulating the

topics that really interest her. The development of such sensitivities will be an aid to mutual understanding at the very least, and maybe also to the lessening of the power of a mistaken reason to take the idea of god seriously.

Mystery: (1) It is sometimes said that god works in mysterious ways. This idea even has textual credentials. It is a very familiar idea. What has not been noticed is how odd the religious use of the idea of a mystery is.

A motley group of people is gathered at a remote country inn. They are enjoying sherry in the drawing room when the power fails, plunging them into complete darkness. The return of the lights reveals the horror: Lady Kirkly has been murdered! Who is the culprit? It's a mystery.

What is the appropriate response to being presented with a mystery? The normal idea, which certainly suits the demise of Lady Kirkly, is that we should get to work solving it. Roll up our sleeves, scour the inn for evidence, for the solution to our mystery is surely at hand. Sometimes we fail to solve mysteries, sometimes we don't. Work and luck are the keys to success.

All of this shows that the normal idea of a mystery is an invitation to inquiry. The typical religious notion of mystery is quite the opposite. When we are told that god's ways are mysterious, we are not being invited to scrutinize them and to dispel the sense of mystery. We are instead being told to stop thinking about them and to acquiesce in the puzzle.

Is the typical religious invocation of mystery benign? I can't see how it is. The squelching of normal human curiosity and of skeptical inquiry into purportedly important ideas needs justification. We should worry that what is often happening here is deflection of interest into the nature of the world in order for inside members of a religion to retain power over people. Not cool.

Even if power is not the issue when a mystery is invoked to end a conversation, the effect of this rhetorical gambit is lamentable. Suppose that a person is wondering about how some natural phenomenon works and divine mystery is presented as an explanation. The implicit suggestion is that it is not our place to investigate this occurrence. But this suggestion should be resisted, even from the perspective of religious belief. Any god worth worshipping will welcome curiosity about creation. The religions that dissuade inquiry should be shunned by both atheists and believers alike.

Suppose someone is distraught over the death of a loved one and god's mysterious ways are offered as a consoling explanation. This should not be received as a salve for the pain. It should be taken as an insult. God has taken someone away and deigns to keep the reasons hidden? Again, this is not a god worth worshipping. Although I am sure that mystery is offered in good faith to soothe pain in such cases, it need not be. It could be done to stop a member of the flock from becoming angry with god and from thinking about whether these religious beliefs are worth holding. These are good suspicions, from the perspective of the godfree. I cannot help but think that sometimes the reasons that these suspicions are smothered in mystery are self-serving and, to that extent, despicable.

Now, there is another sort of reason for which mystery might be invoked in a religious context. It is not the sort of reason that is useful for consoling the bereaved. Nor is this sense likely to be at work when the mysterious is used as a conversation stopper. The suspicions voiced above remain; this new sense should be seen as a rather special and atypical notion of religious mystery. Consider someone who likes a sense of mystery. Such a person might like religious ideas precisely because they make the world more mysterious than it otherwise seems. Perhaps this is an aesthetic attitude—the religiously mysterious is found to be beautiful. Perhaps it is an attitude more distinctly tied to mystery. Regardless, a preference of this sort is perfectly understandable. There is nothing wrong with it. This attitude, of course, cannot be used as an argument for stopping others from inquiring into religious ideas and the nature of the world. Whether someone cultivates a taste and appreciation for mystery should surely be left up to them. Moreover, acquiescence in this sort of stance can easily be driven by a fear of what might be lost by asking too many questions. On this, see *Enchantment*.

(2) Suppose that we put all of the previous concerns aside. There is still something to worry about with regard to religious appeals to mystery. It sits uneasily—inconsistently, one might insist—with religious appeals to the order of the world. For instance, a powerful line of thought supposedly in favor of the existence of some sort of god has been the complex design of

the natural world. Organisms are complicated and clearly designed things; surely such order requires a supernatural designer! We now know that this is not true, but we can put this aside in order to consider the nature of the claim. Its spirit is to turn us toward features of the world within which we find ourselves and to make a certain sort of stab at understanding it. The supposition is that god's hand in her creation is there for us to see, provided that we think about things and come to understand them properly. This, it seems to me, is an honest attempt to understand the nature of the world, and one that has been assessed and shown to be a failure. Crucially, it assumes that the world can be understood and that efforts to understand it are worthwhile. This patently flies in the face of appeals to the mysteriousness of god's nature and workings. I won't insist that religious people can't make either appeals to mystery or to the understandability of the world. I will, however, encourage them to think twice about making these sorts of claims together. Can they really have it both ways? I'm not so sure.

14

N Is for . . .

Nonbelievers: (1) See *Believers (or, My Sisters and Brothers in Disbelief)*.

(2) One of the better labels for atheists. It should be as good as any, but there's one hitch: there is a widespread respect for belief, and hence distrust of disbelief. The result is that this name for atheists brings with it a mildly pejorative overtone that would be nice to avoid. See *Godfree*.

Nonhumans: When I teach introductory ethics, we invariably do some readings on the moral status of nonhuman animals. That is how I insist on speaking (it's pedantic, but it's for the classroom): "nonhuman animals," to help my students keep in mind that we are not speaking of something really radically divorced from us. We are speaking of the animals that we often neglect, at least in our thought about what matters, as opposed to human animals (see *Animals [the Human Ones]*), which we focus on altogether too much. Some religions are culpable for fostering this neglect, even abuse, of nonhumans. Shame on them. I will let you figure out which ones are guilty. Some religions, albeit far too few, have avoided such hubris (see *Humility* for the general problem here). Good for them.

If you are interested in the details about the moral status of nonhuman animals, the usual advice applies: *Pick Up a Textbook*.

15

O Is for . . .

Ockham's Razor: A principle for choosing between rival hypotheses, models, and explanations for some phenomena.

Useful but contentious. The basic idea is that, other things being equal, the hypothesis that makes the fewest assumptions or countenances the smallest number of entities should be preferred. This is arguably the principal intellectual contribution of medieval philosopher William of Ockham (also spelt "Occam").

Consider two explanations of a particular body of evidence. They both explain the data, but one refers to more mechanisms, laws, and kinds of things than the other does. Which one should you prefer? Ockham's razor advises us to prefer the one with the smaller number of moving parts, so to speak. Be intellectually conservative: require extra evidence in support of the extra mechanisms, laws, and entities that the more complicated explanation involves. Until the extra evidence is provided, prefer the "simpler" explanation. (See *Simplicity* for discussion of this slippery idea.)

Why am I talking about this? Ockham's razor has a long history in debate about the existence of god. It has been invoked by both believers and nonbelievers. I'm inclined to think two things here: that this principle is inconclusive, but that it tends to support the godfree side of things. Why? Consider something that we want to explain, such as the origin of the world. Here are two explanations:

(A) God is the origin of the world.

(B) The world arises through natural mechanisms governed by natural laws, the details of which we are still working hard to understand.

Despite the superficial simplicity of the god-hypothesis, it is actually the more complex one, and hence Ockham's razor gives us defeasible reason to prefer the naturalistic explanation. The explanation is simple: the naturalistic explanation recognizes one kind of thing—natural things, governed by natural law, and in principle explicable via natural science and related bodies of inquiry. The god-hypothesis recognizes all of these natural things—it must, since, after all, this is exactly what we are trying to explain. But it explains these natural things by reference to a second kind of thing: supernatural beings such as god. Really simply put, the naturalistic hypothesis explains the nature and origin of the world in terms of one kind of thing, whereas the god-hypothesis explains the same body of evidence by appealing to two sorts of things. Ockham's razor advises us to insist on extra evidence to justify inclusion of more things in our explanations rather than less. So, until we have some sort of extra evidence, or some other sort of consideration justifying the god-hypothesis, we should prefer the naturalistic one.

As I say, when pressed Ockham's razor turns out to be complicated and contentious, so I offer this as a tentative line of thought in presumptive favor of atheism only, not as a definitive one. There are lots of other things to be said in favor of a godfree view of the world, so the case for or against atheism does not stand or fall with Ockham's razor.

Ontological Argument: Some arguments for the existence of god are made on the basis of purely conceptual considerations, as opposed to those that are world-based and hence empirical in spirit. Some purely conceptual arguments are founded on very specific aspects of our lives, such as morality. See *Morality (or, On Loving the Good with and without God)* for consideration of this sort of argument. Other purely conceptual arguments are much more general, and the most famous of these is the so-called ontological argument. Both this general sort of argument and the ontological argument in particular were well worked over by medieval scholars. Now this kind of argument is no longer fashionable. I cannot canvass centuries of scrutiny of this sort of argument, obviously. But I can give you a sense of how it works and of some basic problems that it faces. I will leave it to readers to perform a more nuanced examination of this argument for themselves (*Pick Up a Textbook*), but note: the efforts of scholars over hundreds of years have produced no convincing version of this argument.

The argument, really roughly, works like this: Imagine something perfect in every way—it cannot be improved. This thing must exist, otherwise it would not be perfect, since existence would improve it. Ergo something perfect in every way exists; this is god.

This is an admirable argument in its clarity and singular focus on perfection and existence, the conjunction of which is hoped for by many to apply to the supernatural being called "god." However, there are many problems with this general line of thought. Here are some:

1. The idea of "perfection" is badly handled here. For one thing, objects, etc. are perfect (or better/worse) in specific ways—for example, something can be a perfect knife, a perfect friend, a perfect storm, perfectly awful, etc. It's nonsense to apply all of these ways of being perfect to one thing. Do we really want to endorse the idea of something that is both a perfect knife and a perfect friend? Surely not. Even worse, ascribing all varieties of perfection to one thing is incoherent, as some ways of being perfect are incompatible with others. Consider, for example, what it is to be a perfect adult and what it is to be a perfect child. The problems can be multiplied at will: perfect bachelor vs. perfect husband, perfect friend vs. perfect enemy, and so on. So the very attempt to imagine something perfect in every way turns out to be something that cannot be done, because nothing can be like this. This implies two things: this argument won't work, and god cannot be perfect in every way.

2. This argument, if it worked, does not get you a personal god, but something more abstract (and arguably very weird, given [1]).

3. This argument makes mistakes about the nature of "existence." Here's the jargon: existence is not a predicate, but this argument treats it as one. I don't suppose that this jargon makes the point clearly, so here are the details: if we specify the "way something is" by listing its attributes, existence is not included. To see this, imagine describing something by constructing a list of attributes and then asking whether it exists. "It"

must mean the same thing, in terms of its attributes, whether or not it exists. If this were not the case, we could not ask sensibly whether it exists.

For instance, suppose that you are asking whether a unicorn or a perfect circle exists. To do this, you have to have a specific account of what a unicorn or a perfect circle is. This is what a description of its attributes provides. Then we would ask if something with these attributes actually exists. Existence is not among these attributes. If it were, it would make no sense to ask whether the unicorn or the perfect circle (or anything else) exists. The description of its nature would include the answer to this question. We know that this is not how questions about existence work. We know that figuring out whether a perfect circle or a unicorns exists (or Santa Claus, or leprechauns, and on and on) requires not just an account of what these things are, but also inquiry into the wider world, to see whether it includes them.

If existence were a predicate (to use the jargon), and hence if it were included in the lists of attributes of particular kinds of things, then our questions about whether things exist would be rendered useless. We would be imagining one thing (without the attribute "existence") and then seeing that something else (with the attribute "existence") exists. We could never find out, for example, that unicorns exist. We would imagine unicorns-without-existence, then discover that unicorns-with-existence can be found in the world. Things with different attributes are, of course, not the same thing. So: existence is not part of the way something is. (In case you are wondering, neither unicorns nor perfect circles exist.)

The problem is that the ontological argument represents existence as if it were an attribute just like those that define the nature of a unicorn or a perfect circle. It does this be imagining adding it to our perfect being, as if existence were just like a color or a shape. This means that it misrepresents what it is for something to exist or not exist. These aren't among the attributes that make something the thing it is. Instead, they are, conceptually, ways of representing things with certain attributes—these things are real or not. They, with a fixed identity, either exist or they do not. With regard to reality, to speak of existence and nonexistence are ways of saying whether something is included within the class of things which are real. If something exists, it—defined in terms of the list of attributes which make it one thing and not another—is in that class. If it does not exist, it is not in that class; it's in the class with the leprechauns and ghosts and unicorns and perfect circles . . .

The bottom line is that there are good reasons to think that the ontological argument fails. Note well: these reasons are not exhausted by what I have offered here. Suppose that we accept this failure. Does this signify anything of deep importance? It might be the case that it's the specific considerations—those about perfection and existence—that are marshalled by the ontological argument that are the root of the failure. Perhaps consideration of merely these things is insufficient to demonstrate the existence of god. Fair enough, I suppose, but I worry that there's a deeper problem here. This general method of arguing presupposes that we can draw conclusions about what exists on the basis of ideas that have nothing directly to do with the nature of the world. Can we really draw these conclusions on this basis? Can we really hope to demonstrate the existence of something in the world, so to speak, on the basis merely of examining ideas and not directly examining the world itself? Why should we think that our ideas, and the relations between them, offer this sort of window onto the realm of things that exist? I am very suspicious of this general project. I cannot offer a knockdown argument against it, but I can register my doubts. To the extent that these doubts are warranted, we should be suspicious of purely conceptual arguments for the existence of god. Existential claims arguably need a more direct foundation in reality than this sort of argument offers.

Oratory: Religion has a long history of spoken address and of charismatic speakers. We need not focus on famous examples, such as St. Anthony. The experiences of ordinary believers provide lots of evidence. People seek out moving speeches for their Sunday mornings. Some change churches due to the quality of the church leaders' performances. This is evidence enough of the power of personality in religious oratory.

Fair enough. Enjoy the good speakers and eschew the bad ones. But beware: there are dangers here. Feeling something because of a powerful speaker is not the same as learning something, knowing something, or even being exposed to coherent ideas. The ideas worth having are those that survive the transition from heated oratory to dispassionate, even boring speech and writing. An idea that survives the intellectual scrutiny that clinical settings foster is worth having. An idea worth having only in impassioned but garbled performance is hardly worth having at all.

The fundamental lesson: don't fall for guff because you are impressed by the quality of a speaker. See *Guff*.

Order: It is common, and legitimate, to claim that order—regularity, complexity, what looks like the product of design somehow—needs explanation. In the case of artifacts we cite the mindful behavior of human originators: for instance, engineers designed and built that car. This works to answer our likely question, "Where did that come from?" But note: this is not the only question we might want to ask about order. And for those other questions, this is neither a sufficient nor even a promising answer. If you want a complete explanation of such ordered complexity, then the explanatory demand has only been moved one step back, as the minds and behavior of human beings are themselves very complex.

It is important to have a rough idea of just what order and disorder are in order to understand the issues. Our everyday sense of these things is a good starting place but it can lead us astray. Consider a library. This is an orderly place: every book has a place. Imagine a library with all of the books in their proper spots. Now suppose that a small tornado blows through the library, upsetting all of the books. Order has been destroyed. Now the library is, by library standards, quite disorderly. But in terms of the things that need explanation, this is only relative disorder. There is still a significant degree of order in this messy pile of books. Consider a book: letters are arranged in words, words into sentences, molecules into paper (of various kinds probably) and ink. Wherever there are different kinds of things (paper, ink) there is order. Where there is order there is more complexity than there would be otherwise. Disorder is undifferentiated simplicity. The real question that we are faced with by order, then, is how and why there is ever any deviation from this sort of simplicity. How do there come to be different kinds of things? Their production and maintenance requires energy, as any parent who insists on orderly children's bedrooms knows.

The path of least effort, of the least amount of energy, is undifferentiation and hence complete disorder. Why do we have order instead?

In the case of orderly bedrooms and complex artifacts such as cars, we know that the desired explanation cites the minds and efforts of people. A typical religious move cites much the same thing to explain the existence of order and complexity in general: divine minds and behavior are the source that religion offers. The analogy with human affairs is understandable, and we should all see why this explanatory attempt is initially tempting. But we should all be able to see pretty much instantly why it fails.

To see the details, let's focus just on minds. Minds, divine or not, are always going to be pretty complex. They are significantly ordered. Start with a simple human case. Suppose that you want to explain the complex order of a car in terms of the designers' mental states. A remotely complete account would have to cite the beliefs, wants, cooperative intentions and compromises, and myriad decisions, plans, etc. that constituted the mental history of the particular automobile. Remember, wherever there are different kinds of things there is order. Well, here there are many different kinds of mental states and mind-involving interpersonal interactions. Here there is complex order.

Arguably the problem gets even worse when we try to invoke divine minds to explain the existence of the complex order we see around us. Beliefs, wants, etc. are familiar things to attribute to gods, but presumably few religions wish to limit the mental possibilities for divine minds to those sorts of states that humans exhibit. So a divine mind can be expected to have at least as many different kinds of states as our minds do: it's got to be more complex, not less. And this means that divine mentality cannot be an explanation of the complex order we find in the world. When we cite god's mind as the origin of complexity and order, we don't explain these things at all. We just move the explanatory task from one topic to another. The complex order of the world called out for explanation to begin with; now it's the complex order of god's mind that needs explaining. No explanation of order has been provided.

The problem lies in trying to explain complexity, order, apparent design, etc. in terms of something just as complex, ordered, apparently designed. A real explanation must follow a different path: the less complex/ ordered/apparently designed (and so on) is the only thing that can really explain the more complex. Working down from more to less order, the hope is to reach that which is so simple that it needs no more explanation. In the case of the physical order exhibited by the things that make up our world, constructing such explanations is the job of the sciences. This is how evolutionary biology works, for example: diversity of forms of life is explained through the combination of simpler, more homogeneous starting points and powerful but mindless processes (random mutation and systematic destruction and preservation through competition). Psychology explains how complex mental processes can be carried out by brains, by decomposing them into more simple steps that combinations of neurons can do. And so on, with lots of hard work both behind and before us.

It's understandable if this, when put in such an abstract form, is intellectually unsatisfying. How can simple stuff really amount to life and minds and so on? The details matter: working through the steps can answer this question satisfyingly (for those who do not mean it purely rhetorically). But satisfaction can also be had through realization that it's the only game in town. No explanatory work is done if we move from order to more order. Only the more simple can explain the more complex, in the sense in which this basic question about order is being asked.

Some have held that divine minds are both minds and simple, although my impression is that this is not currently a widely held position. Aquinas held this sort of view. This has the virtue of offering the simple to explain the complex. It has the problem of being incoherent: mentality cannot be simple, for the reasons we have already seen. A simple mind would have no mental states—no beliefs, intentions, etc.—but something with no mental states is not a mind. So no salvation for the typical religious explanation of order lies with this strategy.

Origins: It is remarkable how much religion is marked by accounts of our origins, and hence how much interest in these origins is responsible for our involvement in religion. Divine commands or actions are offered to account for the origin of the universe. The same goes for the human species, and maybe even for individual people. It is not uncommon for religions to encourage us to see ourselves as children of god (see *Adults* for commentary). The gods are held up as the source of moral values.

Sometimes this is interwoven with thought about our species' origins: god has moral authority over us because she is our creator. (These thoughts about values are mistaken: see *Morality [or, On Loving the Good with and without God], Tragedy [or, Despair about the Meaning of Life], Irony [and Meaning in Life],* and *Absurdity [and Meaning in Life]* for discussion.)

Such interest in origins is understandable. Perhaps it's even a mark of laudable curiosity. Religion, however, is not a promising place to look for answers. We know this for some questions, such as the origin of the human species. We know the natural processes responsible for our emergence in the earth's history. But let's put such particular failures of the explanatory attempts of religion aside and turn to religious accounts of origins more generally. For present purposes, take the most basic origin question: why is there something rather than nothing? Obviously, merely saying "God did it" won't do to answer this question: a state of nothing is a state without a god to do anything. Religion and nonreligious perspectives must both face this origin question. For believers, this is to ask why there is a god. That a satisfying religious answer can be given to this question (in any form) cannot be assumed. For this to be the case, the religiously interesting facts that account for the existence of something must be ones that are not available to a naturalistic explanation. This, however, is unlikely. See *Questions* for more general discussion, and see *Ontological Argument* for the most famous failure to provide a religious answer to this sort of question.

The answer to this question is likely to require the intellectual resources of several very difficult fields of study. To a considerable degree it is a question about this universe, meaning that physicists and astronomers have the requisite expertise. But it is also a different sort of topic, so others must also be consulted. For instance, the question could rest on conceptual confusion. Maybe it is logically impossible (as opposed to physically impossible) for there to be nothing. To assess this, astronomers and physicists are the wrong people to ask. This question belongs to the general study of possibility and necessity, which is a branch of logic. This is all hard stuff, so don't expect an answer that you will understand. If you do understand it, don't expect to like it. And if you don't understand it, it should be clear that you likely won't want to put in the work required to get it.

To clear your head of such difficulties, see *Ockham's Razor* and *Simplicity.*

16

P Is for . . .

Paradise (Fool's; or, Whatever Gets You through the Night): Is a fool's paradise better than no paradise at all? If you adopt a godfree life, you give up on eternal life in a supernatural paradise. You might mind this loss. Would you be better off keeping the illusion?

Maybe. It's hard to argue against the consolations provided by the idea of a heaven. For many this idea is bound up with many distasteful ones, meaning that the overall belief system is not, on balance, consoling or attractive. This is the case for the religion in which I grew up. But I recognize that other people might find this very system more worth it than not. I also recognize that other religious illusions might be undeniably seductive. The payoff in relief and maybe even pleasure that comes with commitment to these ideas should not be ignored. People might genuinely feel better with these ideas than without them. To that extent their lives will be better for having these ideas.

Still, a love of truth is no vice. A love of important truths is better than a love of trivial ones. And by the standards of the religious, I presume, truths about the existence of god, the nature of the world, and standards of right and wrong must count among the most important of truths. From this perspective, the maintenance of an illusion cannot be recommended.

Should we be so moralistic as to urge wholeheartedly the loss of comforting falsehoods? I am not so priggish as to think that the truth-oriented life is necessarily better than a religiously inclined one. Some truths are cold and hard. So the issue is more complicated than one might think. Still, to the extent that one loves truth one should be suspicious of comforting illusions. And to the extent that truth is valuable, a life out of step with it is an improvable one.

Perplexity: Many turn to religion for help with their problems. Practical problems are sometimes part of this process, but often it's more intellectual and existential concerns that draw folks to the pews. Fair enough: perplexity is discomfiting, and any port in a storm.

Still, various cautions are worth heeding here. First, religion is a source of false problems, empty anxieties, and these do real harm. For example, there is no hell; turning to churches out of fear of eternal damnation is to use religion to solve a problem that it generates itself. The fear that comes with this idea is a problem that lies at the feet of religion; getting over religion is the best way to assuage it.

Second, religious answers are often only superficially satisfying. In short, they aren't real answers. See many entries in this book for discussion of related ideas: *Origins, Order, Questions* for one cluster; *Morality (or, On Loving the Good with and without God), Tragedy (or, Despair about the Meaning of Life), Irony (and Meaning in Life),* and *Absurdity (and Meaning in Life)* for another.

Does this mean that atheism offers all the answers? Of course not. It offers some answers, but it really offers more hard work than settled questions. There is satisfaction of sorts to be found in tracking the slow progress made with regard to important and difficult questions, but it won't be to everyone's liking. If you go godfree, be prepared to be humble about what you do and don't know (see *Humility* and *Ignorance*).

You should also be prepared for future troubles. The godfree trade old perplexities for new ones. Some find such a life worse than the old, mistaken one. So be it: truth need not be worry-free, but it's truth all the same for that.

Pick Up a Textbook: The means of solving or dispelling surprisingly many of the queries we have about ourselves and the nature of the world—about everything, in other words. Very few people think to do this, however. I say that this sometimes helps to dispel rather than solve our problems, for one of the things that we sometimes discover when we really delve into a question is that our starting presuppositions were so poor that the question really wasn't a good one. Perhaps it was poorly framed. Perhaps it turns out to be altogether meaningless. Perhaps it is really a host of smaller questions to be pursued on their own merits in myriad ways. Whichever it is, to dispel a question is often as good as solving it, at least as a way of scratching the itch of curiosity. For some starters see *Short List of Suggested Readings*.

Even if you think you have it all figured out, it can be worthwhile to pick up a textbook. You're wrong about something. After all, we all are. Cultivating our sense of our own ignorance is an important part of the process of developing the intellectual humility that the complexity of the world demands. See *Humility* and *Ignorance*.

Practical Religion: Some people deny that religion is, either at all or primarily, a matter of holding beliefs that can be assessed in terms of truth or falsity. This would be to see religion as, at its core, a kind of theory (about the nature and origin of the world, about good and bad, and so on). Rather, these people emphasize that religion is something we do. It is essentially practical, not theoretical. Let's put aside religious traditions that clearly emphasize truth and belief (see *Truth [or, Truths]* and *Belief and Doubt* for more on these), and let's consider this view directly.

One of the appeals of this sort of view—indeed, one of the reasons that it is offered as an account of the nature of religion—is how it stands with typical godfree complaints about religion. The central complaint is, bluntly, that distinctively religious claims are false. There are no gods, no souls, no supernatural beings, etc. This complaint treats religion as being centrally about belief and truth. But if this is a misunderstanding of religion—if it's not really theoretical but practical—then this can't be a convincing complaint. Atheists are barking up the wrong tree.

Another source of appeal will be to those who lack conviction in the godly claims made by typical religions but who like participating in religion, or at least in certain parts of religious practice. If religion is primarily practical, then one can, on its face, be pretty religious while renouncing, or at least suspending adherence to, the weird supernatural claims that religions make. People can be religious without being forced to believe false things—yay!

As an analogy, consider the role of hockey in Canadian life (or baseball in American life, or soccer in many other countries). Hockey means a lot to many Canadians. But hockey is not primarily a matter of belief. It's not a theory. It's an activity. It is primarily something that you do, and the relevant beliefs about it are secondary to this core nature. As practical, hockey enters Canadians' lives in many ways: it engages various feelings, action tendencies, and even our reflective attention. Traditions and institutions have grown around this activity, and they too engage Canadians' lives in complex ways.

The view that religion is essentially practical portrays religion in the same way. Beliefs are secondary to its active nature. Its hold on our lives derives not from belief but from various and diverse other aspects of our minds.

So far, so good. But this view of religion faces a dilemma, at least with regard to many claims that are made about the appropriate role of religion in people's lives and in society at large. Suppose, on one hand, that religion is "merely" or "purely" practical. That is, suppose that it is not, at its core, based on belief of any kind. The only relevant religious beliefs are secondary, about religious practice. Hockey is like this: to participate in hockey requires no distinctive hockey beliefs. You need to believe, for example, that the puck is *there*, and not *over there*, to play hockey, because the nature of the practice generates the role for such beliefs. But there is no core picture of, well, anything to which to subscribe in order to be a hockey player. If religion is like this, then its role in our lives is based, ultimately, solely on taste. This is how it works for hockey, after all. As such, it has no grounds on which to assert authority over people's lives. It would not be the case that people ought to be religious because certain distinctively religious claims are true, just as it is not the case that the grounds for playing hockey are that certain hockey claims are true. The reason for participating in either activity would be because, at base, it suits you. Those whom it does not suit are off the hook.

This is a problematic view for most religions, including the well-known major ones. They all claim, either politely or loudly, that people ought to be their adherents. They assert authority over all. So let's move away from this first option and consider a second one. Instead of being purely practical, suppose that religion is impurely practical. That is, besides its distinctive activities it also makes distinctive claims, such that belief in these claims is necessary for one truly to be religious. This would give these religions the grounds on which to assert authority over all: you should be religious because religion has a distinct view of important truths. At the same time, however, any religion that makes such claims opens itself up to their critical examination. You say, for example, that a supernatural being created the world? Let's try to figure out whether this is true by examining the world. You offer particular claims for our belief? Let's see whether we should believe them. And, of course, this option opens up these religions to the lines of complaint typically made by atheists.

Questions of belief and truth are unavoidable for any religion who claims authority over people regardless of whether they want to participate in it. That's pretty close to all religions, so far as I can tell. To insist on the thoroughly practical nature of religion is to give up such claims of authority. I'm fine with that: do your religions and leave the rest of us alone. You can't have it both ways.

Pray: We don't do this.

17

Q Is for . . .

Questions: (1) Do science and religion conflict? Not if they are fundamentally concerned with different questions. Is this the case?

It is sometimes claimed that religion and science ask and answer different questions. What are the questions that religion addresses that science supposedly is silent about? Particular religions have questions to address that are internal to their texts and traditions. Interestingly, these are not necessarily outside the purview of science. Suppose, to use a hackneyed example, that you want to know how many angels fit onto the head of a pin. This question is generated by the assumptions that there are angels and that they take up space. Empirical and mathematical methods are clearly central to resolving this issue: we have to measure the pinhead, devise some sort of estimate of the size of an angel based on textual and other considerations, then do the appropriate calculations. Just how science and religion interact for such internal questions must be assessed on a case-by-case basis.

Arguably the more important kind of question is the kind that we might face outside of a religious context. These are familiar questions: What is the meaning of life? Of death? Where does the world come from? Maybe there are others. For instance, for relations between religion and morality, see *Morality (or, On Loving the Good with and without God)*.

The first thing to observe is that science either addresses these questions or reveals things that are directly relevant to these questions. The theoretical branches of physics and astronomy wonder about our ultimate origins. Biology, psychology, and other sciences deliver information that is relevant to understanding the nature and hence meaning of life and death. Maybe these sciences must be conjoined with philosophy to address these questions directly, but this is a minor modification. We have no strong reason to think that religion addresses important questions about which science is silent.

The second thing to observe is that even if religion addresses these questions, whether or not they are independent of science, it can't answer them. Why this point is so often missed is a puzzle to me. Take the origin of the universe as an example. If god is offered as the origin of the universe, this might seem like an answer, but it isn't. It just moves the question back a step: what is the origin of god? This is no less a question than the one we started with, hence no answer has been given. See *Order* and *Origins*.

The same thing goes for the meaning of life or death. Suppose that god's plans are offered as making our lives and deaths meaningful. This just moves the question back a step: why should we think that god's plans are meaningful? After all, we distinguish between pointful plans and pointless ones in normal contexts, so the mere invocation of a plan does not answer the question. We are left with a question as puzzling as the one with which we started. No answer has been given. For more, see *Tragedy (or, Despair about the Meaning of Life), Irony (and Meaning in Life), Absurdity (and Meaning in Life)*.

The religious believer need not be silent in response to these questions. Obviously a higher order of gods can be offered—God A created this world, and God B created God A—but this moves the issues back one further step without, again, answering them. Moreover this will obviously be unpalatable to monotheists. Alternatively, one can wallow in mystery: god's plans are inscrutable, or god just inexplicably exists. Mystery, however, is not an answer. By normal standards it is a question and an invitation to inquiry. See *Mystery* for discussion.

The most promising route of response is to try, really, to answer the question. Suppose that god is offered as the origin of the universe. To account for god's existence, we might sharpen our focus: perhaps god has specific attributes that account for her necessary existence such that she can have no origin. Now we are getting somewhere. But look at where this road leads: first, if the answer is supposed to be acceptable to a particular religious tradition, the details and method must be acceptable to that tradition. Some traditions will be disquieted by the attempt to reason about these details. Others will reject particular possibilities.

Second, and crucially, the answer must offer features of god that both do the job that they have to do and are not also features of the universe—or, more nebulously, of "being"—itself. Given that the theoretical branches of sciences that study the origins and nature of the world are incredibly complex, this is not something that can be taken for granted. The details of these particular research programs must be reckoned with to show that god can be the ultimate origin of the world in a way that the universe cannot perform itself. This is just to say that the religious attempt to answer this question must conjoin itself with the resources of science if a substantial answer is to be found. And this is just to say that science does in fact answer this question after all: the religious answer will complement and join the view of the world given by the sciences. Ultimately it looks like there is no independent ground to be found for religion. Either it has nothing to say or it becomes part of science (and, probably, philosophy).

For more see *Evidence*.

(2) I am told that many religions have a tight link to science, emphasizing the importance of this way of learning about the nature of the world. Good. The major monotheistic traditions certainly have this sort of history. Good. But now they are not so much concerned with this sort of inquiry. This is bad, and it is not redeemed by the distant historical facts.

More importantly, there is an important pattern here. If we squint and simplify our view of major religions, it's not hard to find a period marked by a combination of faith and empirical inquiry that leads to a divorce at the cost of inquiry. This is revealing. To the extent that this is a real pattern, it shows the centrality of a certain sort of faith to religion (see *Faith vs. Reason*). It also shows its danger, for we should distrust any institution committed to an account of the way things are that won't put in the work to figure out if that's how things actually are—or, even worse, that holds on to such an account despite good evidence that it's false.

It's not hard to see the error here if we think of other topics. Imagine committing to pay a certain amount for your groceries without knowing whether the items in your cart add up to that amount. Imagine insisting that you are in good health despite a doctor's report to the contrary. Or, if that's not strong enough for you, imagine insisting that you are in good health despite having open wounds with bones sticking out of them and blood spraying all over the place. See then say, not the other way around.

Quiz!:

Part One: Short Answer. Each question offers a statement. Say whether it is true or false. Briefly defend your choice; answers should be short enough to be tweetable.

1. There is a god.

    False. See *God (or, Gods), Evidence, Ontological Argument, Who Bears the Burden of Argument?,* and *Supernatural.*

2. A godless life is meaningless.

    False. See *Meaning of Life, Tragedy (or, Despair about the Meaning of Life), Irony (and Meaning in Life),* and *Absurdity (and Meaning in Life).*

3. Without god, absolutely anything is permissible.

    False, but the godfree see values differently from believers. See *Morality (or, On Loving the Good with and without God), Sin, Sacred, Values,* and *Standards.*

4. Atheists do not have souls.

    True. No one does. See *Soul.*

5. Atheists think we are just animals.

    Trick question. Technically true: we are animals, but "just" suggests something lowly. We are wonderful animals. See *Animals (the Human Ones), Apes,* and *Meat Machines.*

6. Atheism offers nothing to those who fear death.

    Hmm, hard one. Sort of true, sort of false. This is the only life there is. In case it helps: there is no heaven or hell, and nonexistence is not to be feared. See *Death, Heaven,* and *Hell.*

7. The godfree think religion is worthless.

    False. We think that it's not all that it's cracked up to be. It's particularly problematic with regard to truth: see *Truth (or, Truths), Humility,* and many other entries. Still, religion enters people's lives in many complicated ways, some of which are good for people.

8. Only religious people value families.

   Laughably false. Or cryably, depending on how you think about it. See *Family and Friends.*

9. God is needed to explain the origin of the world.

   False. Not just false either: the idea of a god is so ill-suited to explain the origin of the world that it's really a nonstarter. See *Order* and *Origins.*

10. Faith is unavoidable, so we might as well be religious.

    Sort of true, but not in a way that helps religion avoid the criticisms of atheism. See *Faith vs. Reason, Reason,* and *Questions.*

Part Two: Essay Question. Answer the following in less than 1,500 words. Failure to respect the word limit is a mortal sin and will be punished with an eternity in hell (just kidding).

Should I be an atheist?

Despite its brevity, the question "should I be an atheist?" is tricky. If pushed to give a brief answer, I would respond "yes," but this would be unsatisfying and misleading in a variety of ways.

Atheism is, at its core, a matter of belief. Or disbelief, if you prefer. The godfree don't believe in the existence of gods. Apart from that, nothing else need unite them. They will tend to have overlapping attitudes about many things, but only some of these are related to their atheism, and the relations are complicated.

If religion were merely a matter of belief, or if our beliefs were disconnected from other aspects of our lives—our behavior, our habits, our communities, our tastes—then we would have our answer: there is no good reason to believe in the existence of gods, so we should not believe. We should be atheists.

However, reality is more complicated than this. Religion is not merely a matter of belief. Our beliefs are not sharply divided from other aspects of our lives. These complexities complicate the answers that we should give to this question.

To get some perspective on these complexities, consider the general form of the question: should I be a _____? Generally speaking, when faced with this sort of question, we consider more than what we should believe. We consider the benefits and burdens of the choice being made. We take into account how the matter at issue enters our lives. Belief is relevant, but it might not be decisive.

For instance, suppose that we were faced with another question: should I be a plumber? Plumbers have plumbing expertise, which means that they have certain beliefs about how plumbing works and certain skills concerning how to make plumbing work. If we have beliefs about plumbing, they should be the ones that plumbers are inclined to have. We should think about plumbing like plumbers do. If they don't think that water spirits make the well work or that prayer will fix our broken pipes, then neither should we.

This, of course, is not what we would focus on if we were really faced with the question "should I be a plumber?" We would hear this as the following question: should I *become* a plumber? And to answer this question, the beliefs are only a part of the story, and probably a secondary one at that. We would look at the plumbing life and see how it meshes with our own—our hopes, our tastes, the social groups to which we belong. For instance, to be a plumber is to be of use to people. That's good. But you will have to fix other people's dirty toilets. That's distasteful to many. Perhaps you come from a long line of plumbers. This can provide reasons both for and against becoming a plumber. Or maybe you associate with people who look down on the trades. To become a plumber will alienate you from important social relations, which is probably bad. And so on.

In short, when answering a question with the form, "should I be a _____?" we need to look not just at what we should believe, we also need to look at the burdens and benefits of making this choice.

So: what are the burdens and benefits of becoming an atheist? We immediately hit a stumbling block when we turn to this question. Just as no definitive account of these can be given for becoming a plumber, so none can be given for going godfree. The reason is that whether something counts as a burden or a benefit will often depend on one's situation, including one's tastes. Since there is considerable variety in both context and preferences among us, there is considerable variety with regard to what atheism offers each of us. Crucially, what is a benefit to me might be a burden to you, and vice versa.

Here is a very tentative list of some possible benefits of becoming an atheist:

1. You lose certain fears—or, at least, you should lose them, if the beliefs really take hold. I once feared hell; I no longer do, because I no longer have the package of beliefs of which this is a part.

2. Many cultivate an interest, or a renewed interest, in learning about the nature of the world, including values.

3. You go from feeling like a child in the universe to having the role of an adult.

4. You lose certain social burdens, such as having to perform rituals, attend church, and so on.

5. You lose certain perplexities, such as wondering about god's mysterious plan, or being bothered about why such a purportedly good divine being is such a jerk.

However, each of these putative benefits either could just as much be a burden, or come with new burdens:

1. Along with the fear of hell goes hope for heaven.

2. Many believers already have an interest in the nature of the world. Many will see the shrinking of the world to include only the natural as a loss, and hence a burden. And hey—learning about all of this sounds like work, which is always a burden!

3. Many want to be children. What's so great about adult responsibilities anyway?

4. Lots of people like rituals and church, along with the stability that such ways of structuring one's life bring.

5. This isn't obviously so great, and there is no shortage of new perplexities to replace the old ones.

These lists could be extended, of course, but my case should be clear. To the extent that we understand the question "should I be an atheist?" as the question "should I become an atheist?" no definitive general answer can be given. And if I were a betting man, I would bet on the list of burdens, for many, being longer than the list of benefits. Becoming an atheist has brought me more benefits than burdens, and this will be the case for others, but I can't promise anything. For those whose social circles pose grave threats, even mortal danger, to atheists, to become an atheist is at least to court ostracism, and at worst to put at risk one's own life. It's hard to see atheism as a beneficial choice to make in such circumstances, despite those being the beliefs that we should hold.

Let's change tack, for there are more complexities lurking in the original question. So far I have been reading "should I be an atheist?" as raising the question "should I, actual me, in the real world, become an atheist?" But we could also read it as the more neutral and abstract question "should one become an atheist?" What should we say with regard to this question? It strikes me as asking about idealized people in idealized circumstances. This, however, is easy to answer: ideally, we should live in accordance with truths about the nature of the world. We have every reason to think that there are no gods so, ideally, one should be an atheist. An ideal world will contain no religion, for it will contain no false beliefs, no lives led on the basis of false beliefs, and no institutions designed on the basis of falsehoods.

This is all very abstract. Does it have any real-life implications? Yes. One of the reasons to ask this abstract question is to shed light on a different one: If we were designing people, what sort should we make? Should they be religious believers, or not? Now, it might seem like this is an equally academic question as the one it replaces, since we don't design people. This, however, would be a mistake. We do design people. At least, those who play a role in having and raising children do. This question, then, has implications for children's education. Should we raise our children to be atheists, or not?

Some of the real-world threats that we face will also be faced by our children. We should not put them in the way of mortal harm, that much is clear. But to the extent that there is an obligation on us to make our children better than us, and to make their lives better than ours, then there is also an obligation not to make them into religious believers. This is not a definitive obligation, but it should be clear that if we continue to raise our children as religious believers, we fail to move their circumstances closer to ideal ones than our own are, and this is worth taking seriously. There are good reasons for children to know about religion, for now at least, but the only reasons there are to immerse them in religious beliefs and practices are unfortunate ones.

Should *you* be an atheist? I can't answer this for you. But there is good reason for you to take the question seriously. You should truly, deeply consider going godfree.

18

R Is for . . .

Reality (or, Realities): What there is.

Philosophers, theologians, and others sometimes give in to a temptation to speak of "realities." There's your reality and mine, there's religious reality and that of science, there's present-day reality and ancient reality, and so on. This is naughty; these people should know better.

Suppose two people speak of their experiences of what is real. One of these people is blind and the other is deaf. Each describes experiences that the other cannot have. We might say that these people have different realities. We can say this so long as we mean it metaphorically. We should not say this, however, if we mean it literally. Each person is open to different aspects of reality, not to different realities. Both of their experiences pick out real things; reality contains both, inclusively.

Indeed, the very idea of "realities" is incoherent, if it is meant literally as a way of speaking of what is real. Suppose that we have a well-worked-out idea of what is real, and then we discover something new. Suppose that we even find a group of people who are attuned to this novel thing. We have not discovered a new reality to go along with the old one. We have discovered something new to add to our now even better worked-out account of what is real. Reality is constituted by what there is. Our sense of what is real should just be our sense of what there is. It makes no literal sense to speak of plural what-there-ises.

There are various sources of the mistake of speaking of realities. One has been essentially presented already: our particular viewpoints are partial and not completely overlapping, so that some people are in touch with aspects of reality—with real things—that others have not encountered, or to which they are, figuratively speaking, deaf. Compounding things are the various sources of error and bias that give us distorted pictures of reality. In principle there is an infinite number of not-quite-right ways that things can seem to people, although in reality our mistakes and distortions tend to cluster in familiar ways. The more that we equate what is real with people's experiences of the world, the more that we will be tempted to portion out different realities one to a person. We might be tempted to count even more realities than this—maybe we would count culturally specific realities, or species-specific ones, or ones for each academic specialty. This would be a mistake. Reality includes whatever there is; there can't be more than one such group of things.

Another source of this mistake is the very ordinary fact that there are different kinds of things. Some things are food, some are not. Some things are living, some are not. Some things are abstract, some concrete. You get the idea. We should not speak of food reality versus not-food reality, etc. Instead we should just accept that what there is is a heterogeneous category. The hard work comes in accurately describing the contours of what there is—in carving the world at the joints, to co-opt an old parlance. Our ideas about the kinds of things there are don't automatically capture the ways things are.

Another source of this mistake is the conflation of truth with reality. Truth is a more slippery phenomenon than reality—see *Truth (or, Truths)* for discussion.

This all matters more rhetorically than substantially. When someone speaks of a reality that the godfree are blind to, it sounds pretty serious since "reality" is a term that we have to take seriously. After all, the alternative is stuff that isn't real, that isn't included in what there is. However, once we reflect on this we should realize that there are no realities portioned off in these ways. Instead there are just the ways things are. This takes hard work to figure out, but in principle it is open to everyone. We cannot legitimately just help ourselves to the title "reality." A place among the various things that are must, in an important sense, be earned.

Reason: Tricky to define, of course. Let's say that a belief is formed by reason when it is produced through at least roughly logical thought processes. Sometimes the input to these processes comes directly from our senses, but sometimes not. For instance, reasoning about abstract topics, such as the idealized objects of geometry, or general moral values such as justice, requires that we step away from the basic deliverances of perception and attend to more rarified and general topics. By contrast, when a belief is formed in other ways—such as mere trust in what other people say—then it has not been formed through reason. See *Faith vs. Reason* for discussion.

Relics: Bodily remains treated as sacred. There are purported pieces—hearts, bones, blood—of holy people to be found in churches all around the world. Since nothing is sacred, these clearly aren't either (see *Sacred*).

There is sort of a secular version of this phenomenon. The bodies (or pieces of them) of nonreligious famous people are on display in various places. Lenin's tomb is the most famous. The resting places of others draw curious crowds. Rock music has generated some famous versions of this phenomenon: Jim Morrison, Elvis Presley.

Still, although this is a worldly version of the relic phenomenon, it is not a thoroughly atheist counterpart. Lenin and Morrison are venerated for various things, but not for being atheists. Religious relics, however, are cherished precisely because of their religious links. And if I'm right that this phenomenon involves treating body parts as sacred, then there could not be nonreligious relics, at least not without incoherence. For atheists to line up at Galileo's tomb, or Darwin's gravesite, or Hitchens' or Hume's final resting place would be peculiar. A moment's acknowledgement would not be out of place, but that would be it. There is nothing magic about these ashes and bones.

Put aside the fame and the mistaken idea that these bits and pieces are magic, and what is left is, to put it bluntly, gross. I hope that those godfree people who seek to reinvent the worthy bits of religious practice leave this particular oddity to history.

Religion: What is religion? I'm not sure that there are necessary features that mark something as a religion. Atheists disagree about whether there is something desirable about religion or not, and at least some of the time these differences stem from disagreements about just what religion is. Presumably believers disagree as well. I'm inclined to bin the idea of religion. I don't see anything particularly worth keeping here.

Many—myself included—associate religion with institutionalized beliefs and practices concerning gods. Some atheists think that there is something worth keeping about churches, canonical texts, weekly meetings, and the like. Maybe there is, but this strikes me as a matter of taste rather than deep need. Lots of godfree people eschew these social trappings of godly ideas just as much as those ideas themselves, without loss. We can, of course, enjoy the aesthetic aspects of buildings, songs, and stories, but there is nothing worth the name "religion" about this sort of engagement with these objects.

I have heard it said, rather vaguely, that religion concerns topics of "ultimate concern," or reality in its "ultimate" form. These ideas are worth a little thought. The idea of "ultimate reality" deserves skepticism. Reality does not come in degrees. Things are either real or not (see *Reality [or, Realities]*). There is no "ultimate" versus "penultimate" or "superficial" reality. This is the wrong way to carve up the things that we find in the world. There are different kinds of things, and different vocabularies for talking about these things. The physicist and the biologist talk very differently about the same objects, for instance. But because they are the *same* objects, one cannot be more real or differently real than the other. So: there is no ultimate reality to contrast with nonultimate reality. There is just reality.

The idea of things of "ultimate concern" can be approached either subjectively or objectively. Let's start with the subjective approach. For something to be of subjective ultimate concern is presumably for it to be of basic or fundamental concern to a person, rather than of intermediate concern. For instance, my attention might temporarily be focused on a coffee cup. It is my immediate concern, but it is not of basic importance in my life. The things that really matter to me—the things that are of subjective ultimate concern—are other things. But I'm a nonbeliever, and there is nothing religious about the idea that some things really matter to me whereas other things matter only fleetingly. This can't be what the idea of religion hangs on.

The same goes, however, for the objective approach. For something to be of objective ultimate concern just is for it to matter on its own, rather than for it to matter because of its relations to other things. Coffee cups, for instance, matter only because of their ability to serve the health needs and tastes of people. But—perhaps—pleasure and health matter in and of themselves. They are, arguably, things of ultimate concern, whereas other things are not. Again, there is nothing particularly religious about this. The godfree can think this just as easily as religious people. In fact, we can think it *more* easily—see *Irony (and Meaning in Life)* for discussion. Really, what we have here is a familiar distinction—that between instrumental and intrinsic value—badly handled by the religious approach to things.

Maybe we could examine other possible hallmarks of religion. I'm inclined to think that certain attitudes are best focused on here—see *Religious Spirit (or, Religiosity; Religion in General; Religion in the Abstract)* for discussion. The bottom line, however, is the same as what is intimated here: there is nothing particularly worth keeping about religion or the religious spirit. A thoroughly religion-free life might not be to one's taste, but other than that it lacks nothing. For those who lack religious tastes, a life without religion can be just as good as a religious life. For those who are displeased, even rankled, by the trappings and idea of religion, a life without it can be considerably better than a religious life.

Religion in the Public Sphere: As I write this, the province of Quebec has unveiled its planned "Charter of Values." Roughly put, this bill would ban certain specified "conspicuous" religious symbols from being worn by employees of the province when on the job. Crucifixes (well, largish ones), turbans, the niqab are all out in this domain, although provincial employees are, of course (I hope it's "of course"!), free to wear whatever symbols they wish to on their own time. Let's put aside the idiosyncrasies of the Quebec charter that make it incoherent and hence unjustifiable and let's instead focus on straightforward bans of religious symbols from the public sphere. Is this something that atheists should wish for? Should we use the law to carve out officially religion-free public spaces? Is this a good road to take to diminish the power of religion, which is something typically desired by the godfree?

It's certainly a tempting idea. And, as we will see shortly, it's technically justifiable, despite the protests about the Quebec version that have been voiced in the Canadian media. But ultimately I don't think that it's something that atheists should want. It's unnecessary, unwise, and, ultimately, contrary to our interests.

We can see both why this is justifiable (technically) and why this is something that atheists should not embrace if we get straight about the fundamental issues. We must distinguish between different ways in which people interact. When I speak with my neighbors on the street, we interact as essentially that: neighbors. The law is there to constrain what we do to each other, but our interaction is not automatically intrinsically mediated by such law. We are neighbors first, co-citizens second. This goes even when I interact with those of my neighbors who work for the government. When we chat at the end of the driveway, they are not operating in their capacity as representatives of the state. They're just the nice people who live a couple of doors up.

By contrast, when we interact with employees of the state on the job, we are operating in a fundamentally different sphere. This is the essentially public sphere, in the official sense of "public" meaning having to do with citizens and the state, not the lax sense that contrasts with "private." In the officially public realm, we are primarily citizens, on the one hand, and representatives of the state on the other. This goes even when I deal with my neighbors in their official capacity. Their identity as my neighbors matters, probably, to the cordiality and personal touches of our interaction, but not to the fundamental nature of the interaction itself, between state and citizen.

The public sphere especially deserves careful attention when we are thinking about liberal democracies, such as the one in which I live, and in which I hope that you live too (not necessarily the same one—I wish liberal democracy for all, not necessarily Canada for all). Official power in such a democracy lies in the autonomous will of the governed (ideally speaking). This means that the state cannot pick favorites among ways of living for citizens in such a democracy. If it did, it would force or nudge a way of living upon some citizens to which they did not autonomously consent. Such an arrangement would be illegitimate by the standards of the ideal of liberal democracy. Such an arrangement is illiberal, in the sense of conflicting with these people's liberty, and undemocratic, in the sense of illegitimately overriding the will of these people for no counter-balancing good reason (political philosophy is, of course, complicated, so lots of details must go unaddressed here: please *Pick Up a Textbook*).

Here, then, is why it is technically justifiable for a liberal democracy to take the sort of position that Quebec is currently seriously considering.

Employees of the state represent that state when on the job. They do not officially represent it when they are off work. It is illegitimate for the state, at least in liberal democracies, to endorse particular ways of living as preferred ones. But this is exactly what is being done when representatives of the state wear overt religious symbols on the job. A representative of the state is endorsing a view of a preferred way of living. This is fine (of course; Of Course!) when off the job and when interacting with people as just one person to another. But it is not fine when on the job and interacting with others as a representative of the state to a citizen of that state. These are topics about which the state must be officially silent. Such official silence is inconsistent with the conspicuous appearance of these symbols in the public sphere.

So such a legislative move is justifiable. However, consider a couple of features of this argument that should render this sort of law unappealing. First, the sort of state endorsement of religion, and hence of views of the kind of life worth living, that is at stake here is very weak. It is one thing for a state to enshrine a particular religion as the state's own—that's grade-A strong endorsement! But when someone happens to wear the niqab or a crucifix that is not an official part of an effort by the state to make a message, through law, with these symbols, then what we have is incidental endorsement at most. Maybe the religion is endorsed by the person who wears the symbol—not even this can be taken for granted; see *A Very Ordinary Day*—but, when the apparatus of law is lacking, that's the end of it with regard to state involvement. This is not a big deal, I should think— rather, it's the kind of messy detail that liberal democracies face on the ground, rather than on the idealized page of political philosophy.

Second, the argument depends on a pretty clean division between the public sphere and the rest of our lives. Maybe such a division is technically there—hence the "technical" justification of this sort of law— but the experience of these spheres involves considerable blurring of divisions. Consider people who use government services. It's one thing for a courtroom or driver's license office to seem, pretty effortlessly, as a specifically governmental place. It's another thing for parents and children to experience daycares and classrooms like this. Instead, these places feel more integrated with our lives, not really distinctly public in the official sense. Consider also the employees of the state. Are we really to expect them to feel purely official when at work, for their jobs to be neatly separated from the rest of their lives? I should hope not, although some significant degree of separation is not unreasonable to ask. The attempt to remove religious symbols from the public domain is an attempt to enforce and make more rigid the division between the public and the rest of our lives, not an effort to acknowledge a state of affairs that already exists on the ground.

Overall the technical justification does not amount to much. Then there is the issue of the consequences to be expected from this sort of law. So far as I can see, it serves no particularly good purpose and, in fact, is likely to bring about bad consequences of various kinds. It *might* serve a good purpose where people are particularly uptight about their interactions in the public sphere. I say that it might, but I don't know of any real places where this is the case. Moreover, such legal sidelining of overt representation of religious identity in places fraught with interreligious tension can lead to inflammation of conflict. Anti-Jewish and anti-Muslim occurrences are not unheard of in Quebec, which has a racially divisive Catholic history. Such laws might carve out a secular public sphere, but at the undesirable cost of increased intolerance through the society at large. A poor trade: no significant gain, but a remarkable loss.

All of this matters, but it is not my principal reason for opposing such legal measures. My godfree interests are a bit more subtle. Nevertheless, the reasons can be put quite bluntly. Throughout most of Canada, religion barely matters. Sure, people observe various faiths in diverse ways, but the effect on society at large is pretty minimal. There are many to whom religion matters a great deal, but our multicultural civility has rendered their tastes, and hence the public powers of their religious creeds, toothless. The state is complicit in this, and quite justifiably so—recall that liberal democracies cannot justifiably hold up one view of the life worth living over others. Since the histories and founding documents of many—all?— major religions call for the shunning or even destruction of outsiders— whether they are otherwise religious or not—the defanging of religion that happens in such places as Canada is a good thing. The light touch of the state generally signifies that, officially speaking, religion barely matters. This is something that atheists should endorse.

By contrast, laws such as Quebec's proposed Charter of Values have the ironic effect of signaling that, by the lights of this particular state, religion does indeed matter. People wear overt religious symbols for various reasons. For some it is done out of devout belief. For others it is habit, or tradition, or purely aesthetic, and so on. For some of these latter people, the religious nature of their symbols barely matters. But legal sidelining of such symbols from the public sphere treats them as all alike, and as all mattering. This, ironically, gives religions in this sort of state more credence than they receive in more silent public contexts. This is not something that the godfree typically want.

I want the effects of religion in society at large to decrease. The idea that legally carving displays of religion from the public sphere would accomplish this is superficial. Religion derives a great deal of its power from belief, from being taken seriously. Laws of this kind do exactly that. When we refuse to take religion seriously, it loses its power over us. Instead of the nourishing sunlight of attention that such legal measures deliver, religion deserves the withering shade of neglect.

Religious Spirit (or, Religiosity; Religion in General; Religion in the Abstract): Particular religions have lots of faults. Many texts that are of fundamental importance to existing religious traditions recommend murder with regard to outsiders. Women don't do very well when we look at particular creeds. Exploitation of fear and hope with wild speculation is virtually everywhere amongst religious codes. How much of the blame for these problems should be laid at the feet of religion in general, as opposed to particular religions? How much is religion itself, regardless of the form it takes, morally problematic? Surely we can differentiate between religiosity in general and particular religions? So: are all the problems that come with religion attributable to particular religious institutions? Is the religious spirit in and of itself morally blameless for these faults, and maybe even recommendable when seen for itself?

Maybe, maybe not. It depends on just what the religious spirit consists in, and this is hard to pin down. I don't have a definitive idea about just what religiosity is, but it's illuminating to run through some candidates.

As a first possibility, maybe faith is central to the religious spirit. Toward any particular thing or idea, we can take various stances. Not all of these will seem particularly religious. A stance of critical reflection, for instance, is not uniquely religious. But a stance of faith, whatever that might mean in a more particular way, seems like a candidate for a religious outlook. Maybe it's all that is needed for the religious spirit.

It this is correct, then there is nothing necessarily laudable about the religious spirit. It seems like a willful refusal to think about what one believes. What's so good about that? Nothing that I can see. (See *Faith vs. Reason* for relations between reason and unquestioning belief.)

At any rate, it's hard to see how faith could be definitive of a religious attitude. I can take an unquestioning stance toward many things—the musical power of Led Zeppelin, the superiority of my nation over others—without this amounting to a religious attitude. The difference between religious and nonreligious faith lies not in the stance but in its object. So, let's move on to another way of characterizing the religious spirit: maybe some topics are essentially religious while others are not. The religious believe in gods and spirits—these are supernatural entities. Accordingly, perhaps the religious spirit consists in a willingness to take seriously the supernatural. To be religious is, essentially, to be superstitious on this view.

If this is correct, then it is difficult to see what's so great about the religious spirit. Either the world includes supernatural entities or it does not. A willingness to believe in such entities seems premature at the very least, and maybe incoherent. After all, consider what "supernatural" means. It means "outside of nature." Are there really any things that are wholly outside of nature—not subject to natural law, and arguably incapable of interacting with those natural things that are subject to natural law? After all, if the supernatural could interact with purely natural things, those natural things would not be subject to natural law at all. Moreover, to be outside of nature is not, in itself, to be worthy of admiration. Evil spirits seem to be common enough as objects of superstition, so this stance is not wholly edifying by its own standards. Superstition is a very weak foundation for a defense of religiosity.

Perhaps the religious spirit is defined not by unquestioning belief or credulity about the supernatural, but rather by emotional tendencies. A case can be made for thinking that the religious have distinctive hopes and fears that are not shared by the godfree. Particular religious traditions offer specific visions of heaven and hell, but perhaps these tap into deeper sources of human concern. While a particular vision of heaven might not be definitive of religiosity, perhaps a desire for eternal life is. Dante's vision of hell is peculiar to a culturally specific brand of Catholic Christianity, but maybe worries about unpleasant lives after death provide the psychological underpinnings of religion in general. To be religious, on this view, is to have specific forms of general hopes and fears.

Maybe. I do not desire eternal life, nor do I worry about eternal damnation, but perhaps atheists can have general forms of these concerns outside of religious contexts. More importantly, even if these emotional tendencies define the religious outlook, it is not clear why we should think highly of them. We should excuse them, perhaps; unrealistic hopes and fears are part of the human condition, after all. But this is far different from thinking that they are valuable, worth having, perhaps even worth fostering. Presumably they are worth cherishing to the extent that they are either realistic or make our lives better. Such suppositions are both pretty dubious. There are no good reasons that I know of to think that life after death is a realistic option for us. Nor is there much of a case to be made for thinking that these hopes and fears make our lives better. I think that they make them worse. (See *Heaven, Hell, Hope,* and *Fear*).

Overall, I'm not optimistic about finding general marks of the religious spirit. There are tendencies worth scrutinizing here, but arguably nothing uniquely definitive of religiosity. Maybe we can see why if we change our point of inquiry. Instead of trying to find some mark that religious systems and attitudes share, let's think instead about how religion tends to enter people's lives. Some people come to religion from nonreligious backgrounds, but this seems to me to be the exception rather than the rule. More typically, people grow up with religion. They enter the world into particular sorts of lives with defining beliefs and, more importantly, characteristic customs. People grow up taking a religious outlook for granted. This is worth emphasizing. Even those people whose lives are only lightly touched by religion tend to grow up in a context that takes religion—its ideas and practices—seriously. The religious stance is as much one of habit as it is of belief or emotion, perhaps more. For more on this, see *Habit, Language,* and *Tradition (or Custom).*

Responsibility: There's an old view that atheists renounce morality along with god. This is false, of course: see *Morality (or, On Loving the Good with and without God).* A correlative of this view is that the godfree embrace a life free of responsibility. The truth, ironically, is the other way around. To be godfree is to accept responsibility for making hard choices, not to relinquish it. Sometimes atheists are chastised for this, cast as arrogant, as playing god. But to recognize that we are the only ones around to face and to make certain sorts of choices is not arrogant, it's grown-up (see *Adults*). And playing god is not a problem if there is no god to insult or usurp by so doing. Which there isn't.

19

S Is for . . .

Sacred: Nothing is, but not for the reason that you think. "Sacred" is an explicitly religious term of moral evaluation. When we give up religion we should give up explicitly religious terminology. That is, we should do this if we mean to speak clearly. We can use "sacred" and other religious moral terms—"sin," "sanctity," for example—metaphorically. But why would we? This risks confusion: people might think the user is a religious believer. It also invites mistakes. For instance, one might think as a consequence of the prevalence of such terminology that religion and morality are inextricably linked. But they are not: see *Morality (or, On Loving the Good with and without God)*. Finally, to use religious language metaphorically strikes me as contrary to the spirit (ahem) of being an atheist. Many of us give up religion with a sense that this is where clearheaded thinking leads. Such clearheadedness, however, is thwarted by the confusing use of explicitly religious terms, at least for purposes that need not be religious. So: let's agree that nothing is literally sacred and let's examine the real moral issues clearly.

Salvation: Some people are born particularly bad. All of us are born somewhat bad. Getting over this is the sort of hard work that is to be expected of human life. There's no salvation to be had from without, except for the efforts of other people. Nor is any salvation really needed.
See *Heaven, Hell,* and *Mercy*.

Sanctity: See *Sacred*.

Satanism: A religion, or group of religions, venerating Satan as godlike if not a god. Atheism is not this. The godfree have no gods. Yet other religions are so opposed to both the idea of Satan and to atheism that they sometimes conflate the two. Please, do us the courtesy of not confusing us with Satanists, at least for the sake of accuracy. Pope Francis made this error on his first full day on the job. In the evening mass in the Sistine Chapel he said, following Leon Bloy, "Whoever does not pray to God, prays to the devil [because] when we don't witness to Jesus Christ, we witness to the worldliness of the devil." To think that not praying to Jesus implies praying to the devil, or to anyone else, is a mistake. To insist on this is to present a distorted view of the life of atheists. We don't pray (see *Pray*). It is really that simple.

In fact, I would rather be confused with Satan himself than with Satanists. Satanists strike me as kitschy and tawdry. Not so Satan: he is widely represented as witty, debonair even. It's a much more flattering mistake. A mistake nonetheless, of course, but still.

That this is a mistake should be clear. Satan is often represented as a seductive maker of promises that look really good but eventually leave you worse off than when you started. But this book, if taken as an attempt to seduce you away from belief, is lame. The godfree life brings both benefits and burdens. Depending on your tastes, the benefits might well be outweighed by the burdens. So be it: the baseline reason to be an atheist is, to be it bluntly, that it's true, and truth's comforts are often cold.

Science: Multifaceted and complex, of course, but for present purposes there are two things to note. For many, the word "science" stands for a body of information. Evolution by natural selection, the heliocentric view of the solar system, gravity, relativity: all are so-called "scientific" facts belonging to this body of information. Fair enough: our first encounters with science are typically with such facts. And these are important facts, as are many others in this body of information, so they are worth knowing, or at least knowing about.

There is a problem with an understanding of science that emphasises the facts, however. Such a view makes it difficult to differentiate science from any other body of information, such as those offered by religions. It also misses the feature that makes science the kind of thing that it is. The facts are the tip of the iceberg, the icing on the cake, the surface that is put on for show to all who are interested. Underneath the surface is a process, to put it simply. This is the scientific method, and it is the real heart of science. The scientific method is various ways of studying the world to figure out how it works. The body of information is what is produced by the scientific method, but this method is what makes science what it is. It is, at its core, what distinguishes science from religion. When we neglect this, we put science, and understanding in general, at risk, despite the familiarity people might have with so-called "scientific" facts (I hate this way of speaking, since these are just facts, but it has its uses.). See *Authority* for details.

There is much that could be said about particular sciences and about the scientific method in general. Instead, here is one feature that is particularly important. Scientists are not only committed to studying the world in order to figure out how it works. They are also committed to double-checking their work—to making sure that experimental results can be replicated, to ensuring that their observations are statistically representative, even to doing their sums over.

This commitment explains a common source of skepticism about science. The results of particular studies are sometimes reported on the news for all to hear. Later, contradictory studies are sometimes reported. Health reporting is a good place to look to see this pattern: eggs are bad for you, then they are good for you. Oat bran (or spinach, or blueberries, or . . .) is held up as particularly impressive, then no longer trumpeted as worth special attention. This is very frustrating to those who think of science as a body of information. The story is always changing! Can't these guys get it straight? They don't know anything, so I won't pay any attention to them.

But instead of being frustrating, this changing of reported results is actually science at its best. A finding has been reported in the news. This is good, and there should be more of it, but it should be done better. For one finding does not necessarily a complete story make. If it's an interesting finding—or even if it isn't—scientists will want to double-check it in various ways. This double-checking often reveals nuances that complicate what has been reported. They sometimes reveal errors. All of this is good: our understanding of the way the world works can only be refined by going through exactly this sort of process. The results that were reported and then taken back in subsequent reporting are like assessing the iceberg from just the tip, the cake from just the icing. The real work is more complicated and going on beneath. Rather than being a source of skepticism, we should be happy that we have such a robust institution for investigating the world.

This is far too brief, of course. There are complicated questions about vagaries of the scientific method, about different methods used by different sciences, about relations between the sciences and, for instance, philosophy. Or religion, for that matter: see *Questions*. As usual with this sort of vast territory, one must *Pick Up a Textbook*.

Secular: From the Latin for "worldly." "Secular Humanism" (see *Humanism [or, Secular Humanism]*) is a synonym for "Atheism" of mixed worth. I prefer "Godfree" (see *Godfree*). The Latin is helpful, however. It makes clear that the appropriate contrast is with things that are "unworldly," to coin an ugly word. More to the point: a secular stance is one that rejects anything supernatural. Most religious beliefs and practices endorse the supernatural, and hence are opposed to secular views, but maybe—just maybe, since the details matter here—some don't. Can there be a secular religion then? Maybe.

Self: A contentious notion to be handled carefully by both secular and religious thinkers.

Much of the religious interest in selves is bound up in the notion of a soul (see *Soul*). Overall, there seems to be a tendency to think of selves as, let's say, personality units of fundamental importance. This is a resistible tendency, however. It is rejected by much of contemporary psychology. The history of philosophy is marked by both its defense and its rejection by, for instance, no less an atheist than David Hume. Among religions, it is interesting to note that Buddhists give up on both the self, at least in this sense, and on gods. This brief sampling of the diverse directions from which this notion is assailed should give us pause with regard to the idea of the self. We cannot assume that the notion of a unified self, one per person, roughly equatable with the idea of a soul, is a defensible idea. Work is needed to see whether it is, or whether instead the self's naysayers are correct.

Short List of Suggested Readings: There is lots to read that is critical of religion. I could bore you with a lengthy list of readings, but I won't. I'll let you do the work yourself, not that it's hard: *Pick Up a Textbook.* Instead I will make a few choice suggestions and let you find your way from there (and from the Internet, and libraries, and booksellers, and so on—signposts aren't exactly hard to find.).

The works of the so-called four horsemen of new atheism (yuck, how I hate these terms)—Richard Dawkins, Daniel Dennett, Sam Harris, and Christopher Hitchens—are well known, widely available, and worth reading. Let me recommend something else: *Why Are You Atheists So Angry?* by Greta Christina. It's short, punchy, funny, angry (of course) and touching.

Instead of Hitchens' own work, try his collection *The Portable Atheist: Essential Readings for the Nonbeliever.* This spans history from ancient times until the present day, and it cuts across cultures and, vitally, religious traditions. There are some classics here, as you would expect, but it's some lesser lights who do the trick best for me. Mark Twain on flies is great! Philip Larkin's selections are ones to grow old with. For those with more academic tastes, Elizabeth Anderson's piece is important, and Ibn Warraq's are downright definitive.

For those with or without academic tastes, how about a novel? Try *36 Arguments for the Existence of God* by Rebecca Goldstein. But be careful—it's a trap! The book has a nonfictional yet highly readable appendix about such arguments. Entertainment and illumination in one package!

You are presently reading my attempt to convey some understanding about what a godfree perspective on certain important (and not-so-important) topics is like. I have deliberately avoided taking an academic approach to this project. Crucially, I haven't named many names, instead trying to focus on the forest instead of the trees. For more scholarly, name-naming looks at similar territory, try two books by Udo Schüklenk and Russell Blackford. *50 Voices of Disbelief: Why We Are Atheists* is an edited collection of pieces by fifty people giving their two cents about various aspects of godfree living. *50 Great Myths about Atheism*, by Schüklenk and Blackford alone, is a one-by-one attempt to dispel common distortions and misunderstandings of going godfree. Good stuff, with lots of references to chase up, both for and against atheism.

It's well worth opening a philosophy of religion textbook. Or two, for that matter. I like David Stewart's *Exploring the Philosophy of Religion*, but I recommend that you get a handful off the shelves of a library and flip through them. The result will be an introduction to hard questions addressed by both believers and nonbelievers, as well as some cross-cultural, cross-tradition eye-opening material. Good stuff for those with the patience for it.

Various organizations around the world collect demographic information about religion. Statistics Canada does it where I live, as do other organizations. Slightly more probing studies are performed in the United States by the Pew Research Center. Regardless of where you live, it's worth looking into this sort of data. It tells you things about your neighbors! I expect that this sort of data collection will only expand in the next few decades. I'm looking at you, Google.

I bet that there's an atheist society near you. Look for websites. They'll have stuff to read, and to say, and to talk about.

That's enough for my purposes. There's lots to read in this list, and it all leads to other things to read. How much time do you want to put into this? I have presented just some directly relevant stuff, but lots of other fields bear on our concerns: biology, geology, astronomy, physics, cosmology, nearly all branches of philosophy, psychology . . . that's a lot of textbooks to pick up. Yet that's what understanding the relevant details requires. If anyone told you this was simple stuff, they were mistaken, or lying.

Sign: Religious believers sometimes claim to see God's hand in the world, such that some events can be understood as divine signs. What should we make of this?

First we should note the different ways in which we use the notion of a sign. Smoke is a sign of fire. That is, because of the causal relationship between fire and smoke, smoke provides evidence of a fire's existence. I take it that, in most cases, this is not the religious sense of "sign." For believers who see God as creator of the world, nothing in particular would be a special sign of god because literally everything is held to bear this relationship to him. This grey hair is a sign of god, this bottlecap, and so on. I take it that the usual idea is rather that some things are more personal messages from God. Their nature is essentially communicative. Smoke happens to signal a fire, but it is not a message from a fire in any literal sense.

Sometimes these religious, communicative signs are relatively benign. For example, something awesomely beautiful might be taken as a sign of God's existence. I have heard the Grand Canyon referred to in this way. More pointedly, sometimes religious symbols or persons are said to appear in some sense such that they present signs. A statue purportedly starts to weep, or a rock structure is claimed to resemble a saint. At other times the supposed sign is not so benign. Is every new disease seen by some group as a divine punishment? It would not surprise me to learn that this is the case. The same seems to go for natural disasters and more personalized misfortunes and successes.

On one hand it is easy to see what atheists should think about such claims. In a godfree world there can be no signs from god. The events in question have some other source, either in human artifice or in nonhuman but natural processes. We need not think that things that appear significant to us are significant in a grander sense. See *Humility*.

On the other hand, this is a phenomenon worth some scrutiny. Suppose that I come home and find a note on the kitchen counter. It reads, "Gone back to work. Love D." It is perfectly reasonable for me to interpret this as a message; it's banal even to point this out. But it's not the piece of paper alone that makes this interpretation reasonable. Think about the framework of my life. I live in a context in which people communicate with each other. One of the ways in which they do this is via language. Some linguistic messages are spoken and picked up through the ears, others are detectable using our fingers, but this one is written by hand and read using one's eyes.

All of this would suffice for me to interpret the note as a message, but further facts are important to the content of the message. I live with precisely one other person, my wife, whose name begins with D and with whom I commonly exchange affectionate messages. Other people do not typically have access to my home. This makes it reasonable for me to see the note as a message to me personally, from a specific person, my wife, informing me of her exact whereabouts, given that I know her place of employment. Or at least it does if it is in my wife's handwriting. After all, we leave a personalized touch on messages of this kind. Someone else's handwriting would leave me confused, wondering about who wrote the message and who it was for.

Atheists see the world as lacking the sort of god who could send messages, be they direct and obvious or oblique and mysterious. At least some religious believers, however, do not see the world this way. Instead, their understanding of the world includes the kind of framework just described writ large. Besides the signs routinely sent among persons, this worldview allows for divine signs. Given this, it is not crazy for religious believers to think that they sometimes see signs of god. It is quite understandable, even if ultimately mistaken.

Nevertheless, there is good reason for the religious to be wary about claims that something is a sign from god. The things that are offered as divine messages can be impressive in certain respects, but they are all woefully puny in their communicative power. The hypothetical six-word note from my wife is clear and direct in its message. Its communicative efficacy is far higher than that of a weeping statue or an epidemic. The message of these sorts of thing is famously and patently unclear. If it were clear, we would all be religious believers, and we would all have the same religious beliefs.

Organized religions should dissuade believers from the tendency to see signs. They are insulting to the idea of a good and powerful god. Either god is so poor at communicating that these are the only sorts of messages he can muster, or he is so mischievous as to toy with believers and to mislead nonbelievers with these confusing and opaque signs. Divine texts are a bit better, but their variety and resistance to satisfying interpretation hardly vouchsafe a powerful or considerate god. The poverty of well-designed messages counts against the existence of the gods typically offered to us. If there are gods sending us messages, they are not gods worth worshipping. For organized religions to encourage their believers, even implicitly, to take putative signs seriously smacks of desperation. It may even be more craven than that, opportunistic exploitation of the hopes of the naïve.

It is no defense to claim that understanding god's messages requires, well, something that the godfree do not have. Perhaps what is needed is just the right attitude: one's heart should be open to god in order to hear his messages. Perhaps it is extensive training in a particular religion that is needed. It does not matter: such claims only prove my point about the communicative shortcomings of so-called divine signs. These sorts of things are not required for human messages. The requisite communicating skills for human messages are easily acquired by little children. We are far better, apparently, than god at communicating. This is why respectable defenders of religion ought to dissuade people from taking this sort of claim seriously. Besides, appeals to attitude and expertise are belied by the many believers with the right sort of credentials who nevertheless see no divine signs. Good for them.

Simplicity: A surprisingly tricky idea. Some are attracted to the idea of god because they think they understand this view of the nature of the world, whereas the story delivered by a naturalistic viewpoint is perplexing at least and, in its details, baffling. Should the apparently simpler view be preferred? Maybe. See *Ockham's Razor* for a more principled application of this idea. The crucial thing to see is that the notion of simplicity is ambiguous. First, something can be simple to understand. This is how the idea of god seems to many. I am inclined to think that this is merely apparent simplicity in many cases—a few questions tend to reveal complexities, even contradictions, in these ideas. What is apparently simple to understand is not necessarily all that simple.

Second, and more importantly, a body of ideas can be simple in its deep structure even when it is difficult to understand. This is the case with naturalistic accounts of the nature of the world. They are very difficult to understand—no simplicity here, in this sense. But they reveal a picture of the world that is simple with regard to the kinds of things that are in the world and that explain its nature and origin. Crudely put, there are natural things in this account only, no supernatural ones. This means that there is no need to explain interaction between natural and supernatural things. This is a good thing, as, when we think about it, the very idea of such interaction implies that everything that we think we know about the world is false, and that science is impossible. (See *Evidence* for discussion.) By contrast, despite being, on its face, simple to understand, in its workings a view of the world that allows for both natural things and god is relatively complicated.

If we stand back from the question of the nature of the world and the existence of god and instead think about more particular questions, we find good reason to be wary of accepting ideas that seem simple to us. We all know that ideas that seem simple to understand—about the origin of diseases, about how machines work, about the motivations of the people around us—are often false, and that ones that are more difficult to understand are often true. The fact that something is, on its surface, easy to believe is no guide at all with regard to whether it is worth believing.

Sin: See *Sacred*. With religion goes sin, but that's not as much as you might think. See *Morality (or, On Loving the Good with and without God)* for discussion of right and wrong.

Sincerity: Meaning what one says. Neither the liar nor the bullshitter speaks sincerely (see *Lies* and *Bullshit*). There are religious liars and bullshitters, but the typical religious speaker is neither. Whatever its faults might be, religious discourse cannot be charged with overwhelming lack of sincerity.

However, it is one thing to feel as if one means what one says. It is quite another to take the proper care about the topics one is addressing. Those religious people who say that they care about truth yet who hold on to articles of faith despite the nature of the world—even in the face of the nature of the world—should be taken to be sincere yet superficial. Their care for truth only goes so far. Real care for truth requires, well, care—double-checking to make sure that one is getting it right, for instance. It also requires openness to learning.

Sincerity without care about getting things right is good. It's just not as good as it could be. Intellectual humility is better, if caring for truth is what we really value (see *Humility*).

The godfree need not charge the believer with lying, or bullshitting, or insincerity. There are religious examples of all of these, of course, but these are special cases, not the defining features of these kinds of discourse.

If we take a wide perspective, we can see that it could be worse. Lack of care about truth is one thing; violent persecution of nonbelievers who insist on the real nature of the world is quite another. Think of the Spanish Inquisition, or the literal claims of far too many religious texts to see where this sort of sincerity gets us.

Soul: We don't have these, in any religiously interesting sense.

In the science versus religion trenches, evolutionary biology gets all the attention. Fair enough: this is interesting and important stuff with distinct relevance to our understanding of our nature and situation on earth. But it's not the only game in town. I have long been surprised at how little attention psychology gets in discussions of religion. What psychologists are learning about the mind puts pressure on the idea of the soul. And, once we think about it, we can see that the soul is of central importance to the relevance of religion to our lives.

Just how should we understand this idea, the soul? Presumably there have been lots of notions of the soul. To canvass them all here would be tediously detailed. Thankfully it's not necessary. We need only ask one question: is the soul supposed to be the mind? We might add qualifications here: "somehow, to some degree," etc., but it doesn't really matter. The crucial question is whether we should think of the soul as somehow involved in thought and conscious experience. Other supposed properties of the soul are irrelevant to our purposes.

Suppose that the soul is held to be, to some degree, the mind. I take it that this is a common way of thinking of the soul. My understanding is that when people hope for their soul to go to heaven after death, they are thinking of themselves continuing to experience whatever good things heaven has to offer, perhaps as if on a really great vacation. They are still themselves, psychologically, on this view. Likewise, when people worry about their souls going to hell, I take it that they are worried that they are going to experience awful things after death, perhaps as if stuck in an interminable and boring philosophy class. On this view, souls are, either centrally or in some small part, the thinking things that we are right now.

If this is the correct way to think of the soul, then it faces a challenge from psychology. Psychology is a young science with a difficult subject matter, but its various resources are revealing interesting and surprising things about the nature of thought. A couple of broad trends in these findings call into question this notion of the soul. First, thinking depends on our brains and bodies in very intimate ways. From one perspective this should go without saying. After all, we are all familiar with the changes in thought and behavior that stem from brain damage due to injury or gradual degeneration due to illness or age. Even more familiar is the loss of certain sorts of experience due to the loss of particular organs. If your eyes are poked out, you won't see anything anymore. With your eyes go visual experiences. But, from another perspective, this can hardly be emphasized enough. It is so easy to think of our minds as somehow separate from our bodies and so difficult to find a satisfying vocabulary to describe links between thought and meat. Still, there you go. If you want details—lots and lots of details—*Pick Up a Textbook*.

The other thing to point out from psychology is that it reveals that we tend to have a misleading picture of our own minds. We tend to think of ourselves as unified personalities, to some degree. Some of us think of ourselves as very unified, lacking thoughts and motivations that evade our conscious attention and hence control. Others of us are more familiar with thinking of ourselves as having sources of ideas and desires that are hidden from us. This can be both comforting and disquieting. But none of us, from the inside, suspect the truth: that our minds are deeply disunified. Thought is produced by a surprising variety of mechanisms, many of them outside of our conscious control. The image we have of ourselves as a unified personality in charge of our decisions and lives is itself a psychological achievement produced by multiple thought processes. These mechanisms, ironically, give us a misleading idea of our own nature.

Here is how these trends threaten the notion of the soul as a thinking thing. Since thought depends on our bodies so intimately, the thing that thinks is the body, not the soul. We should say this even if we are willing to see thought as realized by our active engagement with the world, perhaps involving various sorts of cognitive aids. After all, it is our bodies that engage with worldly resources, which are themselves of course also physical things. Moreover, since thought is produced by a variety of bodily mechanisms, we should see our sense of ourselves as a product of thinking, not as a window onto the seat of thought itself. This sense of self is delivered by multiple mechanisms that are to various degrees separate from and answerable to other mechanisms. Thought is not essentially unified. These trends in the findings of psychology challenge the common view of the soul as a thinking thing independent from the body. Short version: no physical platform, no thought. That means, on this view, no body, then no soul.

Of course, the point about embodiment does not challenge views of

178 • A Is for Atheist

the soul that also insist on the presence of our bodies (see *Bodies*). There still remains, however, the point about the diverse mechanisms that give rise to the appearance of a unified self. This threatens every notion of the soul of which I know.

So far I have been considering views of the soul that, to some degree, equate it with the mind. Let's now consider the alternative: views of the soul that do not see it as the same thing as the mind. On this sort of view, it's a mistake to think of the thinking thing that you are now as persisting after death in either heaven or hell. The soul might persist after death, but you won't experience this. Experience, after all, is part of our thinking lives. With thought goes experience, pain, pleasure, and everything else that comprises our mental lives.

Obviously psychology poses no challenge to this view of the soul. Psychology describes the nature of the mind, and this view dissociates soul from mind. So, believe this view of the soul if you like. But notice: such a view gives us no reason to care about our souls, and hence no reason to care about god, religion, or anything in this vast area. If you are not going to persist, as a thinking thing, in a heaven or hell, then your life as the person you are is confined to your few years on earth. This is exactly how the godfree see—or should see—the limits of their lives. There is no difference between the godfree and the believing perspective at this point. Those religious views that countenance the persistence of the soul after death believe something that the godfree reject, but they share much with regard to the nature of the mind.

To see why we need not care about the soul on this view, consider an analogy. Suppose that when we die, someone collects our left feet and stores them in perpetuity. Perhaps it's the government, perhaps this is what god does—it doesn't matter, for the purposes of the analogy. The point is that if this were the way things happened in the real world, we would not have any reason to care one way or the other about this. I certainly would not care. One *might* care, but people have arbitrary preferences about all sorts of things. And in this case such an attitude would certainly be arbitrary. It is not going to make any difference to us after death (on the assumption that our minds are not even to any small degree our feet). It's a curious fact about the world that this is what happens to our left feet, nothing more and nothing less.

If our souls have nothing to do with our minds, then we have as much reason to care about them and what god does with them after our deaths as we would about our left feet in my hypothetical foot-collection world. It would make no difference to me what happened to my soul—it would be much like any body part that has no capacity for thought all by itself. Some people might care, but this would just amount to a difference in tastes between them and me. We have no reason that I can see why we should care. With this view of the soul goes any reason to care about god and religion that we could have. Imagine a persuasive argument for the existence of god. If our souls are not thinking things, then we have no reason to care about this god. What could it do to us to threaten or persuade us into caring? Worldly rewards and torture are familiar and not enough to do the job, and once we are dead, our capacity for experience is completely gone and god would lose all possible grip on us as selves. He's welcome to the bodily remains, in my eyes. You might differ. *De gustibus non est disputandum.*

So: the soul is religion's downfall. If the soul is somehow, to some degree, the mind, then religion faces a challenge from psychology, since it reveals a quite different view of the nature of thought. If the soul is distinct from our minds, then we have no reason to care about god, other than mere curiosity.

There is an in-between possibility, but not one which any religion of which I know has offered. It is that your soul is *a* mind, but one not continuous with *your* mind before you die. On this view, a thinking thing connected to you persists after death, but it is not you. It is a distinct person. By the standards of this purely hypothetical view, you have as much reason to care what happens to your soul after death as you do about other people in general. Let's be clear: you have never met the person that persists after your death. The soul, on this view, is a stranger who happens to be related to you. If a religion offered this view of the soul, would it give us much reason to care about what happens to us after death? Theoretically a little bit, but not much. We have as least as much, if not more, reason to care about the many strangers—who may or may not be related to us—who are affected by the decisions we make in this life. I say "as much" here, but I don't really mean it. After all, we know of these people, whereas this view of our relation to our souls is purely hypothetical. It is good advice always to think about the effects of our actions on the people who actually exist, rather than on our souls, however we may conceive of them.

Space Travelers: Imagine yourself as an astronaut visiting a newly discovered planet. Picture not the arid rocks or the gassy balls of our neighbors in the solar system but something out of science fiction: a lush world populated by intelligent life. You are curious about this world. You want to know how things work there, what its origins are—all the same things that we want to know about our own world. How should you proceed to find these things out?

Suppose that the intelligent aliens on this planet learn of your curiosity. They approach you with their explanations of themselves and their world. As it turns out, they have not developed principled forms of empirical inquiry. Instead, they explain their situation in terms of stories they have developed about various kinds of supernatural being. They have a very rich set of stories to offer you. The crucial question is this: would you accept these stories as the final word on the nature of the aliens and their world?

Of course you wouldn't. If it weren't you but instead astronauts that you're paying for with tax dollars, you wouldn't expect them to take the alien stories at face value either. Quite the contrary: I'm sure that you would expect the astronauts to investigate the nature of this world directly. The stories might be scrutinized for clues, but they would not be accepted as answering the questions that you have. The alien planet itself will have to answer those questions, not the aliens. The stories would have to earn their explanatory keep. To the extent that they failed to deliver the truth about the nature of this planet, and to the extent that this is what you were interested in, you would disregard them.

The point of this imaginative exercise should be clear. I am drawing an analogy between the situation the astronauts find themselves in on an alien world and the situation we find ourselves in on planet earth. Let me be as clear as possible: the analogy is direct. We humans are in *exactly* the same position on planet earth as the one these imaginary astronauts find themselves in. We have arrived on a planet and we have questions about its origin and nature. The intelligent life forms that are already here offer us stories to explain these things. At this point, however, many of us lose the clear-thinking attitude we evince toward the astronauts. Instead of insisting that the stories that are offered to us match the world, we accept the stories as told and balk when the world turns out to differ. When we do this we are putting carts before horses. We should think of ourselves as intrepid astronauts and insist that the world answer the questions that we have. This means rolling up our sleeves and doing the hard work of empirical inquiry. This means science.

In case you are unmoved by the dispassionate curiosity of my imaginary astronauts, here is another way to think about these issues. Suppose that you have purchased a very old car. It needs repair. It's a lot different from the automobiles that you normally encounter as a mechanic, so you're not sure how the parts work nor how you should go about fixing it. Suppose another person claims to know about this sort of car. They tell you various things which you then try out in your garage. You work really hard with what your friend is telling you, but the words just don't match the machine that is giving you all the trouble. Push comes to shove: will you accept your friend's story as the truth and deny what the car is telling you, or will you disregard your friend's stories as misleadingly uninformed and instead try to learn from the car directly? You and I both know what you would do. It's so obvious that I don't even need to spell it out. The same attitude is worth adopting when it comes to figuring out how the world works.

Various things lead us to fail to take the sensible stance toward our own world that we would expect our astronauts to take toward the alien world and the mechanic to take toward the antique car. I won't canvass them all. Particularly important is, I think, lack of need and even of opportunity to test our ideas about the nature of the world against the world itself. It's notable that religious explanation does not apply to the most mundane and practical of topics, such as how lightbulbs work. There might be rules about operating such things, but my impression is that the religious recognize that this is not the domain for religious explanations. Sober-minded electricians can be devoutly religious, provided that their religious commitments do not interfere with their work. Good thing too, as it would probably kill them (and us).

When religious explanations are tested, they fail miserably. Look into the research on, for example, prayer and medical treatment, and you will see. It's a mistake to think that our stories about the nature of ourselves and world should not be tested against the world. Our lack of need and opportunity make us lazy. Empirical inquiry is difficult, demanding of both effort and time. That doesn't make it second best; it's still the gold standard for measuring our understanding of ourselves and our situation. It just makes it hard. Together we ought to do much better than we currently do to remind ourselves of the centrality of this stance and this work to our efforts to satisfy our own curiosity. Too many of us are encouraged in our intellectual sloth to lose our respect for the only ways we have of figuring out how the world, including us, works.

Spirit: A tricky word. What does it mean? We use it harmlessly all the time: people can be in high or low spirits. A defense of a position can be spirited. In these cases surely we do not commit ourselves to the existence of spirits in any substantial sense. There is metaphor here, perhaps allusion to something we understand but which can be more simply and more enjoyably put using spirit-talk.

This leaves literal use of this idea. The world does not literally contain spirits, at least not in any religiously interesting sense. I take it that there is great overlap between the idea of a spirit and that of a soul, so see *Soul* for further discussion.

"Spirit in the Sky": One of very few half-decent overtly religious songs in the rock and pop genres. So thanks, Norman Greenbaum. Other worthy candidates: the Velvet Underground's "Jesus," Led Zeppelin's version of "In My Time of Dying," "The Ballad of El Goodo" by Big Star . . . "My Sweet Lord" by George Harrison? Pretty good. Blind Faith's "In the Presence of the Lord"? Considerably better. There must be others, but you get my point. There are spiritual themes in much heavy metal music—the first Black Sabbath album rocks!—but it comes off as awfully Hallowe'eny to my ear, hard to take seriously.

Why are there so few listenable religious rock or pop songs? I don't know, and I don't really care, understandably. But it is a significant fact when we take a wider view of religion and art. It's not uncommon for defenders of religion to cite its benefits to society, and chief among these are the aesthetic accomplishments we find around the world. It is true, to a point: there are beautiful paintings about religious topics, wonderful buildings built to the glory of god, and impressive pieces of classical music inspired by, or at least commissioned on behalf of, divine subject matters. Sagrada Familia? Great! The Alhambra? Fantastic! But this is only part of the story. Crummy religious rock songs help us to remember that love of god does not necessarily yield great art. Religion produces bad art at least as much as it produces good art: the crappy churches, paintings, and symphonies tend to be forgotten and not taken into account. Moreover, entire aesthetic traditions are marked by a paucity of religious success. Rock music is a notable case in point, as is jazz: the secular triumphs far outnumber the religious ones here. Maybe the same goes for literature, or at least for certain literary forms. How many genuinely good religious novels are there? Not many, so far as I know.

Let's give due credit to aesthetic accomplishments with religious origins and themes. I will continue to visit the great paintings and cathedrals to be found in Europe when I go on vacation. They are worth our attention, regardless of our religious orientations. But let's not forget nonreligious art—it is just as worthwhile. And when tallying the social pluses and minuses of religion, let's not overvalue aesthetic success. Religious rock music counts against religion at least as much as the interior of St. Peter's Basilica counts for it.

See *Enchantment* for more on godfree reactions to beauty. For more on the good vs. bad consequences of belief, see *Moral Math (or, Good vs. Bad Effects of Religion and Atheism)*.

Spooky: A pejorative term used by atheists to dismiss many of the claims central to religious worldviews. God, spirit, the soul, more specific stories about people rising from the dead or about other sorts of miracles: all spooky, and all thereby suspect. I don't like this term, although I use it occasionally. It's a useful term for capturing the visceral contempt that appeals to the supernatural (god, etc.) can trigger in the godfree. The same sort of contempt is often felt by the religious toward atheists; turn around is fair play. Still, it's a problematic response and therefore a problematic term. To call something spooky is to dismiss something without argument. Our feelings of dislike for certain ideas (for example, people rising from the dead—come on!) are, strictly speaking, irrelevant both to the truth of those ideas and to the various roots of their appeal for many people. While it can be useful, honest, and even friendly to give voice to our dislike of these ideas, for the most part we should avoid this and speak dispassionately about the strengths and weaknesses of religious propositions.

Standards: The yardsticks of judgment.

When we assess things, we use, either implicitly or explicitly, standards of assessment. To say that someone is a good athlete invokes a context by which we, probably implicitly, understand what is being said. We know that cooking proficiency is not part of what is assessed. We know that inability to walk a few meters without losing one's breath is not being praised. We can call these standards "rules" for judgment if we like, so long as we understand this pretty loosely. Whatever we want to call them, our lives are shot through with references to standards, both overt and unnoticed.

Religion provides standards for assessing the quality of people, the worthiness of lives and actions. To sincerely call someone "a good Christian" invokes these standards; so does describing an action as a sin. Religious standards sometimes take people as focal points: Jesus, Muhammad, Mother Teresa, the local cleric, and so on are all offered as measuring sticks and even guides to our conduct. Even when they are not explicitly invoked, religious standards pervade many people's thought and talk (see *Language*).

The consequence of this is that when someone makes a change from a religious way of living to a godfree life, these standards are given up. Sure, there are still things about the actions endorsed by these standards that can be endorsed using faithless standards. There are still things admirable about the exemplars of distinctively religious virtue. But since the standards are, technically, different ones, these actions and people are no longer praised in the same ways. Sometimes this is mistaken for a lack of standards— see *Morality (or, On Loving the Good with and without God), Values,* and *Responsibility* to correct this view.

Since such assessment is important, indeed natural, for us, and since these religious patterns of thought tend to crop up everywhere, it can be discomfiting to make this change. Going godfree is not necessarily easy, and this is one place where considerable effort can be required. Sometimes people try to assuage their discomfort by trying to rehabilitate the religious yardsticks. Consider those who don't like official religions but who deploy new age terminology, or a general language of spirituality. This really isn't on: it's only to retain a religious worldview without going to church. A godfree life involves giving up the worldview. In fact it's more important to give this up than it is to stop going to church. (I would advise against that too, but this might boil down to matters of taste; see *A Very Ordinary Day*.)

Stories: A particularly notable and, frankly, charming feature of many religious traditions and texts is the wealth of stories through which they deliver their messages. The Bible might be an unwieldy and boring text in many ways, but it is also a repository of vivid and entertaining stories. Religious literature is worth noting for its narrative riches.

At the same time, these stories are tricky, as are all stories. Anyone who has reflected on a story knows this. This holds whether the story is an account of actual events or purely a product of the imagination. Stories, perhaps especially good ones, are rich in interpretive possibilities, such that saddling them with one true meaning is not necessarily possible or even desirable. This is good for literary purposes, bad for intellectual ones. Stories are particularly opaque ways of providing us with lessons. When we are interested in the truth or moral defensibility of a message, we need to know what the message in question is. Stories are notably poor ways of delivering clear messages. Guff can hide in a good narrative, and that is a problem. (See *Guff*.)

Enjoy religious stories. At the same time, don't mistake a good story for a defensible idea. Narrative engagement is not at all tied to truth. When we are really interested in truth, we must be committed to extracting putative messages from stories and subjecting them to direct scrutiny. Without doing this we might not learn the lessons at all, or even worse, we might mistakenly accept falsehoods about topics that matter.

Straw Men: A straw man argument is one that sets up a weak caricature of a position and then holds that with the defeat of this deficient version, the real position is defeated. The term draws its point from the contrast between real people and people made out of straw. The straw people are much easier to knock down.

Religious believers sometimes charge atheists with rejecting straw man versions of religion, of god, of particular arguments in favor of the supernatural, and so on. Fair enough; we should not do that. But straw man complaints work both ways in this territory. Religious believers are just as culpable for trotting out caricatures of godfree life. The purportedly intimate link between religion and morality that atheists reject, anyone? See *Morality (or, On Loving the Good with and without God)* for discussion.

Moreover, there is good reason for us all, devout and otherwise, to wonder whether some of these men are really made of straw. There is a lamentable tendency of believers, when discussing ideas of god, the soul, whatever, to change the subject: we start out with one idea which, when challenged, turns out not to really be the idea after all, and the same with the next version (see *Guff* for discussion). My worry is that the first idea (or second, it doesn't matter—the issue is an idea that is given up by the believer as not really the topic) often really is the topic after all. Sometimes the position that is easy to knock down isn't a straw replica of one's position; sometimes it is one's position.

There is a more nuanced version of this problem. We all know the view of god offered by big religions and held by millions of people. God is a superperson, typically a man—God the Father—certainly a being with a mind. But sophisticated theology, espoused by academics, clergy, and some believers alike, often delivers quite a different view. This is an austere god, god as ultimate reality, not a person, not literally something with a mind. This sort of god is not literally compatible with major religious traditions, although maybe it is metaphorically. Regardless, my impression is that people often take refuge in the sophisticated arguments but really endorse the more familiar view of god as a superperson. The arguments, and the alternative views of god, are necessary if one is going to have a chance of articulating a defensible view of god. But the more defensible view, for many, isn't their real view. The absolutely indefensible one is. Straw men are more common, and dearer to the hearts of many, than one might think.

Studying Religion: You might think that addressing how to study religion requires a firm, or firmish, account of the nature of religion (see *Religion* and *Religious Spirit [or, Religiosity; Religion in General; Religion in the Abstract]*). In a sense this is correct, but in another sense this is wrong. After all, why should a good account of the nature of something be thought to be on hand before the study of that thing? Perhaps the nature of at least some things can be revealed only through principled study. Anyway, with regard to religion, I think that the truth lies in the middle: we can study religion with a rough sense of what it is, and we should expect study to refine our sense of its nature.

Importantly, we can, at the very outset, distinguish different sorts of questions and hence different sorts of ways of talking about religious issues. Following general philosophical usage, we can call these levels of discourse *first order* and *higher order* (see *Morality [or, On Loving the Good with and without God]* for the application of this distinction to moral issues). First-order religious questions and ways of talking are about the familiar objects of religious discourse. When we talk about the nature of god, or sin, or heaven, or the soul (and so on), we are asking first-order questions and refining our first-order discourse. By contrast, higher-order questions and ways of speaking are about first-order questions and ways of speaking. Higher-order discourse is discourse about discourse, whereas first-order discourse is discourse about, in this case, such supposed phenomena as the divine and its relations to the familiar and natural.

Before going on, let me ward off a worry. "First" and "higher" are not meant to connote anything evaluative. First-order questions are not necessarily superior or inferior to higher-order ones. This terminology denotes the kind of topic that is being addressed, not its worthiness of such address.

Onward. An important issue is which sort of question we should be asking first and foremost. This is tricky, as it turns out. Part of the reason— indeed, maybe the whole reason—for this is the trickiness we find when we try to say just what religion is (again, see *Religion*). Let's run through some options to see the details.

Some claim that religious discourse is fundamentally experiential. Someone hears voices or sees a vision, then this forms the basis of a religion. Typically it's the experiences of mystics that are emphasized, but these need not be thought to be rare or to be had only by special people. This way of thinking grounds religious discourse in supposedly direct religious experiences that, in principle, could be had by ordinary people. If this is the case, then it makes good sense to emphasize first-order questions. What are these experiences of? Important question, if this view of the nature of religion is correct.

This view is not the only option at hand, however. Experience is a source of beliefs, but some reject the view that this is the primary aspect of religion. For instance, some claim that religion is inherently practical (see *Practical Religion)*. On this view, religious life consists not in beliefs, creeds, etc., at least not primarily. It consists in ways of behaving. Some of these concern overt forms of worship. Others concern our daily affairs—food, clothing, interaction, and the like. Interestingly, the implication for the study of religion is largely the same as in the first case: if this way of characterizing religion is correct, then first-order issues deserve close attention.

There are other options too. Some claim that religion is inevitable. This is the view, perhaps implicit, of those who categorize unbelief as itself a religion. If religion is inevitable, then again it makes sense to emphasize first-order claims, not the second-order ones.

Note that, in each of these cases, I say "if this view is correct," then the first-order questions tied to that view should be emphasized. But are any of these correct? If so, which one? Are there other options. To answer *these* questions is a higher-order matter. It concerns questions about discourse.

Moreover, there are pretty natural higher-order issues generated by each of these particular views of the nature of religion. Consider religion and experience. We have to ask about the trustworthiness of the experiences, rather than just taking them for granted. This is to ask a question about the experiences themselves, not just about what seems to be revealed by these experiences. Or, to continue with the prior example, to assess whether atheism is a religion requires that we think about the things that atheists believe—godfree ways of thinking and speaking—and then compare this with uncontroversially religious discourse. This is to ask questions about discourse, not about the divine, etc., and hence is higher order.

Some claim that religion is neither primarily experiential nor practical nor inevitable, but rather theoretical. It is a matter of forming and holding beliefs that purport to capture the nature of the world in both its natural and supernatural aspects. As with the prior approaches, determining whether religion really is primarily theoretical requires a higher-order approach. However, in this case we have the interesting result that higher-order approaches need to be emphasized anyway. The reason is that, for the topics in question—the origin of the world, the nature of humans, how we ought to act—religion is not the only game in town (which should give us pause about assuming that it's inevitable, I should think). There are well-developed secular accounts of all of the things that religion addresses. To take religion seriously as a theoretical enterprise requires comparison of it with nonreligious treatments of the same topics. Even more importantly, we must assess its strengths and weaknesses with regard to these topics.

All of this might strike you as dull: of course we must ask questions about religious ways of thinking and speaking, regardless of the fundamental nature of religion and religious discourse. Here is the reason that I plod through these details: people who are inclined toward religious accounts of various topics, regardless of their views about the fundamental nature of religion, tend to do first-order work without attending to the higher order issues. Go ahead, take a look at some of the work (see *Pick Up a Textbook*) and you will see what I mean. This way of working puts the intellectual cart before the horse. In this case the image is quite apt: doing so is a mistake that really gets you nowhere, no matter how nuanced the resulting details might be.

Supernatural: (1) For arguments showing that supernatural entities are explanatorily redundant, and hence unnecessary to explain the nature of the world (see *Evidence*).

(2) I am sometimes presented with claims that the super- or nonnatural is needed to explain nature as a matter of conceptual necessity. The argument is something like this: nature—the domain of natural phenomena, natural mechanisms, and natural law—stands in need of explanation. How did all of this natural stuff come about? Since it is natural phenomena that are to be explained, the explanation can't be put in natural terms. If we tried to explain nature in terms of nature, nature would not really be explained. Instead, it is claimed that we need to appeal to the super- or nonnatural in order to explain nature. A supernatural domain—a domain of such things as gods—is needed in order to account for the existence of what we see around us.

Rather than delivering the existence of the supernatural as a matter of conceptual necessity, this line of thought suffers from a conceptual error. It offers the supernatural as the cause or origin of nature. But consider just what is being explained. It is nature: natural phenomena and natural laws.

Among the structuring features of nature and natural laws is time. Time is, by all standards, a feature of nature. It is studied, for instance, by physicists, and physics is a natural science. Now consider the meaning of "origin" or "cause." These ideas have time as part of their meaning. Causes come before their effects. "Origin" means, to put it roughly, "beginning." This might not seem very important, but it is. It implies that it only makes sense to speak of causes or origins or related notions where it also makes sense to speak of time. If temporal notions do not apply, neither do notions that have time as part of their meaning. This means that, contrary to appearances, it makes no sense to speak of the causes or origins of time, and hence it makes no sense to speak of the causes or origins of nature. The very ideas of causes and origins only make sense within the domain to which time applies— that is, they only make sense within nature. So to ask for origins of nature is not to ask a meaningful question. It is instead only to show that one is confused about the meanings of these ideas.

Against this idea I sometimes encounter this retort: causal priority is, it is admitted, temporal priority, but this is not the only kind of priority there is, and it is not the kind that applies to the issue of the explanation of nature. The priority of the supernatural to the natural is conceptual, not temporal, so no error with these terms is being made.

There are at least three problems with putting the relation of the supernatural to the natural in terms of conceptual priority. First, so far as I can see, the supernatural is not conceptually prior to the natural. One thing is conceptually prior to another when the first is part of the meaning of the second. Consider the concepts "marriage" and "bachelor." A bachelor is, by definition, an unmarried man. So "marriage" is part of the meaning of "bachelor" (because it is part of the meaning of "unmarried"), which means that "marriage" is conceptually prior to "bachelor." Now think about the concepts that are really in question for us: "nature" means, well, nature—the domain of natural things. "Supernatural" means, by contrast, that which stands outside of nature. Conceptually, the very idea of the supernatural is derived from that of the natural. Maybe there is a way of specifying the "nature" of the supernatural in a nonderivative fashion, and then of explaining how it interacts with nature. This might answer my present concern, but it still will not demonstrate the existence of a supernatural domain of such things as gods. For details, see *Evidence*.

Second, the idea of conceptual priority helps to pinpoint the very problem that I have already tried to articulate. "Time" is conceptually prior to "cause," "origin," and related notions. This means that, because time is part of the meaning of these concepts, they only apply to domains where time applies. This is nature itself. So, because of the conceptual priority of time to causes and origins, we cannot speak meaningfully of origins (etc.) of nature itself. If we try to do so, we make a conceptual error: we treat the conceptually prior as if it is conceptually derivative or conceptually independent.

Finally, suppose that I am wrong about both of these points. Imagine that the supernatural is conceptually prior to the natural and that time is not conceptually prior to causes, origins, and related notions. Does this deliver the existence of the supernatural as a matter of conceptual necessity? More specifically, is it conceptually necessary that there is a supernatural origin of nature and all the natural phenomena revealed by empirical study of the world? No. The reason is that conceptual priority is the wrong kind of priority to be looking for, if we're interested in explaining the existence of things.

Here is an example to demonstrate the point. "Child" is conceptually prior to "son." That is, "child" is part of the meaning of "son": a son is a male child. But "son" is not part of the meaning of "child": there can be children that are not sons. This means that it makes sense to speak of sons only where it makes sense to speak of children, but it can make sense to speak of children where there are no sons. Now consider me. I am male, so I am a son. "Child" is part of the meaning of "son," but my being a child is not what made me a son. My origin as a son is not to be explained in terms of the concept "child." My origin is to be explained in terms of certain acts of my parents plus facts about biology: these are what gave rise to my existence as a son. The conceptual priority of "child" to "son" is just the wrong place to look if we are interested in my origins. Causal priority is what accounts for origins, but this is different from conceptual priority.

Likewise, if (contrary to fact) the supernatural is conceptually prior to nature, it is not the case that it thereby accounts for the origins of the natural world. Conceptual priority is the wrong kind of priority for this. Conceptual priority does not deliver causal priority. The existence of nature does not require the existence of the supernatural as a matter of conceptual necessity.

Symbolism (or, Analogy, Metaphor): Arguably unavoidable and often desirable when speaking of religion, as with other topics, but very slippery, to the extent that many religious thinkers mishandle it. We should be wary of it. We should, at crucial points at least, eschew it. Be cautious around those who insist on uninterpreted symbolism about religious topics.

One of the ways the religiously minded embrace mystery is to claim that nothing can literally be known or said about god (see *Mystery*). Let's put aside the fact that many people claim to do exactly this and examine this claim. Suppose that this were the case—what options would we have for speaking of gods? These thinkers claim that religious discourse is essentially metaphorical, analogical, symbolic. We have lots of symbols for god, lots of suggestive ways of intimating things about the divine essence, yet no terms that really describe features of god.

On this way of thinking, there is something right about saying that god is omniscient, for instance, but it must not be taken literally. God does not literally know, but there is something correct about thinking of god as epistemically in touch with everything. We should not think of god as literally the creator of the universe, but there is nonetheless something apt about this way of speaking. And so on: if you can say it about god, it should not be taken literally but instead (I hesitate to say "merely," although I am tempted) symbolically.

There is nothing in general wrong with embracing symbolism. There is even lots of useful religious symbolism to be found. Art, for instance, is a ripe place to look for symbols that run the gamut from mundane to wonderful. Certainly it helps to understand all those European paintings to learn that Mary is typically indicated by that particular shade of blue. It is a symbol that tells people something about the topic of the painting. Such instances are legion.

They also show what the fundamental problem is with the present line of thought, that no religious language is literal. Let's think about how symbols work. A symbol stands for something to someone on some grounds. Some symbols work because they resemble their objects in some respect. Take the Christian cross: it resembles the actual cross on which Christ was executed, so it can usefully stand for Christianity and associated specific subtopics, such as Christ himself. Other symbols are useful because of semantic associations. Take the Christian fish symbol. Christ was not a fish, so this does not resemble him. But he and his disciples are spoken of as fishers of men, and because of this association the fish symbol is useful.

Here is the crucial thing: in both of these cases, we can say that the symbol in question—the cross, the fish—is apt because we understand the nature of what is symbolized. The nature of the object of the symbol makes the symbol appropriate.

The question of the aptness of religious symbols obviously arises—it arises with all symbols. Why is it apt to speak of god, metaphorically, as omniscient? Why is it not apt to speak of god as orange? Without access to the nature of god, and hence without literal ways of speaking of god's nature, these questions cannot be answered. Yet no religious thinkers, so far as I know, disavow the issue of the appropriateness of religious symbols. On the contrary, they insist on some as appropriate and shun others as inappropriate, wrong, even offensive. This won't do, intellectually speaking, unless we have direct access to properties of the divine.

What is left for symbolism other than resemblance and semantic association? Some symbols work because someone stipulates what they will mean. Any of us can do this for any topic: let lettuce leaves symbolize atheists, for instance. There is nothing other than my will grounding this symbol. There is nothing apt about it, with regard to lettuce-atheism relations. Other symbols work by convention. We all know that octagonal signs mean "stop." This shape symbolizes this action, but only by convention. There is nothing octagonal about stopping, and nothing in the meaning of the word "stop" that intimates eight-siddness.

In these cases, the symbols are grounded by our wills, individual and collective, not by the things symbolized. Religious symbols can obviously be like this. But in such cases there is no reason to take them as necessarily shedding light on the thing symbolized. To say that god is conventionally represented as omniscient says nothing about whether this is correct. It says something only about how people tend to think of god.

To insist on symbols all the way down is to acquiesce in mystery about divine questions. It is a way of insisting that there are gods and that people must think about them in certain ways without poking too deeply into the question of whether those ways of thinking are true or not. This is at least mistaken, at worst disingenuous and deceptive. Let's insist on clarity here, both about the topics and the ways we have of representing them.

20

T Is for . . .

Thank God!: An inadvertent insult to those whose hard work benefits other people.

Athletes thank god for victories. Musicians thank god for awards. People who have faced accident and illness thank god for renewed health. There is laudable humility here (see *Humility*). But there is also regrettable insensitivity. God did not restore these sick people to health: their heart surgeons (and cancer specialists, and devoted nurses, and so on) did. God did not give out that award: peers, or journalists, or the voting public did. God did not take part in the big game: you did, and your team of coaches and trainers and other supporters put you in position to win. Examples could be multiplied pretty much endlessly.

When god is thanked for things that other people very clearly did, these people are slighted. Credit where credit is due—this is surely part of the nature of true gratitude. To thank god, however well-meaning, is to fail to give appropriate thanks to those who really deserve it.

Tradition (or Custom): (1) A word for the way people have tended to act or think about something. "Habit" and, especially, "custom" are virtually synonyms. See *Habit* for more.

Sometimes people seem to value practices simply because they are habitual, but this is surely a mistake. Traditions, habits, customs are worth preserving only when they are independently defensible. If we do bad things as a matter of tradition, this arguably makes us and our actions worse, not better. Slavery, for instance, was not persuasively defensible when we had living traditions of owning humans as slaves. Habitual racism and sexism make us worse: when we live in contexts that tend to blind us to the equal status of other persons, and that make it difficult for us to live peacefully with these others as equals, the traditions that define these contexts are a blight.

In case you are not convinced, consider a different kind of tradition. There are lots of art traditions. Imagine a particular form of art, or a particular aesthetic device (a musical instrument, say) that is acknowledged by all to produce ugly art. But suppose that a tradition of use of this artform develops somewhere. The tradition does not make the ugly beautiful. It just makes it the kind of thing that people in this place produce as art. To the extent that being steeped in this ugliness warps these people's aesthetic sensibilities, the tradition is aesthetically bad for them, not good. The same goes for moral values and traditions.

Many people take religious ideas seriously and take part in religious practices primarily because they are traditional and have become habitual. But this is no defense of religion. To note the traditional status of religious practices and beliefs is not to answer any questions about whether the religious spirit, for example, is morally defensible. It is only to raise these questions, and perhaps to attune ourselves to the ways in which we might have been damaged or improved by them. I suspect damage here, but the details are complicated. And anyway, it is a desperate defense of religion that relies on custom after faith, emotion, and the supernatural have turned out to be wanting. For more on these see *Religious Spirit (or, Religiosity; Religion in General; Religion in the Abstract)*.

(2) Here is another way to put this worry. Tradition is a moral amplifier. When one is immersed in a tradition, one acquires ways of thinking and acting. These ideas, patterns of thought, and behavioral tendencies might be ones that a person would not have had otherwise—the tradition makes it possible for one to have what we might as well call a particular way of life. Moreover, the depth and rigidity of the tradition make it harder to get rid of these ideas, etc. than it would otherwise have been. That's what tradition does: it shapes us, rather than being a mere adornment of what we already are independently of it.

Suppose that particular beliefs and ways of acting are good. When these are embodied in a tradition, that tradition is a good thing. It makes it easier for people to acquire these habits; it can even get people to have them when they lack the independent motivation for them. It makes these ideas and patterns of behavior harder to shake than they otherwise would have been, and hence it makes these people better than they are individually. Take respect for women as morally equal to men. Lots of people aren't inclined to give this status to women, but a legal and ethical tradition keeps them on the straight and narrow and contributes to them treating women as equal to men. This is a good thing.

But take slavery again, as another example. I mean this in the sense of some people holding others as property, and hence as unable to direct the course of their own lives. Lots of people over the course of human history have joined in with this practice fundamentally because there was a local tradition of slave ownership. Without such habits of thought and action these people would neither have owned slaves nor endorsed this institution. The tradition makes these people worse than their other motivations would have made them, which is just to say that this tradition is a source of evil.

The crucial thing to note is that, for both good and bad patterns of thought and action, tradition contributes nothing in particular of value. The good is made easier to do when people have traditions to encourage them in this, but so is the bad made easier. In a sense, tradition makes the good better and the bad worse. The mere fact that something is traditional says nothing about its value.

Tragedy (or, Despair about the Meaning of Life): Does atheism render life meaningless? Is a world without god a world in which nothing really matters? Of course not, but it's worth some effort to understand the various tempting mistakes that lead us to this worry.

Day by day we want various things. When we get them, we are sometimes satisfied and sometimes disappointed. An important way in which we are disappointed is when we discover that what we wanted wasn't really worth wanting. Think of a purchase that you made after a long period of desire only to discover that the thing you bought was crappy and you will know what I mean. This can sow the seeds of doubt about the worth of all of our wants.

What if none of them are worth wanting? And this worry, in turn, can lead us to seek ultimate foundations for the value of the objects of some desires. Perhaps the things that are worth wanting are the things that god says are worthwhile. Perhaps it is god's perspective, not our own, which is the foundation of real value. This pattern can be found in other parts of our lives. Besides wanting things we make plans. Some plans are worth making, others are not, as we find out to our chagrin. What if all of our plans are worthless? An appealing idea is that god's plans are the foundation of the plans worth making.

The same goes for commitments: we can commit ourselves to worthless things, after all. Are all of our commitments in vain? Perhaps god makes some commitments worthwhile, thereby saving us from worthless efforts.

The pattern repeats for ways of life. We can lead our lives in various ways. There is dedication to a career, or to physical pleasure, etc. Once we work through the details, we discover that not all ways of living are equally valuable. What if none of them are valuable at all? What does it take for a way of life to be worth living? Perhaps it's god's perspective that makes the difference.

This line of thought about ways of living gets us very close to famous worries about the meaning of life. There is something appealing about seeking the meaning of life in god's perspective. The appeal is generated, so far as I can tell, by the all-too-common experience of disappointment with our wants, plans, commitments, and choices about how to live. We get things wrong, but god is omniscient, so surely she gets these things right. More to the point, there is something appealing in the idea that our lives are meaningful to the extent that they line up with god's perspective.

This way of thinking has unfortunate implications for atheism. If god is needed in order to give life meaning, then a godfree life is a way of living that deliberately gives up on the very foundation of what makes life worthwhile. It's even worse if atheists are correct. If god is needed in order to give life meaning, then a universe without god is a universe in which nothing really matters. This would be a tragedy. Is it really the case that atheism implies that the human condition is tragic? That we value, plan, commit ourselves, seek meaning, yet it's all in vain? Maybe. See *Irony (and Meaning in Life)* for reason to think otherwise. For now there is another problem to face.

Our wants, etc. are not necessarily worthwhile, and this can lead us to seek a foundation for the value of our lives in god's perspective. There is a deep problem with this. The source of our search for a foundation seems to be a realization that desires, commitments, etc. are not automatically worthwhile. The overall inclination seems to be to appeal to god's desires, commitments, etc. when trying to find a foundation for life's meaning. But if wants and plans are not automatically worthwhile, then there is no guarantee that god's desires, plans, etc. are automatically worthwhile. If ours need vindication from without in order to confer meaning on our lives, then so do god's. If life is tragic without an ultimate foundation for the value of our wants, then the same goes for the things that god wants.

Perhaps you think that there's something suspicious about this worry. Good—there is. See *Irony (and Meaning in Life)* for discussion. The important thing for now is to realize that invoking god does not automatically answer our questions about what makes life meaningful. If our commitments, plans, etc. need external vindication in order for our lives to have meaning, then life is a tragedy regardless of whether there is a god, for the same thing holds for god's commitments, plans, etc.

This is not the end of the issue. See *Absurdity (and Meaning in Life)* and, especially, *Irony (and Meaning in Life)* for a rosier picture of the prospects of life having meaning.

Transcendence: (1) Going over, or beyond, or behind (around? under? The spatial metaphors can't be avoided here.) what one thinks or experiences in search of something more fundamental (or higher) and, presumably, more important. Going beyond the ordinary for the extraordinary. Going through the merely apparent to the really real.

There is a pervasive interest in transcendence in religious discourse. The world is not what is important; the supernatural realm is. This life is not really important; the next one is. What is before your eyes doesn't really matter; the deep truth behind it does.

Such interest in transcendence is a misunderstanding and undervaluing of our own limits, in a couple of ways. It's a misunderstanding of the limits of our understanding and imagination. It is an undervaluing of the limits of our lives.

The antidote is to attend to the details offered by the world, both through nature and through artifice, and to enjoy the expansion of the mind via the joining in with the world (not the indulgence in the narrowing of the mind fostered by neglect of this world through interest in transcending it). We ought also to recognize the play of our own minds and senses in such enchanting feelings that invite thoughts of transcendence. See *Enchantment*, *Tragedy (or, Despair about the Meaning of Life)*, *Irony (and Meaning in Life)*, and *Absurdity (and Meaning in Life)* for more.

(2) If the tendency to value transcendence is tied to the quality of particular feelings of enchantment—awe, wonder, etc. that one interprets in terms of a transcendent reality rather than the phenomenon in front of our eyes and ears—then it's true that this is given up in a godfree life. Is this a loss? I don't see how. We can still be euphoric, have feelings of wonder, enjoy epiphanies, and so on. What we lose is a particular interpretation of these. Since this interpretation is intellectually indefensible, this seems like no real loss to me. And since we substitute for it greater attention to and understanding of ourselves in the world, this strikes me rather as a gain.

Truth (or, Truths): (1) A feature of relations between ideas (or sentences or propositions or bodies of thought, and so on) and what there is. Some ideas are true, in that they accurately represent what there is, and others are not true.

It's tempting to equate truth with reality, and in a sense this is fair, but in another sense it is not quite right. There are truths about things that, in important ways, are not real. Is it true that Harry Potter defeats Lord Voldemort? Ask any child of a certain age and you will get the simple answer: yes. But are Harry Potter and Voldemort real? The same child will say "no," perfectly reasonably and perfectly accurately. By these standards there are truths about things that are not real.

What is going on here? The child speaks accurately, as we all know. The reason that it is true that Harry defeats Voldemort is that that is the way the story goes. The truth is about the characters in the story. The reason that Harry and Voldemort aren't real is that they are fictional characters, and fictional characters are, by definition and as we all know, not real. They exist as fictional characters; when we say that they are not real, we mean that they are not real people. They are not among the people who exist. They are included in the way things are (see *Reality [or, Realities]* for discussion) as fictional characters, not as ordinary real people.

There are various truths, but there is only one reality. Truth does not line up to reality in a simple fashion, so we must be careful about how we maneuver in this territory.

Is it true that Jesus turned water into wine? Yes: that's the way the story goes. But this occurrence is not among the things that are, at least not in any way other than as a story. It's just as true and just as real as Harry Potter's defeat of Voldemort. This isn't the way the world—the world outside of stories—works. This isn't the way that the things that are work, as we all know when we're careful about thinking about stories compared to thinking about other aspects of reality. In case you're tempted to think of this as a miracle, see *Miracles*.

(2) The concern for truth enters our lives in various ways. Some of the things we do have their point precisely because we think some idea is true. Other things we do don't turn on the truth or falsity of particular beliefs to have meaning. Maybe this is obvious to you. It turns out to be tricky once we attend to the details. Moreover, these points have puzzling links to the ways in which people orient themselves to religion.

Here is the issue: belief in particular ideas is the very foundation of some of our commitments and activities. For example, my life will fall apart if it is false that my wife loves me. So much of what matters for me hinges on the fact that I take this to be true. But other commitments and activities do not have such beliefs as their linchpins. In these cases there is no idea that would rob these activities and commitments of their value to us if they turned out to be false. Consider someone who loves playing the guitar. The value in such an activity does not typically rest on a belief that something in particular is true. What could such a belief be in this case? A person does not have to believe that something is fun in order to enjoy doing it, for instance. In fact it is usually the other way around: our enjoyment of the activity serves as the foundation for the belief. This goes for lots of other things that we do—sports, cooking, painting . . . really anything that is a good candidate for being a hobby, as it turns out.

Now consider religion. Certain varieties emphasize the centrality of belief, and hence the relevance of concerns about the truth or falsity of particular beliefs. This seems reasonable to me. Take a belief that god exists. It matters whether this is true or false. Moreover, the point of certain activities seems to depend on the presumed truth of this idea. Why would you, for example, pray, or celebrate Easter, if it is not true that god exists? There are possible answers to this question—habit, or to join in with others, for instance. However it should be clear that the activities in question don't mean the same thing if these are one's reasons for doing them. The religious activities have their primary meaning in the light of the presumed truth of the belief, and they lose it if the belief turns out to be false.

Or so one might think. The puzzling thing is that many religious people seem unconcerned about the truth or falsity of the fundamental ideas that, from my perspective, seem to be needed to give their religious practices meaning. These people sincerely lead religious lives without taking seriously the question of the truth of what seem to be vital ideas. For these people religion is more like playing guitar or tennis than like love.

Presumably there are atheists like this too—people who just are not concerned about the existence of god and who live godfree lives without a concern for the truth or falsity of this sort of idea. Fair enough.

Here is the crucial thing. Religious believers who see the significance of religious activities in their lives as dependent on the truth of certain ideas can be talked out of religion. If they come to believe that the core beliefs are false, their old habits lose some of their old meaning. This can be very disruptive, even painful. It can also be joyfully liberating. But the same does not hold for those who are immune to questions about the truth or falsity of their ideas. How could you reason about religion with such people? Their religious lives are isolated from such scrutiny.

To a certain extent immunity to concerns about truth and falsity is fair with regard to religion. Religion does a variety of things in people's lives, after all. But the people who are completely unconcerned about the truth or falsity of certain fundamental ideas seem to be missing something.

Maybe this immunity to issues of truth is a form of faith. But we should be clear here: if this is right, it's just one form of faith. The reason is that, for many, it's faith in the existence of god that matters. That is, the faith of many is that a certain idea is true, and that this truth matters. The religious who are numb to concerns about truth aren't just missing something by my external standards, they are missing something crucial by the standards of many of the people and institutions that are dedicated to religion.

For mitigating considerations, see *Belief and Doubt*.

21

U Is for . . .

Uncertainty: It's an uncertain world. Some people seek certainty in religion. This is false hope. Being an atheist involves learning to live with uncertainty. Sorry. See *Ignorance, Hope, Fear,* and *Humility.*

22

V Is for . . .

Values: (1) A change from a religious life to a godfree life involves a change in values. People who make this change will not value all of the things that they used to value, and those values that persist will not be held in the same way. See *Standards* for overlapping ideas.

Consider, as just one example, the way in which individual autonomy and subservience are valued by generically religious and godfree people. Self-direction is partially valued in most religions, but often for a select group of people only. Women fare particularly poorly with regard to the religious treatment of autonomy. Subservience, by contrast, is highly esteemed, both with regard to gods and with regard to certain privileged individuals and groups.

The situation is reversed for godfree people, generally speaking. Autonomy is esteemed, in part because it is unavoidable. In a world with no divine authorities, of course we must run our own lives. Subservience, by contrast, is suspicious. There are no fitting objects for worship, which is an inherently subservient stance (see *Worship*). There are no higher and lower groups of people. There is nothing particularly valuable about subservience, from this perspective.

Of course there are godfree people who want to treat others as unequal, even to make them their slaves; atheism is no inoculation against evil. The crucial thing is that this attitude gets no vindication from atheism. Indeed, the will to power exhibited in such cases is baldly illuminated by a perspective that portrays competent adults as equally deserving to run their own lives (see *Adults*).

Much more should be said about religious and nonreligious treatment of autonomy and subservience. The same goes for lots of other values. See

Morality (or, On Loving the Good with and without God) for general but extensive discussion of religion and moral value.

(2) With regard to absolutely whatever we take to be valuable—life, nature, the Montreal Canadiens—religion and atheism differ, at least with regard to fundamentals. Why does human life matter? Maybe because god says so. But this is to locate the foundation of the value of human life in god's perspective, not in the nature of life itself. The atheist can, for this and other values, say that it matters because of its nature, not because of divine will.

Another answer says that it matters as a run-up to an afterlife. Its value is that of a test. But this is to make the value of worldly life derivative from the importance of the afterlife. Atheists, on the contrary, can insist that this life matters now, on its own terms, nonderivatively.

This pattern repeats for other worldly values. The religious perspective tends toward valuing this world derivatively, secondarily, rather than directly and on its own. A godfree perspective is the most sure way of ensuring that we appreciate the true nature of the things that matter. See *Morality (or, On Loving the Good with and without God)* for extended discussion.

23

W Is for . . .

What's the Case for Atheism?: Not something that I need to provide. See *Who Bears the Burden of Argument?* for details.

The case for atheism is actually many cases about many subtopics. The entries in this book address some but not all of them. The overall effect is cumulative; that's where the real case for atheism is to be found, in these diverse details.

Still, if pressed, here's what I find most tempting as a quick case for atheism. Whatever else the idea of god is, it's an explanatory posit offered to account for the existence and nature of the world. But it's an idea that is increasingly and seemingly inexorably turning out to be unnecessary. The more we—that is, humans in general, using the combined resources of the sciences, philosophy, and maybe other disciplines—understand the world, the less room we find for this idea.

Indeed, we see evidence against at least some notions of god. For instance, take the physical design of human bodies. These are a wonderful mess, clearly designed, and clearly not intelligently designed. We're so weirdly designed that, had we the technical abilities, we would clearly be able to do a better job. So: no reason here to think that a mindful designer produced us. Much more reasonable is that we are the result of a complex, mindless designing process, which is just what natural selection is. See *Meat Machines.*

The combination of the lack of need for the idea of god and the existence of phenomena that work against the idea of god is a large part of why I'm an atheist. I think that the case provided by this combination is correct. I also think that it's dull, and that many people won't like its provisional and difficult nature. Much here turns on waiting for hard scientific work to be done and paying attention to the details. Much also turns on other topics. So it's just a quick case, but it's not a bad one for that.

What's the Difference between a God and an Extraterrestrial?: Easy: gods are typically thought to be supernatural, whereas extraterrestrial beings are typically thought of as part of the natural world. Does this matter? Surprisingly, yes. Here's why.

Let's back up a bit. The issue is our conceptions of gods and space aliens. I don't think that there are any gods, and I have no specific reason to think that there are any actual extraterrestrials, at least of the sci-fi movie kind, but I do have conceptions of these things just as much as the devoted believers in their existence. There are various ideas of both, of course, but our central conceptions arguably work like this: extraterrestrial beings are part of the natural world. This is why they are of potential legitimate interest to scientists, whose business it is to study and explain nature. God, however, is very often represented as the origin of nature, meaning that he is outside of the domain of natural laws and mechanisms. In other words, god is supernatural, not natural. See *Supernatural* for further reflection on possible relations between nature and the purportedly supernatural.

Some might contest this characterization of our conceptions, especially of god, whereas others will find that this is all so obvious that it is hardly worth saying. Fair enough to both. The crucial thing is this: to the extent that this quick characterization of our concepts of gods and aliens is correct, it has implications for how we reason about the potential existence of god.

It is not uncommon for religious believers to think that they have some sort of worldly evidence for god's existence: a weeping statue, the design of the natural world, morality, and so on. But to argue from some worldly phenomenon to the existence of a supernatural god is never going to work. See *Who Bears the Burden of Argument*? and, especially, *Evidence* for discussion. The reason is that inferring something supernatural from something natural either conflicts with things we already know about nature (and hence is false) or really just expands our idea of what nature is, and hence does not deliver the supernatural after all. What people are implicitly doing when they reason from a worldly phenomenon to the existence of god is treating god as if he is part of nature—that is, they are essentially confusing god with an extremely powerful extraterrestrial.

It would be reasonable (but probably not well-founded) to argue from a natural, worldly phenomenon to the existence of extraterrestrials, since our concept of them is a concept of something that is part of the natural world.

Is it rude to confuse god with an alien? Is it blasphemous? Obviously the godfree can say "no" here: there are no gods to be rude to, no divine codes by which anything counts as blasphemy. However, it's a good bet that by some religious standards, confusing god with an extraterrestrial, even tacitly, is at least rude and probably blasphemous.

Who Bears the Burden of Argument?: (1) Put aside the various antipathies between religious believers and the godfree and some points of disagreement will nonetheless remain. For instance, there seems to be lack of consensus about the starting point of the conversation. Many religious believers think that the argumentative burden falls on the naysayers. Many atheists think that the case for god's existence must be made for belief to be warranted. Who is correct?

There is something to be said for both sides. Religious belief is so common that many grow up steeped in it. Since the adoption of a godfree life would be a profound change for these people, uncomfortable in many ways, it is not unreasonable for them to ask for an argument or two in support of this change.

What might an atheist say to answer this request? There are two broad strategies. First, they can make the case against the existence of god. Second, they can point out that, with regard to the truth or falsity of such a proposition as "that god exists," the argumentative burden falls on the religious believer. This is not a special case. The argumentative burden falls on anyone who makes a claim that something exists.

Odd cases highlight the argumentative burden. Suppose that I claim that I have a gold coin lodged into the fleshy part of my torso under my left arm. Without evidence, you have no reason to believe me. You might have no particular reason to disbelieve me either, if I am a generally reliable person, but this does not alter the status of this particular claim. For it to be reasonable to think that this claim is true, more evidence is needed than my report. It is not something that needs to be argued against in order for us to be reasonable in suspending belief in this claim. The argumentative burden falls on the person making this claim.

I have used an odd case to make my point clearly, but the lesson is perfectly general. The reason that evidence is needed to support my odd gold coin claim is not because the claim is odd. It is due merely to possibilities of familiar sorts of misrepresentation of the world—error and deception, broadly speaking. Since we can be wrong or devious about any claim whatsoever, the burden of argument falls on the shoulders of anyone who makes a positive claim. For mundane topics we don't normally have to insist on this, but this is how it is nonetheless.

The burden of argument that falls on the religious believer is to provide reasons that shed light on the existence of god. Let's call these "truth-relevant" considerations. When someone who is a religious believer asks for argument to change her beliefs, it cannot be truth-relevant considerations that she is asking for, at least primarily. It is up to the defender of religious belief to provide those, not the atheist. Instead she is looking for what I shall call "comfort-relevant" considerations. After all, changing one's outlook would have little point if it did not also have effects for one's behavior and prospects, not to mention one's relations to other people. If we are to interpret the believer's request as reasonable, it must be taken as a pragmatic one. She is asking something like, "show me what there is to gain by giving up my religious ways."

Here the atheist has some things to say, as some entries in this book show, but we would be deceiving ourselves and others if we claimed that there are no costs to giving up religious belief. It might well be uncomfortable to do so. The godfree trade religious perplexities for new ones. Depending on your tastes, this might be a gain, but it might not. And this is to say that there might not be a definitive comfort-relevant case to be made for the godfree life. "Might," I say; it depends on your tastes and concerns.

With regard to evaluating truth claims about the existence of god, the godfree are correct about the starting point of debate. Moreover, to the extent that one values truth, truth-relevant and comfort-relevant considerations are one and the same. To insist on comfort-relevant considerations at the expense of truth-relevant ones also has its costs. If you do not value truth, then there will be no talking you into seeing these costs. However, I'm not inclined to take seriously anyone who disavows any interest in truth at all. Such a claim should be treated as a cynical refusal to think about the topic at hand rather than a principled stance that deserves respect.

As it happens, there are comfort-relevant considerations to think that the burden of argument still falls on the shoulders of believers rather than nonbelievers. There are literally thousands of gods on offer in human history, and nobody believes in them all (see *Believers [or, My Sisters and Brothers in Disbelief]*). If disbelief (for example, in Norse gods, ancient Greek gods . . .) needed support, we'd be drowning either in skeptical effort or reluctant belief. But we all accept that we don't need to argue against the existence of these gods—the burden of argument must be for them. This point, however, goes for all gods.

The ordinary religious believer cares about the truth of such claims as "god exists," as far as I can tell. They have been misled about the argumentative burden that defenders of belief face, but this is not their fault. After being raised in a religious context, who can blame them for confusing truth-relevant and comfort-relevant considerations? Once this distinction is revealed, however, we can reasonably expect religious believers to face their dilemma squarely. Do you value truth? If so, then make the case for god or acquiesce in belief just because it's easier to do so. If not, then give up any claims about the truth of ideas about god and expect others to have nothing to say to you about these topics.

(2) Just what must be argued for with regard to the existence of god is often misunderstood. It is not enough to present a case for the existence of god. The case in question must also be shown to be preferable (with regard to truth, not comfort) to accounts of the same phenomenon that do not invoke gods.

For instance, consider those who want to argue that we should believe in god because we have some sort of experience of divine presence in the world. The problem is the paucity of evidence: hardly anything seems like evidence of the existence of god, and the few purported signs we come across are eminently dubious (plus, see *Sign* for worries about this very idea). Never mind, one might say—this is just what we might expect if certain prominent religious traditions are true. The god of the Bible and overlapping traditions, for instance, would want to be known, so he would provide signs of some kind. But he would want to respect human freedom, so the signs in question would be easily resistible. This is exactly what we find to be the case with worldly signs: they are there, but very contestable.

Maybe this is the correct thing to say of the god of these traditions. This does not mean that we have here a convincing case for the existence of god. This account must be compared to naturalistic ones. And, of course, there is plenty to say from a godfree perspective about the world and purported experiences of god. An obvious explanation of the poverty of evidence is that there is no god. The sorts of things that can be said about people who think that they have experienced something divine run the gamut from the commonplace to the findings of empirical psychology: people are wishful thinkers, cultural indoctrination can lead to experiences that are not veridical, experiences are not completely reliable guides to the nature of the world, our cognitive mechanisms are not perfect and can overextend to "detect" (not really, but falsely) agents of a divine sort where there aren't any, and so on.

For present purposes the details don't matter (although they will matter for some purposes). The crucial issue here is the easy availability of naturalistic alternatives to supernatural explanations of the same phenomenon—in this case, the relative absence of worldly signs of god, and the nature of the few purported signs that there are. We are faced with the task of judging the relative plausibility of these explanations. This might seem difficult, but it's in fact very easy: the naturalistic alternative is automatically more plausible from the standpoint of the assessment of the truth-relevant aspects of these pictures of the world. See *Evidence* for explanation of why this is so. Even if one is not convinced about this, it should be clear that the case for god cannot be made without examination of the details of rival explanations of, well, whatever phenomena are thought to offer some sort of grounds to believe in gods.

This means that much of the material available from defenders of religion is not suited for the purpose of actually defending religion. Testimony about how something seemed to you is insufficient as a case for the existence of god. Apologetic arguments about problems internal to a particular religious worldview are likewise not enough. What is needed is not such testimony or apologetics, but the comparison of various interpretations—religious and otherwise—of these cases. Moreover, solutions to problems merely internal to a particular perspective imply nothing about the overall case for that perspective. Suppose that a club solves a problem of contradictions between certain of its rules. This does not mean that those rules are worth obeying, let alone that they have automatic authority over people who are not voluntary members of the club. This is an exact analogy to much of the material that is offered as a case for the existence of god and as a defense of religion, I submit.

(3) Although everyone will acknowledge a need for arguments for the existence of god, few actually seem to be truly interested in this. That this should go for the ordinary religious person on the street is not surprising—they have more pressing things to attend to. But it also goes for the highest ranking members of particular religions, as far as I can tell.

Here is why I think that this is the case. First, most arguments for god's existence are so poor as to be not just bad but not even promising. The more interesting ones are just poor. So for believers to engage in this kind of reflection is directly self-defeating. But it's also indirectly self-defeating. The reason is that the most promising arguments for the existence of god do not deliver the actual gods believed in by most religions. Take the ontological argument, which argues from god's supposed perfection to her actual existence (see *Ontological Argument* for details). If it worked, this argument would not deliver the existence of a supernatural person, or even a mind, that literally wants, creates, or rules the world that we see around us. It would deliver just the existence of a purely perfect thing. Major religions might make lip service to this sort of idea, but such an austere object of worship is not really what they are about. They really offer us a view of god as a super person, as we all know. The upshot is that particular arguments for the existence of god aren't good for extant religions. Extra arguments are needed for the gods that they offer, and these religions don't tend to offer these either, for such arguments are no better than the poor ones that I have already mentioned. Best not to think too much about this sort of stuff at all, I guess.

(4) Everyone recognizes, at least in passing if not in conviction, that the existence of god must be argued for. Far fewer realize that the same goes for other religious ideas. Part of the reason for this is that they fail to realize that the ideas in question are religious ones. Religious concepts have saturated our inherited ways of categorizing phenomena to such an extent that people often don't realize when they are using them (for more

see *Language* and *Zounds!*). These categories have to earn their keep in truth-relevant terms, however, just as much as the idea of god itself.

Examples are easy to come by. Some people disavow explicit belief in god but claim that they are nonetheless "spiritual." But why should we think that this idea is in any better shape than that of god? What is a spiritual topic if not one having to do with values, emotions, the mind, and other things that can more adequately be addressed without the idea of the spiritual? If the spiritual is somehow distinct from values and emotions, explain how. Otherwise the idea has no respectable job to do.

What might a spirit be? A soul? Many who realize that the existence of god needs defense will let the idea of a soul slide by without question. This won't do: souls need just as much scrutiny and explicit defense as gods do. See *Soul* for more.

If there are no gods, there are no sins (see *Sin*). Yet either literally or colloquially, many use the idea of a sin while they would be more circumspect about invoking gods. Even trickier is the flipside notion of sin: the sacred. Without god, nothing is sacred (see *Sacred*). This does not mean, of course, that nothing matters, nor that nothing is of ultimate importance. It just means that the ideas of the sinful and the sacred are not to be taken for granted as the best ways, or even apt ways, for understanding the nature and status of values. See *Irony (and Meaning in Life)*, *Absurdity (and Meaning in Life)*, and *Tragedy (or, Despair about the Meaning of Life)* for a godfree perspective on how things matter.

God is the lynchpin notion in a complex array of ideas. The idea of god gets the attention—rightly so—and hence people are familiar with the call, even need, to argue for the existence of such supernatural beings. The other concepts deserve the same sort of attention. We will all be more likely to fall prey to the mistakes of religious thinking if we fail to insist that these concepts earn their keep. The first step is to develop a heightened awareness of the very need for argument. I wish that I could say that nothing could be clearer, once our attention is appropriately attuned, but this would be undue optimism. There's hard work here, both intellectual and conversational, for all who care about the truth in these domains.

Wholeness: (1) Is a life without religion less complete than it should be? Some religious people think so. Indeed, the apparent problem is so obvious that atheists might genuinely worry about this. Religious people do things, profess beliefs, and describe experiences that godfree people just don't share. Are we missing something? Something important? Are we incomplete by virtue of our disbelief?

Much turns on what is meant by "whole," "complete." When we look at the details, the sense of a problem here disappears.

The simplest thing that might be meant by "whole" is "statistically" whole. Humans do lots of things. If you don't do some of these things, you are not doing some things that humans do. Hence, by this generalizing idea of wholeness, your life is not whole. The problems with this interpretation are obvious. One is that we just can't do everything that people in general do; time and resource limitations prevent this, at the very least. Another problem is that there is no reason to care about this sort of completeness. Consider some of the things people do: murder, steal, own slaves . . . need I go on? A life that does not include these might be a life that does not include all of the things that people do, and hence it is not whole, but it is not a poorer life for it. It's a better life! Besides these dramatic cases, there are activities of essentially neutral value that do not improve a life, nor does their absence make that life worse. You have never pulled weeds? Who cares!

If there is going to be an incompleteness problem for atheists, the claim must be something along the lines that a life without religion is not as worth living as it might otherwise be. Alternatively, one might borrow from another domain and say that a godfree life is less healthy than it could be. There are various problems with this interpretation. One is a version of a problem with the last idea. Once again, finite human lives just can't include all activities that are available to us, even all of the good ones. If I'm going to church then I'm not in an art museum or a concert hall or a library. Something has to be left by the wayside because of our limitations. We can obviously live lives worth living; we just as obviously cannot live lives that include everything that makes life worth living. A good human life is not an impossibly perfect one. That kind of perfection is a false standard by which to judge the quality of our lives.

All of this is, perhaps, unduly polite to the believer, as it leaves open the possibility that religious belief and practice are among the things that make our lives good. This does not go without saying. Why should we think

214 • A Is for Atheist

religion contributes positively to human life? Not just because believers say so. We can all be wrong about the real quality of the things that interest us and the commitments we have; our firm devotion is not a clear window onto the worth of our objects of devotion. The enthusiastic testimony of, say, a Nazi says nothing about the value of the contribution of Nazi goals to a person's life. Likewise with religion. We need a perspective on religion—on faith, on godly ideas, on particular traditions and theistic life in general—that provides a reason to take it seriously as a worthy piece of a good life. Here then is a third possibility for interpreting "wholeness" that addresses this question. Perhaps the religious are open to certain aspects of the world to which the nonreligious are blind. These aspects of the world are important ones, and hence nonreligious life is incomplete in a way that matters.

This understanding of the wholeness challenge to atheists turns on the adequacy of the idea that there is a religious dimension of the world—a supernatural domain, perhaps, if most familiar religious traditions and texts are to be taken seriously. This is a very dubious idea. There is no good reason to think that there is such a domain. That's why arguments about god's existence are so important. If there were obviously a divine aspect to the world, such arguments would have no general importance. But this is not obvious. By extension, we have no good reason to think that religious people are in touch with some aspect of reality to which the nonreligious lack access. And without this there is no meaningful content to the idea that godfree lives are less worth living than religious ones.

There is another problem here. This interpretation casts atheism as an insensitivity, perhaps akin to blindness. But consider literal blindness. Blind people really are out of touch with an aspect of reality. They can't see, so visible things are not part of their experience. But we should not want to say that their lives are not worthy ones because of this. Perhaps they are incomplete ones in a clear sense—a much clearer sense than that which might apply to the lives of atheists. But they can still be rich ones. Moreover, the concerns and abilities of the blind typically fill in for this deficiency. Anyone who can read Braille or who can recognize people from the felt contours of their faces has abilities that I, a sighted person, lack. And hence they have experiences that I cannot have, at least currently, which means that they have sources of meaning in their lives that I am shut out of. Their blindness is not just a deficiency; it is a source of opportunity. Since I cannot avail myself of these opportunities, there is a sense in which my life is incomplete with regard to them. And note: I have said nothing about the other senses, just touch. The possibilities multiply.

All of this should make us suspicious about claims about "complete" or "whole" human lives. The important question is not whether a life is whole, but whether it is worth living. There is no meaningful metric by which we can judge the completeness of a life and by so doing assess its quality.

I am inclined to think that religious participation is a source of many things that make positive contributions to lives. These things are typically not out of reach of the godfree as they are not distinctly religious. Art, community, a sense of purpose, respite from quotidian concerns and fears—religious traditions deliver all of this, but they clearly have secular sources as well. A life without religious concerns is not deficient in any meaningful way.

See *Are Atheists Fully Human?* for worries about the idea of being fully or not fully human.

(2) It can be tempting to think that religious experiences or lives are more full, more whole, than godfree ones. The religious person sees the hand of god, or at least something supernatural, in the beauty of a sunset or a song. Maybe a life with this aspect to it is better than one without it.

At the same time, it's just as fair to think that the religious worldview accomplishes such purported fullness of experience at the cost of rendering our appreciation of what we see around us unduly thin. By seeing god, the divine, the supernatural, etc. in remarkable experiences, a religious attitude too quickly moves the responsibility for the beauty, our awe, and so on from the sunset or the song to something else. The credit is unjustifiably moved from this world to another.

A secular life finds fullness in the depth of this world. This depth cannot be truly appreciated without attending to the worldly details. Our wonder is produced by the sunset and the song; attention to details about these things, and about our reflective experiential capacities in general, typically deepens people's appreciation. Focusing on the world instead of on the supernatural makes these aspects of our lives better, rather than shutting us off from the fullness of experience.

Why Are You Doing This?: Atheists can find themselves in a bit of a bind with regard to how religious believers respond to us. Some want to treat atheism as a kind of religion, or at least as just as much a matter of faith as religion is (see *Faith vs. Reason* for more discussion). Others—or the same people in a different breath—want to treat atheism as very different from religion. This goes especially for public expression of lack of belief, such as this very book. "Why are you doing this?" is a pretty common question about this sort of expression.

Sometimes this is a thinly veiled challenge, even an attack: "Why do you think you have the right to say this sort of thing? Keep it to yourself!" Two answers are available to such a challenge. The first is an appeal to freedom of speech in general: while there are moral limits to free speech, expressions of disbelief are not prohibited by them. To ask whether there is a god, and to claim that you find the proffered reasons for belief wanting, is not at all akin to shouting "Fire!" in a crowded theater.

The second answer is more particular. It is arguably more powerful. The topics that religion addresses—the nature and origin of us and the world, of what is right and what is wrong—are important and interesting. It's reasonable for everyone to want to get these things right. If I can learn things by joining in conversation about them, and if I can prevent people from falling into error with regard to these important and poignant issues, then why shouldn't my contributions be welcome? Surely these topics do not differentiate godfree inquirers from godly ones? The religious and the nonreligious are on equal footing here.

At other times this question should be taken at pretty much face value: "Why are you bothering to express and defend your atheism when it's so unwelcome in a world so friendly to religion?" There are two answers to this. One is a love of truth and a distaste for error. So far as I can tell, religious accounts of the kind of world we live in, the kind of creature that we are, and the kinds of things we should and should not do are shot through with mistakes. These are important topics; short of this, lots of people are interested in them. One reason, then, to pipe up about them is to help people to sort out the wheat from the chaff.

The second answer points to the darker side of religion. Religious beliefs might be subject to error, which is one kind of problem, but religious practices exhibit problematic features of a much more worrying kind. In a word, they tend to be manipulative. Take the Christian tradition in which I grew up. It offered an eternity of hell—of literal torture—to sinners. This is a false fear; there is no such fate awaiting any of us. Some Christian sects virtually ignore hell; good for them! But others make a great deal out of this. Fostering such fears is bullying.

My upbringing also offered heaven—an eternal paradise—to believers. This is false hope. Churches can make more or less out of this aspect of religion. Those that use the hope of heaven to distract people from worldly wrongdoing and, even worse, to give their time and resources to the church are exploitative.

False fear, false hope—why shouldn't people speak up against these, especially when they turn into bullying and exploitation? Why bother? Surely this is the wrong question. Expressing and defending lack of belief protects people—including myself—from the manipulative aspects of religion. And given the long arm of religious ideas and institutions, this is protection worth having.

For more see *Heaven, Hell, Hope,* and *Fear.*

Wonder: I gather that many are drawn to religion, to thoughts of the divine, by a sense of wonder at the world. Well, the godfree wonder too. The world is wondrous. It is mind-bogglingly complex and beautiful, and awful, all on its own, without supplementation by the supernatural. Many scientists, and much of the best science, is driven by wonder at how things work that is turned into painstaking attention to the natural details. It's a wonder that the religious concern with the supernatural does not distort such work, such attention, more than it already does, given the number of practicing scientists who are believers. Overall it's a mistake to think that religion corners the market in awe at the world. The religious and the godfree share this, but exercise it in different ways. To go godfree is not necessarily to relinquish wonder. It is to inform it, and thereby to hone it, by attending to our world.

World (The): There is one of these—the natural world is all the world there is. Religions supplement this with a supernatural world, typically. There is no good reason to do this. Moreover, such a move tends to remove value from this world—the real world, the only world there is—and locate it elsewhere. This devalues nature. A godfree life is one in which beauty, morality, and the meaning of life are all to be found in this world, not a transcendent one. See *Morality (or, On Loving the Good with and without God), Irony (and Meaning in Life), Tragedy (or, Despair about the Meaning of Life), Absurdity (and Meaning in Life),* and *Beauty.*

Worship: A notable feature of religious life is that believers tend to worship their gods, and to encourage others to do so. Sometimes atheists are portrayed, critically, as worshipping things other than gods. At other times the godfree are encouraged to worship gods, either regardless of their nonbelief or as a route to overcome their lack of religion. At still other times atheists are criticized for living lives that don't include worship. Where does the truth lie? Is worship a worthwhile addition to nonreligious lives? Could it find a place there at all?

Before some reflection, here's how it is from the inside of this godfree life: it does not seem to me that I worship anything, so the first criticism is misplaced. The idea of unbelieving worship seems unworthy of everyone, regardless of godly tendencies. And I'm quite sure that my life would not be improved by adding worship to it. I'm pretty certain that this would be a step backward.

Why? Answering this requires a clear view of what worship is. When people go to church and take part in rituals, songs and the like, they worship their gods. When sincere this involves, let's say, reverence, love, and, perhaps needless to say, belief in the target of worship. This suggests a variety of things. First, unless we think that one's mind does not matter and that all that is needed for worship is the public activities, there is no such thing as unbelieving worship. The atheist who participates in worship activities is surely going through the motions, but not really worshipping.

Second, although love and belief are necessary parts of worship, something like reverence strikes me as central and hence the most important part. Given this, there is no natural place for worship in a godfree life. We can see why by reflecting on what it means to revere, to believe, and to love. Obviously I believe in the existence of my wife. I love her very much. Do I worship her? I would say not. She doesn't worship me either (I asked). This means that belief in and love of something are insufficient for worship. Something like reverence is necessary.

What does it mean to revere something? If to revere is merely to admire and respect, then this is insufficient for worship as well. I admire and respect many people whom I do not worship. For worship, reverence must take a servile form. To worship, one must show reverence by abasing oneself. This can be done a little or a lot. It can be done in very overt forms or it can take ritualized and mostly symbolic forms. Whatever forms it takes, worship involves casting oneself as less than and somehow subservient to the object of worship.

This is the chief reason that there is no natural room for worship in a godfree life. There is nothing to which we, as atheists, are inclined to take the servile attitude of worship. Nor would the addition of such abasement clearly improve our lives. It would either be absurd—imagine us worshipping general values, such as beauty—or degrading.

The absurdity that we find here shows another reason why worship has no role to play for atheists. It is most natural to speak of worshipping something like a person. Can we literally worship something such as money, which is not like a person at all? I can love money, and I can orient my life around its promotion, but I'm not sure that I can literally abase myself in reverence of it. It seems to me that I would have to personify money imaginatively in order literally to worship it. Certainly typical religious objects of worship are personified in exactly this way. God the Father, Mother Nature, and whole pantheons of personlike animals and forces await the curious student of comparative religion.

Atheists, of course, don't believe in the existence of such personlike divinities. The things that we love and admire are either actual persons, with whom equal relationships are appropriate, or nonpersons to which we need not make ourselves servants.

Overall, the godfree life involves no worshipping, and is no worse off for this.

24

X Is for …

Xmas: (1) We all know the sensory and thematic overload that comes with the Christmas season. Christmas is everywhere. Maybe it's more avoidable than it used to be in big multicultural places such as the city in which I live, but this is a small improvement at best. One might well think that Christmas must be particularly unpleasant for the nonbeliever. This is partially true, but the whole truth is more complicated and more interesting than this particular sliver.

Yes, the overtly religious imagery and greetings of the Christmas season tend to grate against godfree sensibilities. However, our lives are almost invariably bound up with the lives of believers whom we like and love. This gives us a reason to tolerate Christmas, and even to participate in the greetings and practices. Moreover, there are other reasons to participate, and even to value Christmas. Some people find the customs and beliefs of the Christmas season to be fun. Why shouldn't we enjoy the big meal, the songs, the exchanging of gifts, the well-wishing? Over and above enjoyment, the godfree can even value these things. Increased interpersonal generosity is good regardless of its motives, so we shouldn't be curmudgeons about the Christmassy context of this sort of seasonal giving. In short, the lives of the godfree are intricately bound up with Christmas.

The power of Christmas makes it worth particular attention, but really it's a concentrated version of the general state of affairs in which the godfree find themselves. Our world is one in which religious institutions, images, vocabulary, practices, and assumptions are quite prominent. This can be difficult to recognize, but it is nonetheless the case. Some cases in point: when I do something as innocuous as walk my dog through the residential neighborhood in which I live, I pass quite a few churches. Sometimes, when I sit in my backyard, I can hear church bells. Why religious institutions should be entitled to disturb my peace when I'm on my own property, I don't know, but there you have it. The omnipresence of religion is disturbing to some of the godfree on a daily basis.

And yet ... we live and love people who are devoted to these institutions. This gives us more than a theoretical reason to accept churches in our neighborhoods. And some of us enjoy aspects of religious life. Some nonbelievers like the ritual of attending church. Much explicitly religious music and art is wonderful. When I think of the origins and symbolism of Vatican buildings, for instance, there is much to find disgusting. But as a physical object and the product of genius and craft, St. Peter's Basilica is breathtaking. There is guilty pleasure to be had for the godfree in a visit to the Vatican museums. This gold-adorned world is so evil, and so wonderful! Moreover, there is much of genuine value in religious practices. Many people would be worse outside of their religious contexts, and it is unduly churlish to complain about their good character due to its religious ties.

Godfree lives are hardly, by any measure, religion-free lives. There are good and bad aspects of this. No simple antireligion implications stem from a commitment to atheism. This goes for Christmas and other major religious celebrations too.

(2) So: suppose that you are a godfree person with both reason and desire to celebrate at Christmas. Can you celebrate Christmas? Literally? Wholeheartedly? As an atheist? If not, what should I celebrate?

Yes, you can celebrate at Christmas time. No, you cannot literally celebrate Christmas, given that this is a religious celebration and you are not a believer. However, you can wholeheartedly wish others well, exchange gifts, be merry. Why not? Belief in Christian dogma is not necessary for this. This goes for many other religious celebrations as well. Often genuinely important values are separable from the religious trappings. Atheists should value what is worth valuing, wherever it is found.

There are other things you can celebrate at this time of year. There is, famously, the winter solstice. There's something appealing, to my down-to-earth godfree and northern hemisphere sensibilities, about marking the darkest time of the year and the forthcoming increase in sunlight with festivities. Also, as it happens, Christmas Day is Sir Isaac Newton's birthday. Given Newton's contributions to natural science and our understanding of the world as governed by natural principles, not supernatural ones, some atheists mark "Newtonmas." We can put Newton's Christian beliefs aside without doing too much damage to his legacy.

There's an obvious problem with celebrating Newtonmas or the winter solstice. It's lame; you'll look like a weirdo. I certainly think this is the case; you might as well just join in the Christmas celebrations rather than explain what you're actually celebrating. At the same time, all celebrations look strange, maybe even lame, from the perspective of people who aren't participating. Candles on cakes for birthdays, red hearts at Valentine's, the sparkly falling ball, first footing, and "Auld Lang Syne" for New Year's ... all peculiar from outside the relevant tradition. There's the foundation for godfree contributions to the holiday season here, provided that you cultivate patience and a thick skin.

(3) Christmas puts the best and worst of religion on display for all to see. It is a season of goodwill. Generosity is its defining virtue. We devote lots of time and resources to giving to friends and family. The official giving message of the season extends to strangers. There's something to the idea that we would be better off if the world were more Christmassy year round.

There's something disturbing about this idea at the same time. Christmas fosters greed while it encourages giving. After all, the crowning moment of the season is the event of opening gifts, which is at least as much about receiving as it is about giving. It is a time of year that encourages show over substance. People who don't really believe Christmassy things put up decorations and participate in seasonal practices. People who don't take religion particularly seriously exchange religious greetings and head off to church, perhaps for the only visit of the year. The focus on material goods is hypocritical for a religion whose defining document exalts the poor and criticizes the rich. Christmas encourages attention to symbols and lack of attention to the messages and effects of the symbols. There is not much to admire about that.

The hypocrisy of Christmas is worth particular attention. Giving is the defining habit of the season. However, not all giving is equally good. We see this when we compare the details of our actual giving habits with the defining figures of the contemporary Christmas tradition.

Ordinary people give gifts to loved ones. We might give some money to charity, so our giving is not strictly limited to friends and family, but this is where the effects of our seasonal generosity are most significantly felt.

Compare this with two of the defining figures of contemporary Christmas: Santa Claus and Ebenezer Scrooge. Santa is an indiscriminate giver. Everyone—or every good person, even though this qualification is typically ignored—is understood to get something from Santa. Scrooge, once he experiences his conversion, is a more complicated figure. At first glance, Scrooge seems to be like us. He buys a turkey for the Cratchits, who are part of his life. He gives Bob Cratchit a raise and promises other benefits. But we see, with a second look, that Scrooge is not so like us after all. He does not give, in the first place, to his rich friends and relatives, although he spends Christmas Day with family. Bob Cratchit is not Scrooge's friend, and Scrooge barely knows the other members of the family. Scrooge's giving is sensitive to need first and foremost, and only secondarily is his generosity aimed at family.

There is another figure who defines the Christmas season, of course: Christ. Would Christ be impressed with any of these giving patterns? To the extent that giving involves attention to others' benefit, Christ is presumably pro giving. But Christ was deeply concerned about the poor, while simultaneously being no fan of the rich. Only Scrooge's giving is centrally structured by considerations of need, so we have reason to think that Christ would prefer his actions over ours and Santa's. From this standpoint, it is hard to say who is better, us or Santa. Maybe indiscriminate generosity is better than our family-centric habits. But Santa's activity makes the rich richer just as much as it benefits the poor. Our concerns, on the other hand, are structured first by interpersonal care and then by considerations of need. So maybe Santa is worst of all.

I know Santa and Scrooge are creatures of fiction. The point is not really to see which of us is best and which worst. It is instead to throw light on the hypocrisy of Christmas, which should make it difficult for us all to swallow, regardless of our religious tendencies. Santa is the hero of Christmas, at least in its popular imagery, which is, so far as I know, disavowed by virtually no Christians or Christian institutions. But by the standards of the defining values of Christianity, Santa is morally dubious.

What does all of this mean? Is it a problem solely for Christians? To the extent that it's a problem with Santa from Christ's perspective, yes, clearly. But there is a more important worry here. The Christmas problem arises because of disconnection between Christmas imagery, stories, and habits from the values that are definitive of its grounding religion. When Christian churches encourage rote participation in churchly activities while, perhaps inadvertently, neglecting the official values of their tradition, they create a context that fosters such a gap. This is a phenomenon that can befall any church—or any other sort of group, for that matter.

Why am I addressing this? Shouldn't I prefer a world of so-so Christians rather than true believers? Maybe. However, it seems to me that there is something genuinely valuable that is obscured by Christmas, so I have reason to wish the season to be changed. I have no reason to wish the rich to get richer; I do want the lives of the poor to be improved. Christmas at best indirectly contributes to this, so it calls out for correction.

Moreover, there is the question of why this sort of disconnection between the values of a religion and its most conspicuous appearances arises. I don't know exactly, of course; the reasons here, and elsewhere, must be complicated. But I suspect some morally problematic root causes. Maybe it's easier to get money from demibelievers rather than to insist on true belief before people can participate in church activities. Where such exploitation is at the root of hypocrisy, we have reason to root out the hypocrisy even if we don't agree with the truly held beliefs either.

(4) You will have noticed that I have not referred to Christmas as "Xmas" (except in the title of this entry). This abbreviation annoys some, so I don't mind mostly avoiding it. Some people worry that to speak or, what is more likely, to write of this holiday as "Xmas" is a mark of rude secularization. It seems like a way of taking the Christ out of Christmas, damn it! Well, maybe it is in some people's hands. I have no interest in removing Christ from Christmas, which you will have already noticed, so I don't mind using the full spelling. But the history of the abbreviation is long and harmless (I'll wait while you check the Wikipedia entry on "Xmas"). The "X" comes from the Greek word for Christ and, literally for centuries, has been used as a shorthand way of referring to Christ. This

works for people who know the abbreviation or who know their Greek. It fails to work for those who are ignorant of these things. So, to avoid ruffling feathers, let's be careful with "Xmas." But all the same, (please see) *Pick Up a Textbook.*

25

Y Is for . . .

You: It's not all about you. Some things are about you, but not much, in the scheme of things. You are a member of a fluke species on an insignificant planet among billions of other planets. From the perspective of the universe, you do not matter. This is not the only perspective to take on meaning: see *Tragedy (or, Despair about the Meaning of Life)*, *Irony (and Meaning in Life)*, and *Absurdity (and Meaning in Life)*. A certain amount of self-importance is involved in those religions (which are numerous) that insist that we matter in an ultimate sense—indeed, that gods created it all with us in the middle. Going godfree involves getting over yourself. See *Humility*.

26

Z Is for . . .

Zounds!: If I become an atheist, do I have to give up religious curses?

No. The use of religious language often implies nothing about one's religious beliefs (see *A Very Ordinary Day* and *Language*), and this holds especially for cursing. Atheists may swear with religious words just as much as believers may. You are not a hypocrite for doing so. Religious concepts are found all through our language. We do various things with language. It is more important to avoid religious concepts for some jobs, such as describing the nature of the world, than for others. Cursing is one of these others. This is a good thing: despite being learned, it's my experience that curses are hard to give up once you get used to them.

This can be embarrassing, if one cares not to ruffle the religious sensibilities of the company one keeps. I recently pulled a lamp off a shelf and onto my head, immediately uttering "Jesus Christ!" despite being in earshot of Christian people whom I did not wish to offend. "Jesus Christ!" is close to my heart as a curse. Do we all have preferred oaths? I certainly do, and despite my godfree life some of these deploy religious terminology. "Jesus Christ!" is one, along with important variations: "Jesus Fucking Christ!" delivers the appropriate emphasis for many things, it seems to me. "Jesus!" is short and to the point, and arguably preferable, on both profane and literary grounds, to "Fuck!" "Goddamn!" and "Goddamn it!" are also useful and valuable. "Christ!" and "For Christ's Sake!" have nuances that suit certain moments in which I find myself.

It's surprising how many ordinary curses have religious origins. "Damn!" is a good one, accepted by many, even among the devout. In this case the godly aspects are relatively hidden. Not so with "Hell!" I have always been surprised by the number of people who consider this a potent curse rather than an innocuous one. Still, it's a good one for medium-serious cursing and for lighthearted use in many conversational contexts. I wouldn't want to lose either of these.

I quite like some religious curses that have ironic aesthetic applications. A couple of churches near my home ring quite ugly-sounding bells. It's an "unholy" racket! It's "godawful!" Naturally I don't mean either of these things in a religious sense, but I do mean the aesthetic condemnation quite seriously.

In principle we could substitute defanged religious epithets for rude ones. "Zounds!" is apparently a shortened form of "God's wounds!" but no one would be offended—I assume—by the use of this religious curse in place of "Jesus Christ!" You'll be seen as a weirdo, but not as rude.

The particularly worldly could substitute the religious curses of other languages for those of their mother tongue. "*Tabernak!*" anyone? The French use so many religious curses ("*Sacrement!*" "*Câlisse!*") that the Catholic Church in Quebec once undertook a PR campaign to recover the original churchly meanings of these oaths. Good luck to them. Time might do it, but I suspect that profanity is virtually immune to the cleansing powers of effort. If anything, such PR campaigns teach the non-French these French curses at least as much as they combat their offensive power.

For many atheists, religious curses will be the only religious language they use outside of discussions of atheism. So be it. Not all language is used literally, and this goes for religious language at least as much as it does for other sorts. See *God (or, Gods)* and *Symbolism (or, Analogy, Metaphor)*.

Select Bibliography

Blackford, Russell and Udo Schüklenk. *50 Great Myths about Atheism* (Malden, MA: John Wiley & Sons Inc., 2013).

Blackford, Russell and Udo Schüklenk, eds. *50 Voices of Disbelief: Why We Are Atheists* (Malden, MA: Blackwell Publishing Ltd, 2007)

Christina, Greta. *Why Are You Atheists So Angry?: 99 Things That Piss Off the Godless* (Durham, NC: Pitchstone Publishing, 2012).

Dawkins, Richard. *The Selfish Gene* (Oxford: Oxford University Press, 1976).

Dawkins, Richard. *The God Delusion* (Boston: Houghton Mifflin, 2006).

Dennett, Daniel. *Darwin's Dangerous Idea: Evolution and the Meanings of Life* (New York: Touchstone, 1995).

Dennett, Daniel. *Breaking the Spell: Religion as a Natural Phenomenon* (New York: Penguin, 2006)

Frankfurt, Harry. *On Bullshit* (Princeton: Princeton University Press, 2005).

Gervais Will M., Azim F. Shariff, and Ara Norenzayan, A. "Do You Believe in Atheists? Distrust Is Central to Anti-atheist Prejudice," *Journal of Personality and Social Psychology* 101, no. 6 (December 2011): 1189–206.

Goldstein, Rebecca. *36 Arguments for the Existence of God: A Work of Fiction* (New York: Vintage Books, 2010).

Grayling, A.C. *The God Argument: The Case against Religion and for Humanism* (New York: Bloomsbury USA, 2013).

Harris, Sam. *The End of Faith: Religion, Terror, and the Future of Reason* (New York: W. W. Norton and Company, 2004).

Hitchens, Christopher. *God Is Not Great: How Religion Poisons Everything* (Toronto: McClelland & Stewart Ltd, 2007).

Hitchens, Christopher, ed. *The Portable Atheist: Essential Readings for the Nonbeliever* (Philadelphia: Da Capo Press, 2007).

Levine, George, ed. *The Joy of Secularism: 11 Essays for How We Live Now* (Princeton: Princeton University Press, 2011).

McDowell, John. "Values and Secondary Qualities," in *Morality and Objectivity*, ed. Ted Honderich (New York: Routledge, 1985).

Pelikan, Jaroslav Jan and Clifton Fadiman, eds. *The World Treasury of Modern Religious Thought* (Boston: Little, Brown and Company, 1990).

Pew Research Center, "U.S. Religious Knowledge Survey: Who Knows What about Religion," September 28, 2010, http://www.pewforum.org/2010/09/28/u-s-religious-knowledge-survey-who-knows-what-about-religion/.

Rachels, James. *Created from Animals: The Moral Implications of Darwinism* (Oxford: Oxford University Press, 1990).

Rosenberg, Alex. *The Atheist's Guide To Reality: Enjoying Life without Illusions* (New York: W. W. Norton and Company, 2011).

Russell, Bertrand. *Why I Am Not a Christian: And Other Essays on Religion and Related Subjects* (New York: Simon & Schuster Inc, 1957).

Shafer-Landau, Russ. *Whatever Happened to Good and Evil?* (Oxford: Oxford University Press, 2004).

Stewart, David, ed. *Exploring the Philosophy of Religion*, 7th ed. (Old Tappan, NJ: Pearson Higher Education, 2009).

Vonnegut, Kurt. *Galápagos* (New York: Delacorte Press, 1985).

Yandell, Keith E. ed. *God, Man, and Religion: Readings in the Philosophy of Religion* (New York: McGraw-Hill Book Company).

About the Author

Andrew Sneddon is a professor of philosophy at the University of Ottawa. He is author of *Autonomy, Like-Minded: Externalism and Moral Psychology,* and *Action and Responsibility.* He lives in Ottawa with two dogs and another ape (see *Apes*).